IRENIC APOCALYPSE

STANFORD FRENCH AND ITALIAN STUDIES

editor
RALPH HESTER

editorial board
JOHN AHERN
MARC BERTRAND
ROBERT GREER COHN
JOHN FRECCERO
RAYMOND D. GIRAUD
PAULINE NEWMAN-GORDON

volume XXI

ANMA LIBRI

IRENIC APOCALYPSE

SOME USES OF APOCALYPTIC IN DANTE, PETRARCH AND RABELAIS

DENNIS COSTA

1981
ANMA LIBRI

Stanford French and Italian Studies is a collection of scholarly publications devoted to the study of French and Italian literature and language, culture and civilization. Occasionally it will allow itself excursions into related Romance areas.

Stanford French and Italian Studies will publish books, monographs, and collections of articles centering around a common theme, and is open also to scholars associated with academic institutions other than Stanford.

The collection is published for the Department of French and Italian, Stanford University by Anma Libri.

© 1981 by ANMA LIBRI & Co.
P.O. Box 876, Saratoga, Calif. 95070.
All rights reserved.
ISBN 0-915838-18-4
Printed in the United States of America.

Contents

1 Irenic Apocalypse   1

2 *Revelation*: The Text as Acceptable Sacrifice   22

3 Learning to Read Irenically   40

4 Petrarch: *De Legendo Deo*   84

5 Daily Bread: The "Horrible Mysteries" of Rabelais   107

   Selected Bibliography   139

*For those who helped with and share in
anything which is good in this book:
for Frances and Frank Costa, the Circle,
M.L., Ed Quinn and Brown Kennedy;
for John Freccero, Thomas Greene,
David Quint and Patricia Parker.*

1 Irenic Apocalypse

No one can deny the problem—the horror—at the heart of the *Apocalypse*. Fully three-quarters of the text incarnates images of violent conflagration, physical torture, and the terrors of a "just" judgment, of a reading which is, literally, definitive. The very quantity of such imagery assures us that our ordinary connotation of violence for the word "apocalyptic" is not totally misdirected. But insofar as the word univocally connotes violence for us, ours is a curiously modern and incomplete characterization of the biblical sense. *Apocalypse* describes violence and the tyranny of a mystery; but it means "revelation" and discloses a mystery which claims to create a people who are free and at peace. Yet, whether we turn to the rhetoric of literary criticism, of popular culture or of aesthetics, we find the very fashionable word "apocalyptic," constantly used without any notion of the irenic or "peaceful" signification which it has carried in much of the Western tradition. The contemporary usage of the term, of course, is hardly a problem in itself; to say so would be—if I may appropriate one word and misappropriate another—to initiate a falsely apocalyptic jeremiad against some kind of Western decadence as demonstrated by, of all things, semantic analysis. If our culture and intellectual milieux, in their generally anti-hieratic and materialistic description of existence, have lost sight of Paradise, the first problem for the critic, is that they have lost sight of an important tradition from which they have been constituted, both for good and for ill. Though the need to think beyond this first problem is clear, the present essay in literary interpretation will find it problem enough.

It is axiomatic in history that any object of interpretation can be understood differently, or even in ways that are truly antagonistic, in different societies. This is, for example, what we might call the historiographical assumption of a text like Augustine's *City of God*; to initiate an analysis of the profound differences between the two "cities," the text sets their two interpretations of the same historical circumstances over against each other. Each culture has its own cult, each its own privileged texts and own "best light" for the way those texts ought to be cultivated. For the Christian culture of those who do good works and wait anxiously for the end, and for those who have (to whatever extent and for whatever reasons) imitated the rhetoric of that culture, a particular reading of *Apocalypse* has been a constant and has provided something tantamount to an aesthetic. This is not to say that the last book of the Bible has been the most important or the most popular in the Christian West. Just the opposite is true. Any number of other books, from both Old and New Testaments, have been more often commented upon, preached and proposed as exempla. *Apocalypse* has tended to disappear as a canonical book to the extent that its aesthetic or spirituality was crucial in informing two of the West's most powerful cultural artifacts: liturgy and literature. Typically, it reappears and is quoted verbatim at great length when it is misappropriated. Norman Cohn's *Pursuit of the Millenium* exhaustively documents the phenomenon of the sectarian misappropriation of apocalyptic texts. As aesthetic or spirituality, the more "hidden" presence of apocalyptic in liturgy and in liturgical art would require a separate study to examine adequately. Suffice it to say that the motifs of the second coming, the adoration of the Lamb, and the synoptic apocalypse of the transfiguration had become, by the fifth century, the central ikons in the apses of Western basilicas. They are, all of them, irenic apocalypses: which is to say that the macabre or alienating or problematic give way, in them, to visions of joy and of integration into the divine life.

The presence of apocalyptic in literature is a presence, first of all, of fictions which explicitly raise questions of belief, moral judgment, death and afterlife within other kinds of fictions. Such a presence confuses, deliberately, the reader's assumptions (or assumes the reader's confusions), about the very nature of the fictional. Several kinds of literature would be necessarily included in this general category, from gothic horror to Sartre's *Huis Clos*. But that which I would call the irenic apocalyptic element in literature is again more specific. Whatever may be the particular strategy of its presence in some of the great literature of the West—in Dante, *Piers Plowman,* Erasmus' *Colloquies,* and Calderòn's *autos sacramentales* (to name only pre-modern texts) —it is an apocalyptic in which peaceful images, whose ultimate source is the biblical Apocalypse, are integrally mixed with each text's vision of the problematic, the arbitrary, and the violent. For the purposes of this study, then, the term "irenic" will refer to those images which serve to qualify the violent, seemingly closed-ended, horrific content of the biblical book: images of dreaming, reading, keeping vigil, endurance (*patientia*), repose, eating, superabundance, learning. Insofar as this imagery neither excludes nor replaces the crisis or problem in a given literary text, but is rather an integral part of the representation of such a crisis, "irenic" will refer to a text's rhetorical appropriation of the aesthetic of *Apocalypse*, in which violence and peacefulness are each present and each understood in terms of the other. The resulting figure or type—"irenic apocalypse"—is proposed as the literary type of Christian eschatology. It characterizes that literature which, with whatever other intents, would attempt to describe the legitimate anticipations of Paradise.

Before approaching the biblical text itself to find the ways its "problem" might be appropriated by later writers, it would be well to discuss the nature of any problem as such. The attempt to solve a problem or to re-solve it with respect to another opinion is the attempt at achieving fullness, agreement, concord. Looked at more closely, a solution is the attainment of a moment when that which is lacked is most clearly delineated so that the problem, in no sense removed, can be seen from a "new" perspective constituted, in part, by the linguistic structure of the delineating process itself. Depending really upon one's point of view, the achievement is either great or minimal; but it is there. The terms of the problem are so well understood by those who face it—each understanding each other's language so well (or just well enough) —that there is agreement while the heart of the problem remains. In the context of apocalyptic, "irenic apocalypse" is a moment of fullness of knowledge of which lack or not-knowing is thoroughly, even pre-eminently a part. With respect to everyday problems of knowing, "solution" might be called—in the words of the Wittgenstein who re-subjected the surety of scientific logic to a violently rigorous doubt—"beruhigte Sicherheit" ("calm certainty"). Yet, when the same everyday problems are, on occasion, questioned more deeply, their violently frustrating quality reasserts itself—"die noch Kämpfende" ("the still struggling") —for it was never really absent.[1] In Wittgenstein's notion of the "play of language," all affirmative

---

[1] Ludwig Wittgenstein, *Über Gewissheit/On Certainty*, eds. G.E.M. Anscombe and G.H. von Wright (New York, 1972), no. 357.

statements, all that which we call the indicative "mood," are "instructions about the use of words."[2] It seems to me that this is helpful most of all if we see that such instructions have as their object some reference to an extra-linguistic reality which is, simply, a given—the way things are—with which language must deal and on which its play has some effect.[3] It is through the temporal coincidence of linguistic acts with this "given" that what we call understanding occurs. Wittgenstein says, for example, that it is "wrong" to say "I know that I am in pain" but "right" to say "I know where you touched my arm."[4] Similarly, we might say, "I know I understand" is wrong but "I know when I understood your words" is right. To paraphrase Wittgenstein, Gewissen ist *dies... this* experience of clarity which (when we are honest about our reflection on it) discloses, as well, a lack of certitude concomitant with it. We know this or that only by *learning* to know such experiences in all cases. Knowing the sense of the Johannine visionary, therefore, means learning this experience of peace in the midst of struggle, over and over again. The aesthetic of the biblical text—the way it characterizes itself—gradually becomes the spirituality—the way an individual or community characterizes itself in a religious sense—of the text's readership. We might, for this reason, properly speak of the eighty-six sermons of Bernard of Clairvaux on the *Song of Songs* as an example of its age's *Bildungsroman*.

The certainty of an airtight, logical demonstration by means of any "language game" is not certainty enough. Wittgenstein goes so far as to ask, in this regard, whether or not knowledge "is related to a decision."[5] *Apocalypse* presents knowledge as a decision, insists that a stance of peace in the midst of struggle be either taken or not taken against the world and its truisms. The resulting "knowledge," the text asserts, is a *way* of living over a period of time which, when retranslated into other language or art, is also an aesthetic. One of Wittgenstein's most interesting examples of the problem is the very same one provided by Dante, whose irenic aesthetic will be treated in detail in another chapter. Wittgenstein plays, in an obvious sense, with the logical absurdity of the Christian eucharist. "If one were to say 'This is wine, not blood'," says Wittgenstein, "Catholics would contradict

---

[2] *Ibid.*, no. 36.
[3] W. Donald Hudson in his *Wittgenstein and Religious Belief* (New York, 1975), p. 64, quotes a wonderful example from the *Philosophical Investigations* in this regard: "The procedure of putting a lump of cheese on a balance and fixing the price by the turn of the scale would lose its point if it frequently happened for such lumps to suddenly grow in size or shrink for no obvious reason."
[4] L. Wittgenstein, *op. cit.*, no. 41.
[5] *Ibid.*, no. 362.

him."⁶ Dante goes to the heart of the problem when, in the second canto of the *Paradiso*, he recognizes those who have struggled over a length of time with something so absurd as "bread of angels," who have repeatedly learned the implications of the foolishness of their point of view, who know they do not know or rather only know *when* they believe—those, in particular, are recognized by Dante as trustworthy interpreters. For an interpretation to be truly critical, according to this model, it must remain open-ended, judging and being susceptible to judgment not by the implied gnosticism of a univocal system of verities but (to use the term *in bono*) by a gnosticism based in the confidence that the ambivalent or polyvalent word is adequate, in human societies, to the experience not only of the problematic but of the ultimately unstructurable mysterious as well. To the extent that criticism chooses to ignore the claims of mystery or paradox, or to characterize them simply structurally—as paradox for this particular effect of irony or comedy—criticism risks total imitation of the process of scientific empiricism. To offer structural certainties as effectively closing the matter at hand, even in processes toward an outcome which has been "scientifically" recognized as susceptible to a certain degree of error, does violence to the nature of problems. It is, in Paul Ricoeur's notion of any interpretation "on trial," to ape "the force of public power" which can only apply laws literally.⁷ Reading *Apocalypse* in such a way would be for us to forfeit, as readers, any expectation of the totally "new" which the fiction's context gives every reason to expect; we would ape, instead, the logic of Rome, the violence of whose law the fiction portrays and which it is out to set us against by "teaching" endurance. The irenic text becomes a model for criticism of itself and, because it proclaims the irenic nature of all true solutions in time, for criticism of all texts. But it must be stated in the strongest terms that the open-ended judgment is not unscientific or non-analytical. On the contrary, it is the function of the world which the individual text creates to make its own structures available, and the function of the kind of text which would proffer itself as so contextualized to allow the tools of structural analysis to be readily usable (like algebraic tables) for an acquired tradition of reading it. Thus, we may legitimately even speak of the "dogmatics" of the text. Not only does the text present itself as a new, unique point of

---

⁶ *Ibid.*, no. 239.
⁷ Paul Ricoeur, "The Model of the Text: Meaningful Action Considered as a Text," *New Literary History* 5 (Autumn, 1973), 110. Ricoeur writes: "Neither in literary criticism or in the social sciences is there such a last word. Or, if there is any, we call that violence."

view but, in Ricoeur's words, it presents itself to its adepts (its readership) as an "injunction to think *in a certain manner*" with respect to these new things.[8] The critic who does not center on the analyzable integrity of the problem or verbal sign, as well as on its ultimate ambiguity, is just as suspect as a mystic without dogma.

Umberto Eco's recent study of the poetics of the "open work" is an excellent and usually circumspect criticism of the many modern aesthetic programs of open-endedness. Eco uncharacteristically errs, however, in his lack of cautious judgment with respect to medieval texts or ikons. He cites Dante's line from the *Epistle* to Can Grande to show that medieval allegory, though it can have four senses for a given text, is restricted univocally to four senses. Eco seems too willing to say,"È chiaro che non ci sono altre letture possibili…" and to speak of "regole di univocità necessaria e predisposta."[9] Such a reading does not, first of all, distinguish Dante's particular critical language, his unique "lettura" of Psalm 113 from the fourfold critical structure in terms of which he applies it; it also fails to see the fourfold structure as but an example of the ways one might interpret the open-ended "alleon" or otherness to which, in the *Epistola*, the text's invitation to move beyond the letter is directed.[10] In his references to the frequent reliance of medieval writers on the senses of words given in bestiaries, lapidaries, and other encyclopedias, Eco confuses the cosmological and ideological prejudices of medieval writing with closed-endedness; in short, he sees the imposition of apocalyptic structures but misses their claim of irenic inspiration. Medieval writers seem no more or less determined by encyclopedias and vademecums than are modern composers by their academic training in how to produce aleatory music. Good art will be unique and bad art will be wholly derivative in both cases. But it is important to recall as well that a great number of medieval writers at least *say* they are inspired by the Holy Spirit, the "spirit of peace" who "blows where it will"; they trace their art, at least rhetorically, to a theory of inspiration whereby a true sense of things is made available not only differently to each interpreter but uniquely for that interpreter. Creativity and receptivity is twice open-ended: externally or sensually, internally or spiritually. Whereas Eco, quite rightly, sees no conflict between the modern "substitution" of "un mondo fondato sulla ambiguità" and the "open work" and no inconsistency in a Brechtian "openness" which "si fa strumento di

---

[8] *Ibid.*, p. 114 (italics mine).
[9] Umberto Eco, *Opera aperta* (Milano, 1962), p. 30.
[10] See *Dantis Alagherii Epistolae*, ed. Paget Toynbee (Oxford, 1966), p. 173.

pedagogia rivoluzionaria," he would deny open-endedness to medieval fictive worlds and to medieval ideological fictions.[11]

In literature, then, the problem called "mimetic" is the same problem of knowledge which we have been discussing, confronted on the level of the fictional uses of language. The lack (or, in the myth of a fallen human nature, the loss) which constitutes it is in no way gainsaid by the creation and manipulation of signs. The sign points out that which it lacks. But it also expresses a real, if momentary, clarification of the terms of any distinct problem of describing or naming the way things are in the world. If the ordinary way to "otherness" is by means of signs, the apocalyptic sign is precisely that one which points to, as it encodes a temporal endpoint, an experience which is conceived of, even "now" in the hermeneutic moment, as being beyond language. But the result of such signification could be a horrifying aporia—not knowing at all. In irenic apocalyptic, however, the aporeme—the sign of contradiction itself—reveals new possibilities of knowing in terms of a fruitfulness experienced now, in waiting upon the seemingly irresolute structure. Though analogous to other types of signification, irenic apocalyptic mediates in those instances when the mimetic gap is seen as greatest, when the nostalgia for an edenic language is most acutely felt. That sign of contradiction which is Jonah in the belly of the whale is, in a most "accurate" modern translation from the original, clearly apocalyptic. But it is there the apocalyptic language of tribulation and not-knowing *only*.

> All your waves, your billows, washed over me.
> And I said: I am cast out from your sight.
> How shall I ever look again on your holy Temple?
> (*Jonah* 2.4-5)[12]

The Vulgate's "inaccurate" translation of the same verses, in contrast, is an irenic apocalypse. It was, of course, the definitive translation for Christians in the West for at least sixteen hundred years.

> Omnes gurgites tui, et fluctus tui
> super me transierunt.
> Et ego dixi: Abiectus sum

---

[11] I can think of no better characterization of the fifteen-odd major medieval commentaries on the *Song of Songs* (especially of those supposedly written to be delivered orally in the monastery chapter house) than Eco's understanding of Valéry's "il n'y a pas de vrai sens d'un texte" by way of a paraphrase of W.Y. Tindall: "...un'opera d'arte è un apparato che chiunque, compreso il suo autore, può 'usare' come meglio crede." See Eco, p. 34.

[12] *The Jerusalem Bible* (English edition, New York, 1968).

> a conspectu oculorum tuorum;
> Verumtamen rursum videbo
> templum sanctum tuum.
>
> [All your waves, your billows,
> washed over me.
> And I said: I am cast out
> from your sight.
> *Nevertheless I shall look again
> on your holy Temple.*]

Jerome, it should be noted, knew exactly what he was doing with the text. In his commentary on the book of *Jonah*, he makes specific reference to what is an open-ended, irenic "interpretation" in his translation. Jonah, as Jerome understands the figure, is already spiritually where he would be in fact. Insofar as he is *typus Christi*, Jonah shares Christ's spiritual glory, even though both are in the depths of materiality, in the belly of a human nature.

> "Verumtamen rursum videbo templum sanctum tuum." Pro quo LXX [Septuagint] transtulerunt: "Putasne addam at videam templum sanctum tuum?"... putas interpretari potest igitur, ut sit quasi propositionis et assumptionis, confirmationisque ac syllogismi extrema conclusio, non ex ambigentis incerto, sed ex fiducia comprobantis, pro quo nos interpretati sumus: "Verumtamen rursum videbo..." [The person of Christ is the Father's *templum* though obscured on earth by flesh.] Ex Ionae vero persona, vel optantis, vel confidentis affectu liquido intelligi potest, quod desideret in profundo maris positus videre templum Domini, et spiritu prophetali alibi sit, et aliud contempletur.[13]
>
> ["Nevertheless, I shall look again on your holy Temple." For which the Septuagint had: "Do you think I may ever return and see your holy Temple?"... "Do you think," then, can be interpreted as the final term of a syllogism of proposition-assumption-confirmation, not from the doubter's lack of certitude but from the verifier's faithfulness; we rendered it: "Nevertheless, I shall look again..." In the person of either the Jonah who longs for, or of the Jonah who believes, it can be understood, in the very peacefulness of its affect, that it desires at the sea's bottom to see the Lord's Temple, and that it is elsewhere by the spirit of prophecy, and that it contemplates something other.]

The Vulgate Jonah's is a statement of present hope for future bliss in the midst of an absurdly hopeless situation. All human signification shares that situation to a certain extent and can share Jonah's irenic moment. Wallace Stevens has it:

---

[13] Jerome, *In Ionam Prophetam*, in *Corpus Christianorum* (series latina) LXXVI, p. 398. Translations are mine unless otherwise noted. Notice the pun on Jonah's desire to see the temple: he is already *contemplating*. The pun in Stevens' "Lies," of course, puts a forked tongue in the only earthly paradise many of us recognize.

> The imperfect is our paradise.
> Note that, in this bitterness, delight,
> Since the imperfect is so hot in us,
> Lies in flawed words and stubborn sounds.
>
> (*Poems of Our Climate*)

The time-span of *Apocalypse* is all time, from A to Z; the central, hieratic figure whose name is "Alpha and Omega" collects in himself all the words and languages which are time's narration. The poetry of *Apocalypse* portrays a final untuning of the phenomenal world in which death is simultaneous with a new, indescribable life, when the elements of what we know "now" as harmony or meaning are dissolved and re-structured "then" into new syntax. It is an "end" finely expressed in Dryden's *Ode for St. Cecilia's Day* (and in Handel's 1739 choral setting of the poem):

> The TRUMPET shall be heard on high,—
> The dead shall live, the living die,
> And MUSIC shall untune the sky.

The biblical text repeatedly focuses, however, on a problematical present in which the possibility of a resolution, though "tasted" (*praelibare*) in the way problems are posed, is expressed as still to come. "Now" (to use the problem of the history of John the interpreter as an example), a metaphor of the final "then" is being educed, an understanding of it is being worked through. But "then," an interpretation of the vision of the end has been accomplished and made public. The flux between "now" and several "thens" is a constant and to express that flux rhetorically, as all irenic apocalyptic does, is to image the human need to find all "thens" as proximate to any experience of transformation or (in the case of Jonah) of conversion. The Pauline "then, face to face" is often appropriated in medieval and Renaissance texts, not as a representation of final bliss possessed but as an irenic apocalypse in which the momentarily anticipated paradise grows dim and the problem of the visionary, although clarified in peace, remains as problem. We shall see that John, who is asked to eat the book of his own vision, finds it sweet "now," and "then," once fully swallowed, very bitter. He is imaged as standing in the midst of doubt, menaced by death; but he is looking literally at the dawn: the dawn enthronement of the new King (the Lamb), which Mircea Eliade sees as entirely characteristic of apocalyptic from the earliest Persian texts to Judeo-Christian texts.[14] John's problem is not sloughed off but acknowledged in terms of the superabundant ability of the "kingdom" to fulfill

---

[14] M. Eliade, *Cosmos and History* (New York, 1959), p. 128.

and surpass it: partly in time, because the kingdom is already here, and partly out of time, because the finally lacking will be filled up at the Supper of the Lamb. *Apocalypse*, to use the words of R.W. Funk's discussion of the historical problem in hermeneutics, sees itself as having to "take the risk of history"—to make a powerful statement about the future because of the facts of the past in a present which either trivializes or threatens to destroy the possibility of such statements. That balance in interpretation which (with respect to one biblical text and its influence) we have termed irenic apocalypse, Funk calls "circumspection." "Circumspection seeks to disclose the risk the past lays upon the future, without any thought other than to take that risk upon itself as genuine responsibility for the past, and yet it knows, because it is circumspect, that it may well prove to be either overly cautious or merely foolhardy."[15] Present action can be dynamic, open-ended, with respect to a future its past requires. But the risk in reading history or reading *Apocalypse* (which reads a history) is the risk of misinterpretation understood as lack of circumspection or lack of an irenic point of view. To use Funk's language in a manner which I think might make sense to him, misinterpretation of *Apocalypse* has historically involved being either "overly cautious" (false apocalyptic or false-alarm; the language of "tribulation" alone) or "foolhardy" (false peace, divorced from "tribulation"). Readers have either used the book to defend a static orthodoxy, totally identifying their own readings with God's, or they have seen in the book the justification for a fully achieved millenial life here and now.

Historical misappropriation of *Apocalypse* is the direct result of misappropriation, in one or the other of the above-mentioned extremes, of its irenic spirituality or (on the level of any signifying activity) of its irenic aesthetic. Falsely apocalyptic violence and falsely irenic fulfillment are equally criticized in the biblical text; they are shown to be all the more insidious by appearing as a series of rhetorical doubles which look just like the irenic apocalyptic aesthetic which the text seeks to impart. The languages of legalistic proclamation, inevitability, and sphinxlike prophecy characterize both the maternal Church and Rome the harlot in *Apocalypse*; but Rome's rhetoric and actions are an illusory, violent "twin" of the church's, because Rome lacks an irenic center for its law. It might well, on the other hand, seem harmless to those who already possess the "glorious freedom of the sons of God," to buy meat from butchers who specialize in food previously slaughtered as sacrificial victims on the altars of Roman gods. But this

---

[15] Robert W. Funk, *Language, Hermeneutic and the Word of God* (New York, 1966), p. xi.

self-assured freedom is an illusory, irenic "twin," because it fails to see the total difference between such eating and the Supper of the "Lamb who was slain" as a victim of expiatory sacrifice. The supposedly peaceful and free experience of the saved community systematically denies, in this context, any problem, any unplanned-for struggle at its center.

As aesthetic problems, the simultaneity of peaceful and violent imagery as well as their false "twins" are discussed by a variety of contemporary critics, some of whom explicitly refer to the Book of *Revelation*. In his introduction to a collection of essays by various authors entitled *Apocalisse e Insecuritas*, Enrico Castelli defines the temptations of scientific objectivity as a kind of false "paradise" of security which refuses to admit of risk. The necessary risk, says Castelli, is to embrace simultaneously that which appears to occur discretely and successively. "…per cogliere un'armonia bisogna che le note si succedano secondo un ordine che non può essere rovesciato, e d'altra parte bisogna coglierle *simultaneamente* perchè l'armonia svanirebbe, in caso contrario."[16] The necessary risk (historical as well as critical) is to define the "immediate"—one's work in the present or the work of art as "presence"—as a form of mediation pointing, not to myself or my problem or my need to be fulfilled, but to a struggle between time and significance in which I am unavoidably implicated either as present to this moment or to this sign. This might be clearer by way of contrast. Modern advertising furnishes some of the most debased, falsely irenic "twins" in the endless series of beer commercials which inevitably focus on the moment *after* some great labor or work has supposedly been accomplished; the scene is always crepuscular and closes in "irenic" fulfillment. *At the end*, one drinks one's beer by the hearth and, at most, spins a yarn about the day's "struggle." But there is no struggle in the advertiser's aesthetic, only a subliminal reference to it; a comfortable fiction of struggle produces a succession of falsely irenic

---

[16] "Premessa" to *Apocalisse e insecuritas*, in *Archivio di Filosofia* (1954, II), p. 3. The Castelli passage continues: "Il simultaneo è il contrario del succedaneo…" Better, I think, would be to think of the simultaneous *in terms of* the successive, different from but not (as "contrario" implies) opposed to it. The problem in early Christian hermeneutics is glossed by H. de Lubac's *Histoire et esprit* (Paris/Ligugé, 1950), p. 179, where he asserts the "literal" and "spiritual" senses of a text "…sont en continuité, non en opposition."

In his essay, *The Sense of an Ending* (New York, 1968), Frank Kermode seems to approach Castelli's observation and in similar terms. He speaks of "concord fictions" as those which teach the experience of simultaneity (pp. 133, 144). Kermode discerns the irenic moment, but thinks of it as outside the given genre of apocalyptic which he consistently associates, in the aforementioned volume, only with terror and desolation.

images and words. The proffered word becomes electronically available *in malo*. As Castelli puts it, some cultures provide more and more occasions when "...non ha più senso mantenere una parola se non è conveniente mantenerla... E la voce del verbo 'ingannare' è una voce 'ingannevole,' così che non si sa più cosa significhi ingannare..."[17]

Falsely irenic "deception" is a principal theme in Harold Bloom's study of Blake.[18] Although (with the exception of "Auguries of Innocence" which he calls "positive" apocalyptic) Bloom does not see the irenic elements in Blake *as* apocalyptic, he makes Blake's attitude towards "false" peace very clear. In eliding the "Songs of Innocence" with pastoral tradition, Bloom shows how, for Blake, such pastoral innocence is naive, unfinished, egocentric. "The purity and wisdom of the child or natural man is... not the reflection of environment, but a self-consuming light that momentarily transforms natural reality into an illusion of innocence."[19] Bloom shows, as well, that the late, fragmentary "The Everlasting Gospel" ("evangelium aeternum" in *Apoc*. 14.6) is an aporeme or sign of contradiction which ironizes the falsely irenic, closed-ended "moral virtues" and proclaims the divine, universal, and unplanned-for forgiveness of sins.[20] It is in a similar vein that Umberto Eco discusses three possible critical responses to the problems of any culture. In his *Apocalittici e integrati*, the "apocalyptics" condemn the possibilities of culture with a false violence born of real alienation or separateness from any "other"; the "integrated" accept all possibilities with a false passivity devoid of any critical struggle with or concern for the "other." Though his book deals almost exclusively with modern texts—including the electronic media's texts—Eco's characterization of a third critical stance takes its language from the heart of Christian tradition. Responsible critics are, for Eco, "the Pentecostal integrated" or "the parousiacal" who announce, in the context of the age's horrors, an evident joy. They are, in the terms of this study, irenic apocalyptics. The joy they announce is—Eco borrows (perhaps unintentionally) an explicitly irenic image from

---

[17] Castelli, *op. cit.*, p. 5, footnote 1.
[18] *Blake's Apocalypse* (New York, 1965).
[19] *Ibid*., p. 30. Bloom re-translates "innocence" as, literally, "harmlessness."
[20] Both Blake and D.H. Lawrence have equal difficulty in seeing Christ as God precisely because of his enlightened involvement with all of reality. Blake, more theological, denies immaculate conception in order to put his irenic apocalyptic Christ in touch with the world's evil. Lawrence's *Apocalypse* (New York, 1931) sees no irenic element in the biblical text and therefore keeps Christ, a gnostic figure, out of its fictional, hysterical thrall. But then Lawrence makes no serious attempt to read the book; he rather writes a fiction in reaction to it which holds us in thrall with his love of this physical world over and against all visionaries.

Revelation—a "nuptial" joy.[21] Although he makes no reference to the long interpretative tradition according to which apocalyptic newness and peace are seen as the work of the Holy Spirit—a tradition which the present volume will discuss in detail—Eco calls the authentic critical stance "pneumatic."

No critic writing today has more seriously confronted and scrutinized the reality of violence than René Girard. In *La Violence et le sacré*, he shares the ideological concern of *Apocalypse* by seeing the necessity of facing up to the violence which is at the heart of man's communal existence. Violence is tied to a desire which manifests itself as "triangular": desiring the desire of another, desiring in which the terms of the desire are already closed and codified.[22] The triangularity, it ought to be pointed out, most often occurs within ourselves, prior, in some sense, to its claim on others' desires. When my desire is to recapture, for example, a "good" experience with, let us say, someone whom I love: when I desire *that* experience and materialistically associate it with a certain place or time or even food, the terms of my desire are so codified—I desire my own expressed desire so well—that my frustration at not attaining its terms is geometrically greater than the everyday occurrence of simply not "finding" what I want. The seemingly inevitable frustration of a fantasy life turns to a violence which is directed initially against the self; if the codified fantasy or desire necessitates enthralling another's desire, the violence which results is passed on. The more clearly social analogue to the above model is the violence which is born of sycophantic imitation or jealous rivalry; its rhetoric manifests itself as a kind of dogma which sees and permits no way beyond the letter: the letter quite literally "kills." It is to disarm the literalism of ideologies which might routinely turn criticism into violence that Girard writes, "le meilleur Freud n'est pas plus freudien que le meilleur Marx n'est marxiste."[23]

Girard's analysis is centered on the ritual violence by which human institutions and religions seek to limit the constant threat of individual and communal eruptions of violence. Girard seems out to define, without mentioning it as such, the structure of a humanly integrating or irenic apocalyptic. Based upon some unique, founding sacrifice, the secondary or ritual sacrifice can only succeed, says Girard, if it

---

[21] Umberto Eco, *Apocalipticos e integrados ante la cultura de masas*, trans. A. Boglar (Barcelona, 1968), p. 383.
[22] René Girard, *La Violence et le sacré* (Paris, 1972). See also the special number of *Esprit* dedicated to Girard's thought; in particular, Eric Gans, "Pour une esthétique triangulaire," *Esprit* 11 (November, 1973), 564ff.
[23] See Alfred Simon, "Les Masques de la violence", *Esprit, op. cit.*, p. 515.

open up an experience of peace (what I would call the irenic) while simultaneously grasping the still really violent. Either the naïveté of complete peace or the obsession with violence, in or out of ritual, would dis-establish the human community. Both, as we have already observed, are kinds of alienation. It is for this reason that the key in Girard to cultic acts, or to cultic communities like the "saints" of *Apocalypse*, is the perception of "difference." *Knowing* the difference between the self and the sacrificial victim (knowing its real value, its purity or "acceptableness") and therefore knowing the need for one, and *allowing* sacrificial violence to open up to an irenic moment— these are the acts of perception or recognition which maintain the community. They are crucial to the survival of the cultic community—which is to say, the community of them that *know* and *allow*—and also effect, though not so definitively, the larger social mass in which the cultic community lives. "...cette violence collective [choosing the victim, recognizing the victim] peut vraiment constituer une espèce de résolution; elle libère les antagonistes de leur haine réciproque, elle apporte vraiment la paix."[24] As in the case of the Johannine reading of the imperial ritual of Rome, in which the saints' failure to recognize and, hence, legitimize a cultic act of conformity is paid for in blood, not perceiving true difference (not knowing and not allowing) means that cultic sacrifice will breed murder. The most crucial differentiating activity, therefore, and the one for which *Apocalypse* is both narrative and ritual text, is recognizing the absolute uniqueness and acceptableness of a sacrifice which puts an end to the constant spilling of an endless number of victims' blood. For Girard and for *Apocalypse*, there are two such sacrifices: the "humbled and contrite heart" (*Psalms* 50.19) announced in the Old Testament culture still characterized by the *lex talionis*, and the life and death of Christ which Girard calls the "donné évangélique."[25] In *Apocalypse*, the former is possible only because of the latter; Christ's sacrifice is final and continually expiatory for those who know the true nature of the victim and who therefore allow one of many terrible deaths by crucifixion to become the irenic meal, both "now" and "then," in which the once slaughtered victim is simultaneously alive and consumed.

The "resolution" and "peace" of which Girard writes is irenic apocalypse, not only in the text-ritual of the "Lamb which was slain" as

---

[24] "Discussion avec René Girard," *Esprit, op. cit.*, p. 530.
[25] "Discussion...," p. 556. On the self as victim, not only spiritually but in a literal, physical way, see p. 553: "Il n'y a de bonne réciprocité qu'au prix d'un renoncement total à la violence, c'est-à-dire de l'offrande de soi-même comme victime."

received by the "seven Churches" in confrontation with their own violence and the world's, but also in the make-up of the larger society and in some of its texts, its literature which seems on the surface quite secular.[26] But the ritual or fictional text cannot, of itself, bring peace, no matter how irenic its aesthetic. As we have already seen in the context of cultic actions, the representational or secondary sacrifice must be perceived and received in a certain manner in which, first of all, its uniqueness and difference are clear. Girard notices that the community which wishes to continue its experience of true peace does so by means of taboos directed at the sources of interpersonal violence and by a punctilious renewal of the original sacrificial victimization over and over again.

> La pensée religieuse se fait foncièrement ignorante du mécanisme qu'elle cherche à reproduire; elle s'efforce donc de tout copier aussi exactement et complètement que possible. C'est d'ailleurs pourquoi elle reproduit et doit reproduire des traits qui appartiennent non seulement à la résolution mais à la crise—celle-ci étant inséparable de celle-là—provoquant de ce fait entre les prohibitions et les rituels des contradictions objectives que les cultures d'abord, puis de nos jours les anthropologues s'efforcent souvent de nier ou de minimiser.[27]

Girard is correct here, except for the problematical—"foncièrement ignorante du mécanisme qu'elle cherche à reproduire…" The ritual or fictional mechanism is indeed unknown as experience—thus, the necessity of repeating the ritual (as the Byzantine liturgy puts it) "again and again" or "insistently." But, in another sense, the same mechanism is known *as experienced*. The entire epistemological basis for the act of "finding out" (chercher) the salutary or interpretative process is based on past experience of it which has been "learned," codified into definite usages (ritual), dogmas (theology), metaphors (literature) which the initiate and, especially, the adept cannot afford to ignore; this is so at the least because the same usages are one warning against the explicit elitism of the totally idiosyncratic "reading."

The process of knowing and allowing is internal, with respect to a particular community. It can, however, be observed externally, its mechanisms known, when one who knows and allows chooses to investigate the phenomenon for the group's benefit. Ritualists or

---

[26] Speaking of the Greek stage as cathartic substitute for the ritual altar, Girard points out: "Tant que l'institution fonctionne comme catharsis, même sous une apparence totalement désacralisée comme c'est le cas de la littérature, elle demeure dans la sphère du sacré." See Simon, *op. cit.*, p. 525.

[27] "Discussion…," p. 533.

theologians can be said to perform such a function. Once the difference between internal and external points of view becomes a problem for an observer *outside* the group itself, the question which needs to be posed is to what extent that observer sees his writing as having an ethical responsibility: to the "text" he reads, to an already defined readership (the teacher and the class) or to a readership which he urges into defining itself along with and in terms of his care for this text. The old presuppositions of scientific objectivity have little place in such observation; anthropologists have found, for example, their scientific work less "accurate" in those situations when ethics was not considered and when their relationship to a specific group became tenuous. They found, indeed, that their alienated knowledge triggered violence. In interpreting the structures of any process, the point of view of the pure observer, the voyeur, is violently closed-ended because essentially self-induced.

If there is a literary analogue to the salutary moment of the community's reception of the unique ritual victim as other and as irenic, it is the moment of understanding (as opposed to understanding generally speaking) when the critic's act of interpretation is simultaneous with his recognition of the total otherness of the text. It is the very ambiguity or open-endedness of forms of mediation like liturgical usages and literary metaphors which can lead to the unknown and unprepared-for experience. But this possibility depends, as Girard realizes, upon an exacting representation, "orthodox" we might call it, of an initial irenic moment. The danger in ritual sacrifice is that the victim and the irenic moment become obvious, domesticated, "undifferentiated" (Girard's term) from the community's normal life or even from its legitimate self-concern.[28] The danger in criticism, by analogy, is that the text and the moment of understanding become just as

---

[28] Girard goes so far as to apply his sense of the danger of undifferentiation to the various movements in the United States which have stressed racial consciousness: "Quand les noirs se réclament de leur négritude, ou les italo-américains de leur italianité, je ne crois pas que ce mouvement corresponde à l'affirmation de différences vraies; je crois au contraire qu'il constitue un moment dans l'intégration à la société moderne." (See "Discussion...," pp. 546-47). Though abject poverty and enforced ignorance must be fought in no uncertain terms, the fact remains that the truest "difference" was in the ghetto. Or, to put it another way, true difference will remain only when a people can be both innocent as a dove and serpent-guileful (and when these two emphases can be in real conflict with each other). Political freedom, perhaps, is being able to choose one's ghetto, and not having to conform oneself to a mass culture's acceptable definition of "difference." As Girard says, "a price will be paid" for the kind of approximate "reciprocity" which will permit the world to recognize and accept only surface differences of blacks or italo-americans. I would call that price—the abandonment of those true differences which may have meant being victimized—a-gnosticism.

ordinary and non-problematic, or that the focus of critical anxiety become not the text but the critic's sense of self. The critic must maintain, in his writing, the crisis of the given text; he must "need" the text in order to write about it and create an anxiety for that text as the representation of something crucial and unfindable without it. This is, at least, the explicit critical example of *Apocalypse* in which the text represents itself as just such an interpretation of the vision/text which is its origin.

Apocalypse is the fiction which narrates the tension of the historical situation of that community which does good works and waits for Christ to come at the end. It defines that tension as being sacred. The genre of apocalyptic and the *Apocalypse* above all, says Ernst Käsemann, "...first made historical thinking possible within the realm of Christianity." While the community waits, there arises in time "...the need not merely to proclaim the Kerygma of Jesus, but to narrate it." The paradigm is already available in the response of an earlier covenanted people to an historical manifestation of God's acting definitively for them—when, for example, Israel came out of Egypt. Käsemann points out that "Apocalyptic, as the Jewish haggada of the Passover shows, cannot refrain from recalling past history of salvation and damnation if it would seek to keep hope and warning alive... again and again [apocalyptic] has to recount the sacred story to a new situation and from a new experience."[29] Because the Christian *Apocalypse* represents the end of history or parousia, its tension offers a narrative theory for the text which is oriented to a certain end, but to an end which cannot be adequately spelled out. Insofar as it is known, its quality affects most of all the narrative's focus on the present. So that fulfillment, properly speaking, or resolution or "the way the story turns out" is both now and to come; it is present to all parts of the seemingly diachronic text.

Apocalyptic origins in the Old Testament are abundant and reasonably clear from the simple point of view of form-criticism. The prophets, especially *Ezechiel* and *Daniel*, are universally recognized as containing apocalyptic elements; the Christian churches have historically placed these two prophetic texts liturgically alongside *Revelation*, not as mere glosses but as unique, vatic utterances in their own right. E.M. Cross notices, too, the importance of *Job* for later apocalyptic.[30]

---

[29] "The Beginnings of Christian Theology," in R.W. Frank, ed., *Apocalyptic* (*Journal for Theology and the Church* 6, New York, 1969), p. 34.
[30] See R.W. Funk, ed., *Apocalyptic*..., p. 163. Klaus Koch's *The Rediscovery of Apocalyptic* (Studies in Biblical Theology, second series, 22) (London, 1972), p. 25, provides a convenient list of the form-critical characteristics of apocalypses:

In *Job*, the old clarity of deuteronomic history, of royal and prophetic lines, is gone; God seems hidden, its path through history untraceable. The accent of the book is on man's ambiguity and doubt in the face of the unknowable and unnameable. Ambiguous language, whether from Job's pile of shards or from his God's whirlwind or, indeed, from his friends (who are, in turn, falsely irenic and falsely apocalyptic), reveals a dread of not-knowing at the heart of any covenant which constitutes the "present" crisis which apocalyptic always describes. R.W. Funk sees a similar analysis of ambiguity in the New Testament, but in the imagery of the Kingdom which, in the gospels and in *Revelation*, has already arrived. In the unnoticed person of Jesus, the Kingdom come is a surprise, most of all because it has already been "here" for thirty-odd years. "...the ephemeral mustard plant is both a burlesque of, and serious satire on, the mighty cedar as a symbol of the Kingdom."[31] Nor does the present Kingdom clearly root out the ambiguity of continuing evil in continuing time—the time between the unnoticed and glorious comings, between Christ's resurrection and the Christian's universal resurrection of the body, between the possibility and necessity of interpretation and no more need to "interpret" as such. *Revelation* is, then, the apocalyptic text which attempts to address a specific readership which believes in the Kingdom come but waits for it to come again over an increasingly long period of time and in ever greater physical suffering. Its narrative fictions embody an aesthetic/spirituality which would teach its readers to unmask, in fact as in fiction, the whore whose name is "Mystery" with a mystery of their own. The whore's mystery is the easy way out; though it present itself as sophisticated and intellectually complex, it simply demands its votaries to accept the fact that materialistically determined time, in which evil is axiomatic, is the only human dimension. The mystery of *Apocalypse* is intellectually available to all people, but it presents itself as extremely difficult to adhere to; though a

    a) concern with the course of history and the last things
    b) the vision-audition of the revelatory secret either from God or from some "angelus interpres"
    c) interpretation of the secret *for* the reader
    d) expectation of a near end, which will be horrible and catastrophic
    e) paradisiacal salvation of those who keep faith
    f) concern for the ultimate fate of all people, even those outside the community
    g) revelation of a heavenly "history" which goes on simultaneously with but is hidden from earthly history and which will finally incorporate it
    h) a crucial mediator: Son of Man, Messiah, angel
    i) a state of glory revealed, in which those saved from death are, most often, as "the stars of heaven."

[31] *Ibid.*, p. 184.

mystery, it is only hidden, in a total way, behind the false self which inhibits conversion.[32] In the text's confrontation of ideologies, the mystery of the whore, which hides its perversity and sure violence under the guise of complexity, is represented as being doomed along with the physical death which its logic sees as so invincible. As one medieval commentator on *Apocalypse* writes, "Babylon ['Mysterium'], id est *confusio*"; the text, he says, points to "Jerusalem" (the *mysterium ecclesiae*) or *revelatio*.[33]

Before turning to the text itself, some brief mention of the differences between the genres of apocalyptic and prophecy seems in order. The two often occur together, as in *Ezechiel, Daniel* and *Apocalypse* itself. But prophecy is, above all else, speech; it presents itself as the transmission of God's will received in direct, spoken message. Apocalyptic, on the other hand, is the ritualization or conscious textualization (the letters to the seven Churches) of God's will received in indirect symbolic vision. As a more consciously literary statement, apocalyptic is an interpretation of the source rather than a direct utterance from the source. Rather than inviting another interpretation which descries the specific content of a specific future event, the more open-ended apocalyptic genre urges an interpretation which would reveal a more general outlook on the future because what is known of the end has definite implications for the present.[34] Quite logically, therefore, there arises a confusion over those prophetic or oracular utterances which refer to eschatological events. The paradigm for any post-New Testament prophecy, in a Christian sense, is that the irenic context of *Apocalypse* has turned its own violent, eschatological prophecies into the narrative of the victory's being won "now." The problem for a figure like Joachim of Flora (XII c., whom Dante praises as "di spirito profetico dotato") and for Dante himself is that all true Christian prophecy must be irenic as *Apocalypse* is irenic: which is to say it must be ecclesially oriented, prophecy for those who are still-struggling and imperfect. To lay total prophetic claim to the end, in the present, is millenialism: a form of literalism which led many early Church fathers to question or reject the canonical status of *Apocalypse*.[35] As we have already seen, millenialism is

---

[32] Northrop Frye applies similar distinctions to Blake in *Fearful Symmetry* (Boston, 1962), pp. 45ff.
[33] Haymo of Halberstadt, *Expositio in Apocalypsim*, in Migne, *PL* CXVII, col. 1144.
[34] See Klaus Koch, *The Rediscovery of Apocalyptic*, p. 47.
[35] Some of the Greek fathers, in particular, who had to contend with the excesses of such millenial sects as the Montanists, rejected the book of *Revelation*. Since they were also quite capable of making stylistic comparisons between *Revelation* and the Johan-

Apocalypse's falsely irenic twin; one looks very much like the other and to distinguish them often requires the most careful use of rhetoric. Even Paul seems to have met, initially, the same fate of being misappropriated as Joachim of Flora may have much later on. The Paul who added the totally novel word *eirene* to the ordinary Greek epistolary greeting (*charis*) sought to maintain the tension between "now" and "then."[36] G.F. Snyder has shown, however, that the letters to Corinth and Thessalonika try repeatedly to correct misunderstandings resulting from the "literalization" of Paul's irenic apocalyptic language. "They heard Paul say that the end is at hand. What Paul meant to say was: we can live in a community expecting the end."[37] The former is the language of prophecy; the latter, an irenic apocalypse.

In the notes on the text of *Apocalypse* which follow, it will be obvious to the reader that I have not attempted a scientific analysis which would reconstruct the text's historical contemporaneity; nor have I taken into account the many abstruse problems of symbology and numerology which have always made even the most gifted critics reluctant to engage in a line by line commentary.[38] Because my concern is the irenic apocalyptic tradition as it is alive for later literature, I will focus on the irenic imagery which seems to me to be central to the biblical text and try to understand the ways the later tradition received such imagery. The proper text for my consideration is the Vulgate. It is the language of the Vulgate, whatever its real inaccuracies, that becomes architectonic for writers in the West until the mid-Renaissance. It is the Vulgate's rhetoric that all the medieval expositions of apocalyptic meanings confront and gloss. If these medieval commentaries can be said to have a common denominator, it is their insistence that *Apocalypse* is, most of all, about the Church. As early as

---

nine gospel and "catholic" Epistle, they argued forcefully against apostolic attribution. The question of specific attribution still remains among scholars; but the Greeks have long since accepted the text into the canon. See "Apocalypse" in Vacant and Mangenot, *Dictionnaire de théologie catholique*, pp. 1467-70.

[36] For *eirene*, see Arndt and Gingrich, *A Greek-English Lexicon of the New Testament* (Cambridge, England, 1957), p. 226.

[37] "The Literalization of the Apocalyptic Form in the New Testament Church," *Biblical Research* 14 (1969), 17. In Thessalonika, for example, many in the community seem to have stopped working for a living. Snyder comments: "He [Paul] did believe reliance upon work was detrimental to anticipation of the Kingdom. He had to say both. The difficulty of his position was that he had to encourage them to work without denying his radically disjunctive eschatology" (p. 18).

[38] For a commentary which takes all modern linguistic and archeological scholarship into account, see the edition and commentary of J. Massygberde-Ford for the Anchor series of the Bible (New York, 1975) which concludes, incidentally, that the greatest part of the text is probably not Christian at all.

the Augustinian or pseudo-Augustinian "expositio," the commentator interprets the entire apocalyptic drama as taking place *in ecclesia*. The figure of John is read, in the "expositio," as Ecclesia; the woman "in the act of giving birth" is clearly a sign for "now": "...per omne tempus quotidie parit Ecclesia in prosperis et in adversis... semper enim in cruciatibus parit Ecclesia" ("...daily and throughout time, the Church gives birth whether in prosperity or in adversity... the Church is constantly experiencing the pangs of childbirth").[39] As the commentator suggests (and as we shall see), her birth pangs and postpartum exile in no way alter the sweetness of her act or the invincible innocence of the "new man" whom she has brought into being or the example of invincible innocence which the text repeatedly urges on its careful reader.

Irenic apocalyptic is present in the other genres which make up the earliest Christian "litterae." The well known *Shepherd of Hermas*, itself a kind of apocalypse for the community at Rome, is a second-century text in which beasts and temptresses are overcome by an ageless Lady Wisdom—surely the Ecclesia—who invites the visionary to an irenic life of sinlessness. The Lady, the first of many irenic Wisdom figures in Western literature, uses much the same kind of invitation (apocalyptic/irenic in its implication) as Beatrice would use against/for Dante much later: "Act like a man!"[40] In the lyric poetry of Prudentius, the whole burden of the lovely "hymnus ante somnum" is to convince the pious reader that even reclining to sleep at the end of a workday can be an imitation of the irenic dynamism of Christ's life and that of the saints. Prudentius' chief example is that of John in *Apocalypse*, whose irenic sleep produces the vision of the Lamb.[41]

---

[39] Augustine (attrib.), *In beati Ioanni Apocalypsis expositio*, in Migne, *PL* XXXV, col. 2434.
[40] *The Shepherd of Hermas*, ed. R. Joly, in *Sources Chrétiennes* 53 (Paris, 1958). See Dante, *Purgatorio* xxxi, 68.
[41] *Liber Cathemeron* VI, in *Corpus Christianorum* (series latina) CXXVI, 32.

2 Revelation: *The Text as Acceptable Sacrifice*

> Apocalypsis Iesu Christi, quam dedit illi Deus palam facere servis suis, quae oportet fieri cito: et significavit, mittens per angelum suum servo suo Iohanni, qui testimonium perhibuit verbo Dei, et testimonium Iesu Christi, quaecumque vidit. Beatus qui legit, et audit verba prophetiae huius: et servat ea, quae in ea scripta sunt: tempus enim prope est. (*Apoc.* 1.1-3)
>
> [The Revelation of Jesus Christ, which God gave to him to reveal openly to his servants, concerning that which will happen very soon: and he signified it, sending it by his angel to his servant John, who bore testimony to God's word, the very testimony of Jesus Christ, to whatever he saw. Blessed is he who reads and hears the words of this prophecy: and keeps to them, at the service of the things written herein: for the time is near.]

The prologue or epistolary greeting of *Apocalypse* sets up a chain of revelation from God to humanity: from the Father to the Logos and thence, through an angelic medium, to the servants of God in the *ecclesia* and, specifically, to John the "revelator." It is important to note that the seemingly missing term here, in view of much of the exegesis of later Christian writers, is the Spirit. The incarnate Logos is, in the text, the very possibility of interpretation of the mystery concerning Him which is to be shown. He is also the person who verifies or testifies for all attempts (however misdirected) at understanding it. His person is then both the content of the revelation and the reader's or hearer's most convincing witness to that content—as the rhetorical doubling of the Vulgate insists: "Apocalypsis *Iesu Christi*, quam dedit *illi* Deus palam facere servis suis..." A further doubling is even clearer. Christ is called the "testis fidelis" (1.5) and identified with a "testimonium Iesu Christi" (compare, "Apocalypsis Iesu Christi") the very testimony which John's "testimonium... verbo

Dei" seeks to reflect and communicate by textually anchoring his written word to the unwritten Word, his unbloody witness to that bloody act of witnessing by which the Logos lays claim to being both "faithful and true" (3.14). But insofar as the Logos' signifying activity is a constant, dynamic presence for the community which is its object, there is a pneumatic link in the revelatory chain as well. The fact that the community is being continually filled with truth, as a result of its continual interpreting of the Logos' unique act of witnessing, is the Spirit's place in the text and in the hermeneutic model it offers. Grammatically, that presence is codified by the use of the present participle in sequence with a verb which indicates the Logos' completed act in time: "et significavit, mittens... servo suo Ioanni."[1] Further on in the text, John's particular interpretative moment will be said to have occurred when he was "in spiritu" ("en pneúmati," 1.10); the very notion of "testimonium" as an act of witnessing will be glossed pneumatically: "Testimonium enim Iesu est spiritus prophetiae" (19.10).

The book's representation of a procession of signifying and interpreting activity does not stop at the visionary but goes on to John's readers and to the hearers of the readings, whose interpretations can be just as "spiritual" and just as original (in terms of proximity to the source) as John's. The author underlines the point with the rhetorical formula of makarism: "Beatus, qui legit et audit verba prophetiae huius..." But the final words of the formula go further: "...et servat ea, quae in ea scripta sunt..." The text insists that the reader "keep to" its words not because they are absolutely final but precisely because they are, according to Matthias Rissi, "provisional and unprovable" words about the end, trustworthy only because of what the reader knows of their ultimate guarantor.[2] The reader's adherence to the particular way this revelation is expressed is, itself, a "testimonium" which shares the quality and, hence, the trustworthiness of Christ's testimony. If Christ's witnessing to the truth necessitated sacrificing

---

[1] For an example of what one very early commentator does with the pneumatic problem in *Apoc.* 1, see Primasius Hadrumetinus, *Commentarium in Apocalypsin*, in Migne, *PL* LXVIII, col. 796. Later on, Richard of St.-Victor will completely identify the Spirit's presence in the text with the fact that the text is for the churches. The letters, he says, are for the seven churches which are the seven "spiritus" already worshipping before the throne; these, in turn, are the seven gifts of the Holy Spirit given to preserve the churches in their present trials. See Richard's *In Apocalypsim libri septem*, in Migne, *PL* CXCVI, cols. 695-700. For a modern recapitulation of the idea, see the article on "Revelation" in Karl Rahner, *Sacramentum Mundi* (New York, 1968-70).

[2] Matthias Rissi, *The Future of the World* (Studies in Biblical Theology, second series, no. 23) (London, 1972), p. 25.

his life, the readers and hearers of the letters to the seven churches are confronted, in the reading act itself, with the necessity of their own martyrdom. A "martyr" means a "witness"; the Greek text has "mártys" for "testis" and "emartýrēsen" for "perhibuit testimonium." *Apocalypse* points out to its readership, therefore, that those of them who have been or will be physically killed are not the only true martyrs. Understanding the revelatory text and adhering to its expressed tension between warning and comfort are a "testimonium" or martyrdom which the reader, like the figure of John, can achieve while still physically alive. We have already noted that one of the ways Christianity became a capital crime was by its refusal to make the public gesture of an acceptable sacrifice; Christians refused (in Girard's terms) to play down the real difference between themselves and the society at large. To neutralize that difference by offering the holocaust of incense on Roman altars or by eating the meat of Roman blood sacrifices would have meant denying the uniqueness of their God's expiatory death. Rather than urge its readers to a falsely irenic and private faith in a context of outward conformity, or to a falsely apocalyptic hope for a militarily restored theocentric nation (characteristic of later Jewish apocalyptic), the Johannine text urges a physically broken and minority church to see itself and all its activities as living in imitation of a unique, acceptable sacrifice. Only Christ *had* to die violently. The physical violence imposed upon the martyrs by Rome (a violence which *Apocalypse* refers to in terms of total revulsion) is a gratuitous perfection of the mimetic conformity with Christ which already exists in the community insofar as its members constantly imitate—from the "death" of conversion to the selflessness of "serving" a privileged text—the one acceptable sacrifice. It is in this sense that John's text for the churches, selfless before and at the service of the vision it would represent, and the reader's reading of it, which must be at its service, are both imaged as acceptable sacrifices, "testimonia" of the spirit if not also of the body. Such a notion contradicts the long popular idea that physical martyrdom had to be replaced, for Christians, by an irenic equivalent, in the form of the monastic movement, only after the great persecutions had ended. Rather, to do a scientific *Rezeptionsgeschichte* of the letters to the seven churches would be to study the ways in which the concept of martyrdom connoted, along with its more obvious sense, a life of irenic patience, both before and after the cessation of physical persecution.

> Ego Ioannes frater vester, et particeps in tribulatione, et regno et patientia in Christo Iesu: fui in insula, quae appellatur Patmos, propter verbum Dei, et testimonium Iesu: fui in spiritu in dominica die, et audivi

post me vocem magnam tanquam tubae, dicentis: Quod vides, scribe in libro... (*Apoc.* 1.9-11)

The Vulgate is particularly precise in its use of the key word *patientia*. The Latin verb *patior* and its cognates express a variety of meanings associated with the ideas of suffering, undergoing, being afflicted with. In grammar, the "modus patiendi" or passive voice permits descriptions of most actions to be perceived as affecting a subject as well as being affected by a subject. As we shall note in a later chapter on Petrarch and Guillaume de St.-Thierry, it is this passive voice which figures so prominently in any rhetorical analysis of mystical or vision literature to the extent that it suggests an irenic mood made up of suffering and the root word's other principal sense: getting through, lasting, being firm and unyielding in the face of suffering. One quite negative connotation for *patientia* is extremely interesting in the context of the present study; it is a connotation of indolence or want of spirit, as in Tacitus' "in patientia firmitudinem simulans."[3] The very range of the word's usage seems to have recognized the danger of a falsely irenic "twin," a situation which looks like a real union of suffering and endurance but which is only timidity or evasion. Medieval commentators of *Apocalypse* are quick to note that the Vulgate places rhetorical stress on *patientia* by placing it after the two extreme terms of which it is the proposed resolution.[4] The situation of John and of the churches is precisely an irenic apocalypse, as we have defined the term: the simultaneous experience of peace and violence, of integration and disintegration. The text's structural representation of its own context might, then, be legitimately restructured in the following manner:

tribulatio	*patientia*	*regnum*
suffering →	patience	← blissful kingdom
(violence)	(endurance)	(peace)

Revelation's narration of the vision itself begins with the figure of John as an example of the manner in which interpretative activity can be an acceptable sacrifice. The identity is first established between John and every faithful reader; he is "frater vester" and finds himself in the same problematical situation as does his readership. "Frater," says Richard of St.-Victor, not "magister," because the text, which will be filled with so many figures of authority, does not wish to frighten

---

[3] See Lewis and Short. *A Latin Dictionary* (Oxford, 1907).
[4] Richard of St.-Victor, *In Apocalypsim*..., col. 703. See also Haymo of Halberstadt, *Expositio in Apocalypsim*, in Migne, *PL* CXVII, col. 949.

off the reader.⁵ Just as God's resting, in *Genesis*, from the labors of creation contains the idea that there is a divine activity of retrospection, admiration and blessing, in that moment of repose, so John's sabbath-repose in the penal colony at Patmos turns into an activity of discernment.⁶ But discernment or "diacritics" and the visionary text which becomes publicly available for other readers are the direct result of a sacrificial death. John's response to the blast of the trumpet is to turn around ("et conversus sum," 1.12) towards a vision which is, at first, unbearable. It "kills" him: "...cecidi ad pedes eius tanquam mortuus" (1.17). This first of many "doubles" in *Apocalypse* is a double *in bono*; it bloodlessly imitates the slaying of the Lamb, not to confuse the uniqueness of the Lamb's sacrifice in a violent way, but to be an irenic example of what Haymo of Halberstadt glosses as "mortification." "...quia electi imitantes vestigia passionis Christi etsi moriuntur mundo, vivunt tamen Deo."⁷ It is the saints' selfless dying to the world, recapitulated in John's literal conversion and falling down "dead," which is both violent and peaceful, an acceptable sacrifice because of the faithfulness of its imitation of the original sacrifice of Christ and also because it recognizes the differences between the two. It is a sacrificial death which results in a new life, indeed, a new identity. Haymo refers the reader to *Galatians* 2.19: "Christo confixus sum cruci. Vivo autem, iam non ego, vivit vero in me Christus."⁸ John is revived, in *Apocalypse*, by the touch of the one who was once dead and who is now alive, by the one who, in other words, passes on the possibility of experiencing the seemingly illogical movement from death to life.⁹ The exhortation to fearlessness, "Noli timere" (1.17), involves no naïve bravado but is logically consequent upon the new man's irenic endurance of both death and life as completely present to him. He is told to write what he sees, to offer the seflessness of his

---

⁵ Richard of St.-Victor, *In Apocalypsim...*, col. 703.
⁶ *Genesis* 1.31, 2.1-3: "God saw all he had made, and indeed it was very good... He rested on the seventh day after all the work he had been doing. God blessed the seventh day and made it holy, because on that day he had rested after all his work of creating." The neo-Platonic equivalent of this irenic combination of God's repose and activity is in Plotinus, *Enneads* V.8.8.: "Plato... represents the Creator as approving the work he has achieved: the intention is to make us feel the loveable beauty of the archetype and of the Divine Idea; for to admire a representation is to admire the original upon which it was made."
⁷ Haymo of Halberstadt, *Expositio...*, col. 959.
⁸ *Ibid.*, col. 959.
⁹ The Western church ritualized this "touch" of *Apoc.* 1.17 (common, as well, to apocalypses in *Isaiah* and *Daniel*) in its introit hymn for Easter Sunday: "Resurrexi, et adhuc tecum sum... posuisti super me manum tuam..." See *Liber Usualis* (Tournai, 1947), p. 778. The text in *Apocalypse* reads, "Et posuit dexteram suam super me..."

interpretative activity for the community's benefit, even though he is fully aware of the ways in which both he and his text, already victims *in bono*, will be repeatedly victimized *in malo*.

Most of the rewards which are promised to the faithful are examples of an apocalyptic accent on the supernumerary. Everything associated with the momentarily revealed kingdom of bliss is so "new" that it is beyond measure, beyond conceivable expectation. The saints will be given a new name (2.17) and a new song to sing (5.9); they will learn the Messiah's new name and the hidden identity of the New Jerusalem (3.12). That they will in every way be filled up is particularly evident in the book's many alimentary metaphors which culminate in the irenic meal of the Lamb. The just will eat from the tree of life (2.7), eat a hidden manna (2.17); the Laodiceans who wait for Him faithfully will eat with the Lord (3.20). It is evident that the intention behind any use of a particular food is a key to its superabundantly fulfilling quality. Just as eating manna (or the manna "hidden" until the final gathering of the twelve tribes) is giving thanks to God for mercies shown to the people, so, as we have already seen, eating food offered to idols ("idolothytes," 2.20) is failing to take seriously the crucial differences among many blood sacrifices. The former will be the food of a transformed, risen body; the latter pollutes the body and leads only to death. The principal punishment mentioned in the text is a "second death" (2.11); it is conceived of as an eternal incompleteness or lack of fulfillment in which the resurrected body is deprived of the total newness of bodily life which is its supernatural right.

The visionary scene at God's throne is one of constant *vigilia*, worship without cease: "et requiem non habebant die ac nocte dicentia: Sanctus, Sanctus, Sanctus..." (4.8). The liturgical character of the entire irenic frame into which the narration of apocalyptic violence is set has convinced a number of critics that *Revelation* is itself a liturgical text whose words attempt to associate the churches' communion meal with the heavenly banquet of the Lamb in which communication and communion are one and the same thing.[10] Were this the case, how-

---

[10] See, for example, Pierre Prigent, *Flash sur l'Apocalypse* (Paris-Neuchâtel, 1974), pp. 25-27, as well as his longer *Apocalypse et Liturgie*, Cahiers théologiques 52, Neuchâtel, 1964. In commenting on 4.8, Richard of St.-Victor contrasts the blissful "then" with the irenic "now" and points out their common denominator. "Quod autem dicit, non habebant requiem, minime designat laborem. Hoc est nimirum summe et perfecte quiescere a Creatoris pia laude numquam cessare... Et jam in via (licet tenuiter) praegustant coelestis harmoniae jucunditatem qua plenarie saturabuntur in patria." ("For when it says, 'they had no rest,' it hardly means physical labor. Never ceasing from giving fervent praise to the Creator is without doubt the highest and perfect repose... On the way home, they have a foretaste (albeit slightly) of the joyfulness of heavenly

ever, it would even strengthen our focus on the biblical text as an irenic expression of both fullness and lack. By the same vehicle—language—with which it opens up to a celestial liturgy occurring simultaneously with it, the text points out its lack and the fact that it, while anticipating a future which will have a constantly present "morning star" (2.28), must "now" wait for that star through a long and problematic night. The text requires the reader to notice, first of all, that the nature of keeping vigil is itself extremely ambiguous. The phrase which describes the saints' worship, "they had no rest by day or by night," is used as well to describe the painful fate of those who worship the beast of the sea (14.11). In a quite literal fashion, the only thing which waiting upon a false god can bring, in *Apocalypse*, is some unsatisfying embodiment of the terms of waiting itself—restlessness. In an essay entitled "Apocalissè e Insecuritas," Maurilio Adriani discusses the idea by comparing the stories of Penelope waiting for Ulysses and of the virgins who keep their lamps trimmed waiting for the bridegroom in *Matthew* 25.1-13.[11] Penelope at Ithaca fills up the weave of time cyclically, repeatedly doing and undoing the woof and warp of a problem which expects a solution in terms it already completely knows. Waiting upon the idol or fantasy which one represents to oneself can move, according to Adriani, from aporia (indecision) to aphasia (silence) to ataraxia (inaction). Aphasia, in particular, claims our attention in an essay about the literary contextualization of eschatological language. The disfunction, in some sense, of language's normal dialogical operation seems the inevitable result of defining a problem in a closed-ended fashion or of defining language itself, because of its self-referential or cyclical nature, as incapable of making phenomena satisfactorily "present."[12] The preparation of the wise virgins in the Gospel story, however, centers on a present which actually expects the totally new. Their symbolic/ritualistic waiting is not only structurally correct (both wise and foolish virgins have brought

---

harmony, with which they will be totally saturated once they arrive home.") See *In Apocalypsim...*, col. 752.

[11] In *Apocalisse e insecuritas*, ed. Enrico Castelli for *Archivio di Filosofia* (1954, II), pp. 21-33.

[12] Another difficulty, of course, is distinguishing such aphasia from the silence which is chosen precisely because it speaks eloquently to a given problem. The two can look as exactly alike as the two forms of *vigilia* or as two kinds of repose (*otium*) which will be discussed in a later chapter on Petrarch. In Dante, for example, the problem of aporia, rather than leading to paralysis, is acted upon by the poet's presenting in *Par.* xxxiii the conundrun of squaring the circle; the poetry would be interpreted even inasmuch as the problem is unsolvable. Logical impossibilities are, at the end of the *Paradiso*, possible fictions.

their lamps) but really adequate to the unpredictable nature of the bridegroom's coming. He comes in the middle of the night and it is because the wise virgins have oil to trim their lamps that they can lead him into the wedding hall, into the experience for which it is impossible to prepare.

The worship before the throne seems to be unbroken and beyond all problems. Yet, because the apocalyptic visionary observes that worship from the point of view of the still struggling community, it involves real crises.

> Quis est dignus aperire librum, et solvere signacula eius? Et nemo poterat, neque in coelo, neque in terra, neque subtus terram aperire librum... Et ego flebam multum, quoniam nemo dignus inventus est aperire librum... Et unus de senioribus dixit mihi: Ne fleveris: ecce vicit leo de tribu Iuda, radix David, aperire librum, et solvere septem signacula eius. (5.2-5)
>
> [Who is worthy to open the book and to break its seals? And no one could open the book, neither in heaven nor on earth nor under the earth... And I wept greatly, because no one was found worthy to open the book... And one of the elders said to me: Do not weep: behold the lion of the tribe of Judah, the root of David, has won the victory to open the book and to break its seals.]

The problem of who will break open the seven seals is simultaneously threatening (John weeps over it) and already solved.[13] The lion of Judah is announced as having already conquered (past tense: *vicit*) in a way which is definitive; the irenic covenant, in the frame vision of *Apocalypse*, has already been established. To look at this notion in a somewhat different context, we might say that what can only happen at the end of Shakespeare's history plays—the return of peace and reordering of society by means of the prince's words—happens in both the beginning and end of *Apocalypse* and sets the determining mood for the entire narrative. The paradox of all irenic apocalyptic literature—a paradox it shares with liturgical literature—is that the moment of dramatic catharsis is simultaneous with the moment of covenanting or reintegration. Even before the victorious appearance of the lion of Judah, the throne has been described as surrounded by a rainbow (*Iris*, 4.3), the sign of God's covenant with the chosen people which first appeared at the end of the crisis of the flood in *Genesis*. For René Girard, that rainbow of peace between Noah and

---

[13] The crisis is, in other words, ritualized. A similar ritual moment occurs in *Purg*. viii, where Dante images a serpent threatening souls about to rest for the night; the serpent is immediately thwarted by two guardian angels. The entire scene, down to a multitude of the smallest verbal details, is Dante's dramatization of all the key parts of the liturgical hour of Compline.

Yahweh signals not only "...la résolution de la crise" but also, after the apocalyptic violence of the flood which erased all real differences, "le retour de la différenciation."[14] In *Apocalypse*, the crisis is certainly resolved, but what particular act of clarification or "differentiation" is there? The text's answer is to make it dramatically evident that the crisis was resolved in a way which the reader least expected. After leading the reader to expect a lion, it is a lamb, mortally wounded, which appears to break open the seals: "Agnum stantem tanquam occisum..." (5.6).[15] The new covenant is clarified not as the work of a militaristic Messiah but of a God who is at the same time the most vulnerable of men. Haymo of Halberstadt's gloss on the rainbow around the throne is clearest of all, in spite of (or because of) his fanciful logic. He takes the Greek accusative of *iris, irin*; just add one more sound, he says, and you get "*irini*" (*eirēnē*) or "pax."[16] He explains that this literally "irenic" vision of the Lamb before the throne shows how the peace of universal propitiation came about. It happened because the divine nature ("sol") entered into or shone on human nature ("nubes imbrifera") and produced the new marvel of propitiation, the rainbow of Incarnation.[17]

Irenic abundance is, perhaps, most evident in the book's image of the final gathering of the saints. The "144,000 sealed" (7.4) is certainly a complete number, the number of all of Israel's tribes. But following quickly upon them into the kingdom is the far more ambiguous "turbam magnam, quam dinumerare nemo poterat ex omnibus gentibus, et tribubus, et populis, et linguis, stantes ante thronum..." (7.9). The impossibility of an expression adequate to the supernumerary results in the list of generic synonyms which is logically without end. The list in 7.9 could have just as well included *et verbis*; Rabelais, more than any other writer in the irenic mode, carried the notion to its rhetorical consequences. One group which is singled out from among the immense gathering is the company of martyrs already physically killed and waiting under the celestial altar. Their request to be avenged is responded to irenically, at least insofar as they are told to rest ("dictum est illis ut requiescerent," 6.11) and to wait upon the accomplishment of other good works which will mean martyrdom for others

---

[14] "Les Malédictions contre les Pharisiens et la Révélation évangélique," *Bulletin du Centre Protestant d'Etudes* 3 (June, 1975), 6.
[15] Says Richard of St.-Victor, *In Apocalypsim*..., col. 756, "Leo est magnus, agnus est parvus... leo per potentiam majestatis: agnus per mansuetudinem."
[16] *Expositio*..., col. 1006.
[17] *Ibid.*, col. 1005. Haymo recapitulates in more general terms in col. 1060: "...et sol iustitiae carnem assumpsit, reconciliatio facta est mundo."

who will perform them. The text would seem to emphasize here that blood vengeance, if it can be a divine act, is always the wrong act for humans. By pointing instead toward the suffering of believers who do no violence and whose acts continue to bring about the advent of a final, divine justice, *Apocalypse* distances itself from any rhetorical assumption of the world's falsely irenic desire for "just" satisfaction. As Girard puts it, referring to the New Testament as a whole: "Loin de prendre la violence collective à son compte, le texte la rejette sur les vrais responsables."[18]

The opening of the seventh seal introduces image upon image of violence and torture for which the whole book and the word "apocalyptic" have become well-enough known. Yet the first thing mentioned in the text is a silence of "almost half an hour" (8.1). Many medieval commentators agree on this moment as an entrance, in time and only for a time, into the heavenly contemplation which goes beyond any functions of language.[19] It is an irenic moment, as is the penultimate experience of the seventh seal when John (like Ezechiel in the Old Testament) is asked to eat the substance of his own revelation.

> Et accepi librum de manu angeli, et devoravi illum: et erat in ore meo tanquam mel dulce, et cum devorassem eum, amaricatus est venter meus: et dixit mihi: Oportet te iterum prophetare gentibus... (10.10-11)
>
> [And I received the book from the angel's hand and I devoured it: and it was sweet as honey in my mouth, and when I had eaten it my stomach was embittered: and the angel said to me: It is necessary that you prophecy again to the nations...]

For the writer to eat, in a way which will be finally nourishing, is to share in the acceptable sacrifice of the Logos. In irenic enjoyment of both the power to reveal and the content of that revelation, John must also accept the apocalyptic consequences of ingesting and fully digesting God's word. For sweetness to turn to bitterness in the stomach is for John's problem (and the reader's) to be frighteningly reconstituted at the very centre of the experience of nourishment; it is reconstituted in the commission to preach a private revelation publicly: where misinterpretation is usual, where the ambiguity of language is

---

[18] "Les Malédictions...," *op. cit.*, pp. 14-15. Bernard of Clairvaux reads the slain martyrs under the altar in a completely irenic fashion when he assigns to their "requiescere" the words of the secure soul's sleep in the Lord, the Compline *Ps.* 4.9: "in pace in idipsum dormiam et requiescam." The line and the situation in *Apocalypse* which it glosses recall other citations from the psalm: "Irascimini et nolite peccare... Sacrificate sacrificium iustitiae" (*Ps.* 4.5-6). See *De Diligendo Deo*, in Migne, *PL* CLXXXIII, col. 464.

[19] See, for example, Haymo, *Expositio...*, col. 1044: "...*aliquid* de superna quiete percipit" (italics mine).

most sorely trying, and where language can be easily appropriated, perverted from its original ends. Words are always bitter-sweet, says Richard of St.-Victor, because they must be put into action.[20] Immediately after John's eating, there follows in the narrative a prophecy of "two witnesses" (11.3) who will preach and who will be killed for the powerful ways in which they use language. Lest the reader miss the connection between all faithful acts of witnessing and the sacrifice of the Logos, the prophecy concludes: "Et corpora eorum iacebunt in plateis civitatis magnae, quae vocatur spiritualiter Sodoma, et Aegyptus, ubi et Dominus eorum crucifixus est" (11.8). They, too, will be raised on the third day.

In *Apocalypse*, the faithfully spoken or written or read word entails suffering and selflessness, even when initially experienced as joyful or satisfying. Rupert of Deutz collates the story of John's eating with that of the apocalyptic whore in *Isaiah* 23.16 in order to provide an adequate description of anyone who appropriates the word to "sing" the self, to call the self to mind, rather than to point to the other. In doing so, Rupert provides a most powerful image of the falsely irenic "twin" which is mimetic of the structure of irenic apocalypse but lacks its substance. He refers, he says, to those who have accepted the "philosophia huius mundi."

> De talium sapientia dicitur in Isaia sub specie meretricis: "Sume citheram, circui civitatem, meretrix oblivioni tradita. Bene cani, frequanta canticum, ut memoria tui sit"... Nam et idcirco meretrix, idcirco oblivioni tradita est, quia canit non ut Dei sed ut suimet memoria sit. Et hujus quidem cantilena nunc interim *et in ore et in ventre suo* dulcis est tamquam mel—"favus" enim "distillans labia meretricis"—sed postmodum in fel aspidum convertitur ei.[21]

> [Of such people Wisdom speaks in *Isaiah* in the figure of the whore: "Take up a harp, go about the city, you whore, abandoned to oblivion. Sing well, repeat your song so that it may be a memorial to yourself"... Now concerning the whore and concerning her being abandoned to oblivion: (it is so) because she sings a memorial to herself and not to God. And though this ditty is sweet both in her mouth and in her stomach the while—"a dripping honeycomb are the lips of a whore"— afterwards it turns into a viper's poison for her.]

Rupert is equally insightful in his notes on the command to John to measure God's temple (11.1-2). To the extent that the sacrificial text is for others rather than for the self, it becomes authoritative and worthy of imitation. Rupert reads the "calamus" with which John is to

---

[20] *In Apocalypsim...*, col. 791.
[21] Rupert of Deutz, *De operibus Spiritus Sancti* (tome II), IV.13, in *Sources Chrétiennes* 165, 1685 B, C (italics mine).

measure the temple as the text of *Apocalypse* itself. It has become the standard of measurement with which the edifice, both external and internal, of an individual's covenant can be tested.

> ...postmodum quippe ab exilio revocatus, et viva voce rursum Evangelium praedicavit, et calamo scripsit, metiendo "templum Dei et altare et adorantes in eo," quia videlicet in verbo Evangelii corda singulorum qui per fidem sunt templum Dei, in quibus Christus ipse "per" eadem "fidem inhabitans" altare est, quasi metiendo determinantur.[22]
>
> [...later, clearly, returned from exile, he preached the Gospel again publicly, he wrote with a pen (*calamo*), measuring "God's temple, altar and the worshippers therein," for obviously it is according to the Gospel-word that the hearts of the individuals who are God's temple by faith are, as if by measuring, tested—the hearts of those in whom Christ himself, "indwelling by that same faith," is the altar.]

Not only is *Apocalypse*, in other words, an ascetic text, but its ascesis becomes the aesthetic—by means of words and images—to which the reader must calibrate his reading, his words, and his life if he is to make an acceptable sacrifice, if he is, therefore, to *know* apocalypse as irenic. It is a terribly large claim for any written text to make. But that which Enrico Castelli terms the "insecuritas" of the world of images is the problem which most insistently urges people to interpret, to orient themselves with respect to the multiplicity of relations of which words and all signs tell them.[23] For the author of *Apocalypse* to ask that the sacrifice which is his text be "kept to" (*servare*) in the sacrifice which is any faithful reading of it, is a very pointed case of the general notion (so important in Book XI of Augustine's *Confessions*) that "insecuritas" or doubt—if not turned into despair or complacency—is (for good or for ill) the same as the attention toward or waiting upon (*vigilia*) the real which is constitutive of one's very experience of time. When one interprets signs, orienting oneself in some definitive way, one's reading becomes the more crucial because it is then constitutive of one's personal history and of the way that history effects other unique histories.

The woman "clothed with the sun" (12.1) is in a situation so analogous to that of the seven churches that it would be needless to demonstrate at length the univocal reception of her as an ecclesial figure in the exegetical tradition. But it is important for our purposes to note that hers is the irenic apocalyptic experience, as the first chapter of *Revelation* conceives of it: "in tribulatio, et regno, et patientia."

---

[22] *Ibid.*, IV.11, 1683A.
[23] "Premessa" to *Apocalisse e insecuritas*, for *Archivio di Filosofia* II (1954), pp. 3-5.

34   *Irenic Apocalypse*

> clamabat parturiens et cruciabatur ut pariat
> ....
> et draco stetit ante mulierem, quae erat paritura:
> ut cum peperisset, filium eius devoraret. (12.2, 4)

[she cried out giving birth, she suffered that she might give birth... and the dragon stood before the woman who was just about to give birth: so that when she delivered he might devour her son.]

The rhetoric here, especially the use of the future participle (*paritura*), focuses on the moment of birth as exact midpoint between the terrible pain of labor and the joy of seeing (despite the draconic presence which threatens to intervene) a reigning king come into the world. Richard of St.-Victor remarks that the dragon wishes to devour this newborn infant because every good work being worked through is apt to be mistook, misappropriated "instantaneously," before its natural evolution is accomplished and it can be a really "saving" work.[24] Even though "the rest of her seed" (12.17) will have to endure a physical persecution that cannot be eluded, the woman retreats from the dragon into a solitary "desert" (12.14) which is, paradoxically, full of nourishment.

> ...et mulier fugit in solitudinem ubi habebat locum paratum a Deo, ut ibi pascant eam diebus mille ducentis sexaginta. (12.6)
>
> [...and the woman fled into solitude where she has a place prepared by God, that she might be fed there for 1,260 days.]

In what is one of the earliest texts for the debate between the active and contemplative lives, the irenic center of the community's experience is preserved here in the midst of outward torment.[25] Feeding for a time in a "locum paratum" must remind us of the pastoral genre and of all the ambiguous language of false peace so often associated with it. The pastoral flock can either be "innocent" of any genuine problem or doomed, in its closed-ended world, to endless feeding on the problem of self-referentiality; or, as in *Apocalypse*, its solitary wandering can truly nourish because it involves the same kind of sacrifice as that of the "Lamb which was slain." Part of the purpose of Petrarch's *De Vita Solitaria*, to be discussed in a later chapter, is to explore

---

[24] *In Apocalypsim*..., col. 800. Haymo of Halberstadt makes the ecclesial application of this idea when he says that, "now," the church gives birth to saving works "every day" (*quotidie*). *Expositio*..., col. 1082.

[25] An earlier model for the text seems to be the flight of the bride into the garden of nut trees in *Cant* 6.10. See André Feuillet, "Le Cantique des cantiques et l'Apocalypse," *Recherches de Science Réligieuse* 49 (1961), 321-53, especially 335ff.

the thin but important lines which separate these possibilities one from another.

In the latter third of the text, as the crisis of the final time comes closer in the eschatological narrative, the number of seductive "doubles" increases. The beast of the land is especially insidious because of the similarity of his mediation to that of the Lamb. The literary vehicle is parody and it is used to set in relief the extent to which signs can look alike and their contents be radically different. "Et vidi aliam bestiam ascendentem de terra, et habebat cornua duo similia Agni..." (13.11). The beast looks like a lamb but speaks like a dragon; it works miracles; it is specifically deceptive ("Et seduxit habitantes in terra...," 13.14); its votaries are marked with the mark of the beast rather than with the blood of the Lamb. In a terrifying reversal of the typology of Passover, those who *are* marked with paschal blood will be killed by the beast.[26] Perhaps most problematical of all, the beast of the land mimes the selflessness of the Logos' constant pointing to the Father by putting all its eloquence and wonder-working at the service of its master, the beast of the sea. In a similar fashion, the harlot Babylon/Rome is a debased double of God's city, Jerusalem, in two principal respects. Jerusalem is, first of all, the only eschatological city because it is the site of both old and new covenants and, as *typus ecclesiae*, the "place" where irenic *patientia* is in the process of building a lasting *regnum* out of its own *tribulatio*. But the harlot is characterized as reading the city's irenic suffering as if it were actually what it is most evidently: total defeat and powerlessness. She celebrates a triumph of her own city by parodying Old Testament language about the chosen city's suffering. Whereas Jeremiah had said: "Quomodo sedet sola civitas plena populo: facta est quasi vidua domina gentium" (*Lam.* 1.1), the harlot says: "Sedeo regina: et vidua non sum: et luctum non videbo" (18.7). She is an anti-Jerusalem in a second sense. Whereas Jerusalem is the city where the most crucial "commercium" has taken place and still takes place—the "commerce" between God and humanity, an economy opened to all by the "exchange" of the Incarnation—all the merchants and shipmasters of Babylon are engaged in the conspicuous consumption of a long list of sensual delights which includes "the souls of men" (18.13). Rather than drinking the blood of the Lamb irenically, their peace is to drink the wine of the harlot's

---

[26] They are also, because they lack the beast's mark 666, forbidden to buy and sell. What some critics see as "an economic boycott against Christians" (*Oxford Annotated Bible*) is, as well, a withering comment on what the bestial sign really validates: business and not salvation or "salvation" by the false emperor-god's face stamped on Roman coinage.

fornication (18.3) which is, in all senses, their illicit commerce with her.

Each of the saints' eternal rewards is portrayed as partially available to them "now" because of the irenic point of view which they patiently maintain: "...quoniam servasti verbum patientiae meae..." (3.10). They have, in other words, not given ground either to the despair of utter "tribulatio" or to the soporific of an easily grasped "regnum." In its realistic attitude toward the necessity of linguistic mediation, *Apocalypse* urges adherence to a *"verbum* patientiae meae," to the selfless manipulation of signs which are neither completely revelatory nor powerless to reveal but which reveal in part. When an "eternal Gospel" (14.6) is promised the saints, therefore, it would be inconsistent with the logic of *Revelation* to think of that Gospel as a totally different "book" from the New Testament *evangelia*. But how is the newness of an eternal Gospel available "now" and how can it be consonant with John's strict warning not to add or take away anything at all from his own book (22.18-19)? *Apocalypse* seems to be especially anxious that the structure of revelation as received not be capriciously or idiosyncratically fragmented. As an interpretation in the present tense ("Ego Ioannes [sum] frater vester...," 1.9), it offers to the future the terms of a problem, already re-viewed irenically, as the only terms which maintain the problem's integrity and which, therefore, ought to be interpreted anew. Only after the reader has attempted to receive the text on its own terms—answering sacrifice with sacrifice, patiently "serving the word of its patience"—can he work toward an interpretation which is idiosyncratic in an authentic way and not mere solipsism. As it is most clearly analyzed in the medieval exegetical tradition, it is the reader's faithful act of reading (not the content of a specific interpretation), necessarily involving his unique history and secret "commerce" with the Word, which "tastes beforehand" and therefore shares something of the nature of the *Evangelium aeternum*. The *Apocalypse*, faithful to the text/vision which it represents, sacrifices itself to obtain the benefits of the "new" Gospel of which it is a necessary structural part. If the word is not to be only a cipher applied, it must be, as well, a gesture offered at a personal sacrifice and because of a communal affirmation. I sacrifice, according to *Apocalypse*, my limited control over the signifier for the benefit of its future as text by simultaneously requiring that my gesture be received and known for what it is and by allowing this gesture to be interpreted as another will interpret it. The New Testament "evangelia" are, therefore, in the process of become the "Evangelium aeternum" or heaven's gospel, in which all lack will be filled up and the necessity of narration will cease.[27] Henri de Lubac describes with great care the way medieval interpreters approach the New Testament, their own writings, and the "eternal gospel." The faithful reading even knows a superabundance or fulfillment "now."

> Le sens spirituel, dans sa teneur authentique, est véritablement un "sens plenier"... C'est Lui [the Spirit] qui donne au Chrétien lisant l'écriture "ea quae sunt plenitudinis sentienda"; Lui qui introduit "à la plénitude évangélique, à cette "plénitude du Verbe" que St. Grégoire distingue de la simple "plénitude du livre," comme objet non d'une science morte mais d'une vivante intelligence.[28] C'est tout le Nouveau Testament, compris comme le déroulement intégral de l'économie chrétienne jusqu'au dernier jour, qui lui [the interpreter] apparaît encore comme orienté vers une réalité qu'elle [the interpreter's reading] *a charge de signifier en la préparant*, servant ainsi d'intermédiaire entre la loi ancienne et "l'Evangile éternel."[29]

After the final destruction of Satan, the world as a conceivable world, our world, is no more. The pantokrator says: "Ecce nova facio omnia" (21.5). But the new is also in some sense analogous to the old, the filling up and perfection of the old. Because it is sung by the saints in celebration of the final disappearance of evil, the old song of Moses can now be called the "song of the Lamb" (15.3). The female figure of the church is no longer escaping into a desert to save her life; now, she is "paratam, sicut sponsam ornatam viro suo" (22.2), entering the city where she may "accipiat aquam vitae, gratis" (22.17). The revelatory book itself, which has been in a constant situation of vigil, waking through the night's terrors in endurance and anticipation, now ends with the advent of a "stella splendida et matutina" (22.16) and of a city in which there will be no night at all (21.25). A thousand-year binding of Satan, however, is described and ritualized in *Apocalypse* as preceding the end. The binding and the "millenial" hope which has always been read in it are an attempt at realizing "now" that the unimaginable freedom of "then" is, in part, defined by the possibilities of present "free" action—which is to say, of irenic action. In a world inevitably

---

[27] Ernst Käsemann sees the eternal gospel very much in terms of its function "now" as irenic narration, rather than of its indescribable function "then." The eternal gospel announced in *Apocalypse* is the necessity of a continual narration which represents, vis-à-vis the New Testament "evangelia," what the gospel narratives represent vis-à-vis the primitive Kerygma which is, according to G. Ebeling, "a manifold interpretation from the start." See Robert Funk, ed., *Apocalyptic*, in *Journal for Theology and the Church*, no. 6 (New York, 1969), pp. 34 and 49. The problem in not striking a balance between "now" and "then" is, as in so many heterodox appropriations of the eternal gospel, to look for the New Testament to be surpassed in its authority by some other "book."

[28] *Exégèse médiévale*, pt. I, vol. 1 (Paris/Ligugé, 1959-64), p. 358.

[29] *Histoire et esprit* (Paris/Ligugé, 1950), p. 217.

filled with satanic violence, such a momentary foretaste is not only irenic in a strict sense but also, perhaps, one of the most human, sympathetic moments in the text. The millenium seeks to convince the saints that they can act differently, in a significant way, from the merchants who willingly fornicate with Babylon/Rome. Indeed, a ritual binding seems necessary *because* the saints are so close to being the same as the merchants. Both their desires for the "happy life" (to use Augustine's deliberately ambiguous phrase) are as alike as they are different, because both groups live in the same suffering world. The binding must be seen as but one part of an immensely complex process of differentiation, along with oaths, taboos, and special forms of piety, which *Apocalypse* enjoins. It shows that the miraculous, the new and the unforeseen can be the objects of a human hope based in the real, even in that reality which will (Satan will again be loosed "modico tempore," 20.3) resist and erode the creativity of such hope with respect to its manifestations in time and in material things. A thousand-year binding of Satan is really, in terms of the way one medieval critic has read the entire book, the freedom, at the least, not to have good actions be immediately devoured by evil. For Richard of St.-Victor, the thousand years is however long it takes the saints to become saints, for their action to bear irenic fruit: "Tanto ergo tempore Satanas ligatur, quanto justorum perfectio consummatur."[30] The Old Testament type, the "thousand year" day of Yahweh in *Psalms* 90.4, specifically compares the millenial moment to the *vigilia* of a single night.[31]

The question of millenium is a thorny one theologically and historically for it clearly represents some kind of rule of the just in time and is narrated in a book which seeks, to a certain extent, to collapse the distance between "now" and "then."[32] The formation of powerful spiritual institutions rather than powerless ones seems the most egregious human error in the history of millenialism. The powerless

---

[30] *In Apocalypsim...*, *op. cit.*, col. 854. Richard seems to refer, as well, to 22.11-12, "...et sanctus, sanctificetur adhuc. Ecce venio cito, et merces mea mecum est, reddere unicuique secundum opera sua."
[31]   Quoniam mille anni ante oculos tuos
         Tanquam dies hesterna quae praeteriit,
         Et custodia in nocte;
                    (*Ps.* 90.4)
[32] As Richard characterizes the treatment of time in *Revelation*: "...quia et praesentia cito discedunt, et futura cito succedunt." *Ibid.*, col. 694. According to Pierre Prigent, *Flash sur l'Apocalypse* (Paris/Neuchâtel, 1974), pp. 101-02, "Maranatha" (22.20) is a grammatical pun in Aramaic. In the written text, without any verbal stress, it can either mean Come! Lord (imperative: "marana/-tha") or The Lord is come! (indicative, perfect tense: "maran/-atha").

model is closest to the Old and New Testament types which culminate in *Apocalypse* 20.7-10 with the helpless but ultimately victorious encampments of Israel against the armies of Gog and Magog, of the new church against Rome's empire. Jaroslav Pelikan points out another side of the problem which was particularly acute for third-century believers who expected an immediate millenium. The extreme position was that of the Montanists and, later, the Donatists whose millenial church had to be, necessarily, sinless.[33] Augustine argues, instead, for an irenic church, one in which the converted soul gains a type of earthly paradise but is not sealed off from the world's evil, one in which the church's perfections and lacks would co-exist until the second coming. Millenium is, then, identifiable with irenic apocalypse as long as the "problem" remains, not in secret but out in the open. Falsely irenic misappropriation occurs when absolute perfection is seen to take place in time, usually in terms of some secret revelation; the perfect state can be fleshed out, quite juridically, in advance, because it is already known and does not wait upon unexpected transformations which are the true millenial possibilities in *Apocalypse*. It is for this reason that Origen equates the millenialist fallacy with the fallacy of literalism. He calls those who seek to achieve in time the delights of the resurrected life "solius litterae discipuli."[34]

Apocalypse ends with the simultaneity of the Lamb's wedding feast taking place in Paradise and of the New Jerusalem descending in very close focus on earth. It is evident that Paradise is being accomplished in the "body" of all the nations as well as in the personal body which will be raised, restored to psychosomatic wholeness, and remade anew on the last day. Though the lack of a temple in the New Jerusalem looks proleptically for the time when the mediation of human language will be unnecessary, the text has spoken clearly enough on the subject. The Lamb which was slain as an innocent victim of violence inaugurates a culture—in *Apocalypse*, a readership—which accepts the irenic meal/sacrifice as the Lamb's definitive self-revelation for them. In doing so, they are asked, as well, to accept the text's sacrificial hermeneutic as their own.

---

[33] See Pelikan's *The Finality of Jesus Christ in an Age of Universal History*, Ecumenical Studies in History 3 (Richmond, Virginia, 1966), chapters 3 and 4.
[34] See H. de Lubac, *Histoire et esprit, op. cit.*, p. 103. For Augustine's idea of millenium, see *De Civitate Dei* XX.8.1.

3   Learning to Read Irenically

> Every loving act of definition reverses the retreat of attention to the word and returns it to the world.
> William Gass, *On Being Blue*

The title is intentionally clumsy. But the "parts of speech," as linguistic structures, were taken seriously enough by medieval writers so that coupling an isolated participle with another verb (specifically described but expressed "infinitely") could be seen as a very limited context for what we commonly call meaning. The word "learning" is both artificial and contingent for most medieval thinkers; it exists merely to permit humans to indicate a concept, itself contingent but readily experienced in a particular act of cognition. According to the grammatical logic of the participle, "learning" indicates *this* act going on, in process. Much more complex contexts commonly occur in spoken and written language; phrases become sentences. The severely restricted title of this chapter would question many modern critics, including literary critics who examine language exquisitely contextualized, for taking up Ockham's Razor against the revelatory possibilities of grammar, syntax and rhetoric on behalf of a scientific nominalism divorced (as Ockham's was not) from a language which insists on the necessity of expressing that which is experienced as completely inexpressible and, simultaneously, as never fully expressed. The closed system of signifiers which the structuralist analysis sees as a given text does not exhaust what can be called a process of signification for which that system, properly applied, might help constitute the legitimate hermeneutic boundaries. Interpretation and signification, as reciprocal processes, are neither "materially" nor "spiritually" determined, neither, that is, determined by the linguistic structures which initiate them nor by a totally subjective inspiration; yet they involve (for medieval critics and for some contemporary critics) both nature and spirit.

Dante, in comparing his pilgrim to Narcissus in the third canto of the *Paradiso,* sets this problem in extreme relief. Poetic language in the *Paradiso* characterizes itself as being in the extreme, the uncommon situation of moving further and further away from nature, from any thing of which language attempts to proffer an experience.

> e io, per confessar corretto e certo
> me stesso, tanto quanto si convenne
> leva' il capo a proferer più erto;
> ma visïone apparve che ritenne
> a sé me tanto stretto, per vedersi,
> che di mia confession non mi sovenne.
> (*Paradiso* iii.4-9)

[and I, to confess myself corrected, reassured, raised my head as much as was meet for speaking out; but a sight appeared which held me to itself so tightly so to see it, that I remembered none of my confession.]

The ordinary uses of language are befuddled as never before and Dante, confronted here with a new "vision" to interpret—signifiers whose power to signify seems extraordinarily weak—falls into a very specific philosophical error: "per ch'io dentro a l'error contrario corsi / a quel ch'accese amor tra l'omo e 'l fonte" (ll. 17-18) ("At which I ran to the opposite error from the error which ignited love between the man and the fount"). The extreme terms of this "errore" are radical realism and radical nominalism. Dante-pilgrim, who is a poet and therefore wise to words as fictions, makes the nominalist mistake; whereas Narcissus had totally identified the reflection in the fountain (the signifier) with a "real" signified and desired it as such, Dante turns away fron the signifiers before him as mere reflections because he presumes a different "ground" for (the) meaning. Narcissus is drowned; Dante sees nothing: "e nulla vidi..." (1.22). Both the theories of language as totally alienated from true meaning and of language as completely, ultimately narcissistically claiming it are dead ends. Beatrice, redirecting the poet's gaze towards the vague faces which have appeared, corrects his error with a philosophical assertion about the general nature of "signifiers signifying" in the order of being.

> *vere sustanze* son *ciò* che tu vedi
> (l. 29, emphasis mine)

[*that* which you see are *real things*]

The singular "ciò" stresses the collective or general *act* of signification for which Beatrice—we might call her a moderate realist—here claims ontic status. Signs, metaphors (still less the terminology of medieval metaphysics) are not that which they signify, but, for Dante, their acts of indicating (their *ens qua verbum*) are "vere sustanze." Language is no more, but no less, than that. Meaning then, even in this fiction's extraordinary situation of moving beyond the sphere of the moon, is not to be found only within language or only behind language but through linguistic *acts* themselves; Dante will "speak with, hear and believe" (1.31) the signs presented to him (they turn out to be saints) because they are—even inasmuch as they are fictive moments vis-à-vis the pilgrim's journey and fictions vis-à-vis the poet's text—the only "real things" he has.[1] But the first move of Dante's eyes, away from a nothing or an absence which must finally alienate, is to the light of Beatrice's eyes. Beatrice, returned to her lover in *Purgatorio* and specifically represented there as both an exemplary and idiosyncratic Christ-event in the life of the poet-pilgrim, here concatenates two of the most important theological images for the Christ in order to reassure Dante that the world of signs and signifying activity cannot finally be alienating, that interpretation itself is not only possible but salutary.[2] The incarnate God as both Logos and Phos (Word and Light) is the crucial mediate term for Christian history. Beatrice, whom Dante learns (in *Purgatorio* xxx-xxxi) to read in terms of that history, participates as word and light in Christ and is the crucial mediate term in Dante's history; by a logic of participation which Beatrice has already defined as ontological, Dante must now learn to read these new signs in the heaven of the moon in terms of his unique history which is still in process. These signifiers—they are both lights and words ("qui rilegate...," l. 30, "bound up" at this place in the book of the universe) —will be crucial mediate terms for *this* point in his journey. Interpreting them is by no means easy for Dante, and their act of signification readily falls away from his experience of it, "come per acqua cupa cosa grave" (l. 123) ("like a heavy thing [disap-

---

[1] As Augustine simply put it in *De Doctrina Christiana* XI (Migne, *PL* XXXIV, col. 100): "...bonorumque ingeniorum insignis est indoles, in verbis verum amare, non verba." ("...it is a notable habit of people who are both intelligent and good that they love the truth in words, not the words themselves"). All translations, including those from Dante's text, are my own.

[2] On the theological senses of Beatrice's coming at the end of the *Purgatorio*, see Charles Singleton, *Dante Studies 2: Journey to Beatrice* (Cambridge, Mass., 1967); see also my article "Dante as a Poet-Theologian," *Dante Studies* 89 (1971), 61-72. An excellent summary of the Athanasian metaphor of light, so important to both eastern and western Christology, is Jaroslav Pelikan's *The Light of the World* (New York, 1962).

pears] in dark water"). But because that act really exists in the order of being ("come... *cosa*" is the simile the poet uses), it participates as an illucidating word, however tenuously, in the act of the Christ who does not permit any proferred word-light not to signify. Such is Beatrice's conclusion:

> Però parla con esse e odi e credi;
> ché la verace luce che le appaga
> da sé non lascia lor torcer li piedi.
> (ll. 31-33)

[So speak with them, and listen and believe; for the true light which fulfills them does not permit them to stray from Itself.]

My purpose in this chapter is to demonstrate that the acts of signification and interpretation are, for Dante, processes characterized by a simultaneity of irenic and apocalyptic elements. Though these elements so dominate the poem structurally (from *Purgatorio* xxvii through the *Paradiso*) as to warrant the description of a new genre, our understanding of them must take into account not only grammatical and rhetorical structures but also "structuring": the text's account of its own context or, to paraphrase Renato Poggioli, *the* theory alleged for *this* avant-garde. A point elaborated in the first chapter is worth recalling here: that which we term "aesthetics" is analogous to "spirituality" for the Christian Middle Ages; for the specific context of those who are "looking for the end," aesthetics is analogous to the spirituality of "patience" in *Apocalypse*. *Apocalypse* is both an aesthetic manifesto and an ascetic one. Form in Dante's text—which I take to be the application of grammar to rhetoric in the *terzarima*—cannot, therefore, be finally divorced from *formation* insofar as the *Commedia* is explicit about the need to justify its status as fiction in terms of its vocation. I in no way presume here that it is possible to know an author's intention in a written text; I do presume, however, that the phenomenon of writing is intentional by nature and that writing can disguise intentionality somewhat more thoroughly than can speech. The crucial distinction to be made is not so much speech *versus* writing but rather language as proffered (its ascetic) in this or that manner (its aesthetic) to be diversely interpreted *versus* language as sheer information, generated to be used univocally. There are many stages along the way between an epic poem and a computer print-out and my purpose here is not to engage in a general polemic over the relative authenticity of texts with respect to their disguised or discovered contexts. For the poet of the *Commedia*, though, the need to provide a context for interpretation (but not *the* context for *an* interpretation) is a mode of authenticity for the text itself and is rooted in the ascetic-aesthetic of *Apocalypse*, a point of view which Dante-pilgrim acquires at the end of the second *cantica*. Such a mode, to put it another way, seeks to overcome a materialistic threat implicit in the gods' gift of the written word in the much-discussed passage in Plato's *Phaedo*. Writing (and all other ikons) will only be a "remedy" for the spoken word if its fictions succeed in inviting that vital interpretative act which had always, by means of mysterious signs and portents, connected people with meanings that were perceived as transcending the finitude of the very signs which revealed them. Writing which does little more than reiterate the principle of identity ($3 = 3$, rather than 3 means...) has the important virtue of greatly extending the complexity of a given problem by measuring and conserving all its terms, but it hardly remedies the lack of meaning with respect to that problem. Dante's fictions are alleged to be both generated and interpretable according to a context which invites, indeed demands, the ultimately idiosyncratic reading of carefully structured "mysterious" signs. Paul Ricoeur has written with similar distinctions in mind: "...the meaningful patterns which a depth-interpretation wants to grasp cannot be understood without a kind of personal commitment similar to that of the reader who grasps the depth-semantics of the text and makes it his 'own'."[3]

Almost without exception, the several detailed studies of Dante's use of *Revelation* in the final cantos of the *Purgatorio* focus on those textual echoes relating to the world's dissolution, violent attacks on the elect, the corrupt papacy as harlot, captivity in "Babylon" by the French giant, the advent of Antichrist—in sum, the apocalyptic imagery of *tribulatio*.[4] R.E. Kaske, however, in an exceptionally informa-

---

[3] Ricoeur's extraordinary article was of the greatest help to me in trying to think about an apocalyptic hermeneutic: "The Model of the Text: Meaningful Action Considered as a Text," *New Literary History* V (Autumn, 1973), 91-117. The quote is found on p. 116.

[4] For a general reading of *Purgatorio* xxxff as apocalyptic in the traditional sense, see Nicolò Mineo, *Profetismo e apocalittica in Dante* (Catania, 1968), and G.A. Scartazzini, *Dantes Vision im irdischen Paradiese und die Biblische Apokalyptik*; other studies attempt to coordinate the biblical and Dantesque images with the poet's political or historical ideas: Alois Dempf, "L'Apocalittica di Dante" in *Apocalisse et insecuritas*, ed. E. Castelli for *Archivio di Filosofia* (1954, II), 93-102; Luigi Tondelli, *Il Libro delle Figure dell'Abate Gioacchino da Fiore*, 2 vols. (Torino, 1953), and M. Reeves and B. Hirsch-Reich, *The "Figurae" of Joachim of Fiore* (Oxford, 1972), attempt Joachimist readings. Charles Singleton is most sensitive to other possibilities of apocalyptic in his *Dante Studies* I, II (Cambridge, Mass., 1965-67). While the passage through the wall of fire in *Purgatorio* xxvii initiates the irenic mode in a special way, it is not lacking in the earlier cantos and in Dante's other works. In the *Epistles*, for example, the language of *tribulatio* is directed against the Florentines who apparently have no fear of the "second death" (*Epist.* 6.21; *Apoc.* 21.8); Dante's political ideal, however, is expressed irenically: after insuring that

tive essay,[5] points much of his exegesis of Dante's apocalyptic language at an irenic resolution of both the political and spiritual aspirations of the poet. Not only is the enigmatic DXV to be read as Christ himself, argues Kaske, but Dante's symbol is a specifically liturgical—hence, irenic—"heralding of the Savior."[6] Kaske also points out what should be obvious—but has not been for most scholars—about Dante-pilgrim's point of view in these cantos: "Dante's own role in the allegory, then, is that of the elect who in the final time will remain free from domination by the Antichrist; and this role seems supported by an analogy between Dante as beholder and recorder of the apocalyptic drama within the *Purgatorio*, and John the Evangelist as beholder and recorder of the Apocalypse..."[7] It is my contention that the pilgrim's most important discovery in the terrestrial paradise is the irenic context for apocalyptic. In *Purgatorio* xxvii ff., the manner in which general salvation history and Dante's particular salvation history are proffered as texts to be read by him is *ecclesial*. It is in the church "now," the locus of Joannine waiting and patience and nourishment that the body of the "saints," threatened by the world's violence, can come to maturity and their interpretative acts, threatened by the world's logic or indifference, can become privileged.

Dante's trial by fire in *Purgatorio* xxvii culminates an ascetic process directed by and towards Beatrice who will come to him in the *carro* of the church. Though Vergil spurs Dante on through his rite of passage with the promise of Beatrice (ll. 35-36), it is Matelda whom Dante first meets. The glance back towards an unrecoverable, Edenic human nature is necessary, I submit, not so much to underline the differences between Eden and "now" but to emphasize important elements of analogy and continuity between them. Beatrice will call Dante by name (*Purgatorio* xxx.55) to a new life, a newness produced by the

---

the vineyard will be trampled out in justice, Henry VII of Luxembourg will marry his long-suffering bride, Italy (*Epist.* 5.22ff; *Apoc.* 14.14-29; 19.7). See *Dantis Alagherii Epistolae*, ed. Paget Toynbee, 2nd edition (Oxford, 1966). Cf. R.E. Kaske, "Dante's DXV," cited below in f.n. 5; and Barbara Nolan, "The *Vita Nuova*: Dante's *Book of Revelation*," *Dante Studies* 88 (1970), 51-77.

[5] "Dante's DXV," in *Dante*, a collection of critical essays, ed. J. Freccero (Englewood Cliffs, 1965), 122-40.

[6] *Ibid.*, p. 130; cf. p. 124, f.n. 2.

[7] *Ibid.*, p. 132. See, for example, Beatrice's charge to the poet in *Purgatorio* xxxii.103-05: "Però, in pro del mondo che mal vive, / al carro tieni or li occhi, e quel che vedi, / ritornato di là, fa che tu scrive." ("Therefore, for the sake of the world which lives for ill, fix your eyes now upon the chariot and make sure you write that which you see"). Cf. the description of John the Evangelist in *Paradiso* xxxii.127-29 which explicitly reads *Apocalypse* as a narrative about the history of the church.

effects of the historical fact of Christ's life on human nature itself. The experience of Matelda in Eden recoups the history of human nature so that Dante can be clear about just what is new. Irenic fulfillment would be self-deception without a problem or promise in terms of which such fulfillment is seen to bear significance; irenic "ripeness" would be the artificial, unsatisfying ripeness of a literary hothouse unless the fiction create a context which represents the long, problematic history of the pilgrim's seed. Dante's literary style must confront these new demands on it in a special and obvious way because the fiction has it that the second coming of Beatrice—now in the context of the saved community's history—"was" the source of a new insight for the poet.

Dante has used many literary genres in fashioning his epic. After the rite of passage to a maturity which Beatrice forces the pilgrim to own, a new form or genre will dominate the text and subtend other genres (including the pastoral in Eden) which now have to represent a new experience of time and narrate a new kind of pilgrimage—no longer a trip to an exotic world but a trip back home.[8] This "supergenre" is irenic apocalypse. It is announced while Dante, Vergil and Statius are still struggling to pass through the wall of flames; the singing they hear from the other side becomes fully clear when they emerge.

> Guidavaci una voce che cantava
> di là; e noi, attenti pur a lei,
> venimmo fuor là ove si montava
> "Venite, benedicti Patris mei,"
> sonò dentro a un lume che lì era
> tal che mi vinse e guardar nol potei.
> (*Purgatorio* xxvii.55-60)

[A voice from beyond guided us; and we, listening to it alone, came out there where one ascended: "Come ye, blessed of my father," sounded from within a light which was there, such that it overcame me and I was unable to look.]

---

[8] It is in *Purgatorio* xxvii, after the pilgrim's entrance into that irenic point of view which recapitulates Eden and quickly surpasses it, that the imagery of pilgrimage is definitively revised:

> E già per li splendori antelucani,
> che tanto a' pellegrin surgon più grati,
> quanto, tornando, albergan men lontani,
> le tenebre fuggian da tutti lati,
> e 'l sonno mio con esse...
> (ll. 109-113)

[Because of the pre-dawn brightness which rises the more pleasing to returning pilgrims the more they are less distanced from home, the shadows fled on all sides and my sleep fled with them.]

Dante's use of the quotation from the end of the long eschatological section of *Matthew* 25 defines the co-extensiveness of the saved, ecclesial community "now" with its identity "then"; Christ's greeting to the blessed at the end of time here greets the pilgrim on his way to meet, in the midst of time, Beatrice in the church. As is the case with many citations from scripture in the *Commedia*, this quote is incomplete rhetorically and it is for the reader to supply the second half of the greeting. "Venite, benedicti Patris mei, *possidete paratum vobis regnum a constitutione mundi...*" (*Matt.* 25.34). Christ's words refer to heaven, the third Eden, the third garden which the pilgrim will eventually enter; that "kingdom" has been "prepared from the foundation of the world," in terms, that is, of a natural history begun in the first Eden, the first garden, at which the pilgrim glances briefly; but the "regnum" which Dante enters in *Purgatorio* xxvii ff. is the church as Beatrice manifests it, a second Eden, a second garden, the mediatrix of a reformed natural history bearing supernatural significance.[9] There is thus no nostalgia on the part of the pilgrim for the perfection of Eden, even in the poet's extravagant use of the pastoral genre to describe it. The irenic point of view subtends the pastoral because it adds to it, just as Dante's Statius adds to his Vergil historically, possibilities for human nature literally undreamt of in Eden—Milton notwithstanding. Dante's dream of Lia and Rachel, though "in" or passing through Eden, is ecclesial insofar as it images a *reformed* human nature marvelling at its new possibilities, enjoying a new reality which is added to, as their fruition, human virtues in the order of nature and the old covenant with Israel in the order of supernature. Dante wakes to the pastoral Eden from a repose which is watched over by a single shepherd, a *pastor ecclesiae*, into which the "old" Vergil is now conflatable only because of the presence of the "new" Christian

---

Dante here reverses the pilgrimage metaphor from a limited, goal-oriented one to a universal one in which pilgrimage is a constant process, and "true home," rather than any concrete relic or image, is the goal: a no-where and no-time which are partially available "now," "here," because of the unique ecclesial relationship to all of time—genesis to apocalypse—which Beatrice, coming "here and now" in the church for Dante, will incarnate. For the Pauline extension of this figure of the pilgrim church to all of Israel, see *Hebrews* 11.15-16.

[9] The Church as garden in all senses is attested to widely, especially in the tradition of commentaries on the *Song of Songs*, e.g., *Cant.* 4.12: "Hortus conclusus soror mea, sponsa" ("An enclosed garden is my sister, my bride"). See, as a thirteenth-century overview of the tradition, Thomas Aquinas, *Scrip. in Sententiis*, "Prologus" in *Omnia Opera*, tom. VI (sec. ed. Fiaccadori, Parma, 1856) (New York, 1948). For the social character of the second garden, see the notion "Plantatio Ecclesiae" in Thomas, I *Sent.* 16.1, 2; the "seeds" first planted there, says Thomas, were the "fideles primitivae ecclesiae."

Statius.¹⁰ This conflation, like the conflation of the first and second gardens (Eden and the church), like the conflation of Lia and Rachel, of Matelda and Beatrice, would emphasize that there is no absolute discontinuity—although they are different—between the order of nature and the order of grace: a doctrine which Dante expresses most fully in Statius' mouth in *Purgatorio* xxv-xxvi. For Dante-poet, the same conflation is true (Vergil and Statius represent it) of secular and sacred letters. The irenic genre, in this sense, both recapitulates and adds to the other genres. It is noteworthy that, while Dante dreams irenically of the newness of the church, whose remote origin is in the *felix culpa* of Eden, Eden itself, according to Matelda, was the true (if hidden) aspiration of the pagan poets. "Quelli, ch'anticamente poetaro / l'età de l'oro e suo stato felice, / forse in Parnaso esto loco sognaro" (*Purgatorio* xxviii.139-41) ("Those who in antiquity fashioned songs about the Golden Age and its state of felicity dreamt, perhaps, of this place in [their] Parnassus").

The dream, then, irenic and ecclesial in both its content and its context, is able to illuminate because it is born of the "work" of contemplation, described (as Dante will describe contemplation elsewhere) as looking at the stars, idly ruminating:¹¹

> Sì ruminando e sì mirando in quelle,
> mi prese il sonno; il sonno che sovente,
> anzi che 'l fatto sia, sa le novelle.
> (*Purgatorio* xxvii.91-93)

[Thus ruminating, admiring them, I was seized by sleep; sleep which often is aware of what's new before the fact.]

Knowing what's new before history has completed its course is not any longer the function of the isolated, revelatory dream which both

---

¹⁰ In the pastor-flock image, as in the dream of Lia and Rachel, temporal emphasis is placed on the irenic side of irenic apocalypse, on the fulfillment which active feeding brings and because of which that feeding, with hindsight, is valued:

> Quali si stanno ruminando manse
> le capre, state rapide e proterve
> sovra le cime avante che sien pranse
> tacite a l'ombra, mentre che 'l sol ferve,
> guardate dal pastor ch'n su la verga
> poggiato s'è e lor di posa serve;
> (*Purgatorio* xxvii.76-81)

[Like goats quietly ruminating, silent in the shade, having been quick and nimble upon the heights before they were fed, guarded, while the sun burns down, by the shepherd who leans himself on his crook and keeps them in repose;]

¹¹ See *Paradiso* x.131-32, *Purgatorio* xvi.99, and the play on *templo/contemplo* in *Paradiso* xxviii.53, 57. Cf. J. Freccero, "*Paradiso* x: the Dance of the Stars," *Dante Studies* 86 (1968), f.n. 12 and 56.

Dante and the author of *Apocalypse* received from the traditions of the ancient world. Such knowledge is "now" the common irenic experience of the struggling church (*ecclesia militans*) which the *exemplum* of Dante-pilgrim represents: "...però li è conceduto che d'Egitto / vegna in Ierusalemme per vedere, / anzi che 'l militar li sia prescritto" (*Paradiso* xxv.55-57) ("for it is granted him that he come from Egypt into Jerusalem in order to see, before he is discharged from his warfare"). The point of view of "anzi che...," knowing or tasting ahead of time, is the foundation of the very notion of an eschatology. For Dante's pilgrim, acquiring an ecclesial point of view alone permits the experience of the "last things" to be integrated—such is the fiction—into the context for the proffered word which is the text we read.

All the themes we have touched on so far with respect to this irenic context are fully realized in the poet's manipulation of the image of seeds. Examining this imagery will demonstrate Dante's insistence that the continuity already observed between the order of nature and the order of grace also embraces the revealed *eschata*. Just as the church "overlaps" Eden in Dante's experience, so Paradise, the third garden, overlaps the first two and, in its turn, both recapitulates them and adds the totally new.[12] Both the *Apocalypse* and the *Commedia* closely identify the church "now" with the heavenly church. Beatrice's coming as a bride both for the Christ-griffon and for Dante recalls the bride of the *Song of Songs*, universally interpreted as the church in history, and the heavenly city in *Apocalypse* 21.2-3 which is described as a bride.[13] In both the Dantesque and Johannine accounts, the eternal descends into and is available to the temporal.

> Et ego Ioannes vidi sanctam civitatem Ierusalem novam descendentem de caelo a Deo, paratam, sicut sponsam ornatam viro suo. Et audivi

---

[12] Such overlapping is in no way unique to Dante. It is stressed in *II Corinthians* 5.1-5 (Jerusalem Bible translation):

> For we know that when the tent that we live in on earth is folded up, there is a house built by God for us, an everlasting home not made by human hands, in the heavens. In this present state, it is true, we groan as we wait with longing to put on our heavenly home over the other; we should like to be found wearing clothes and not without them. Yes, we groan and find it a burden being still in this tent, not that we want to strip it off, but to put the second garment over it and to have what must die taken up into life. This is the purpose for which God made us, and he has given us the pledge of the Spirit.

Cf. *I Cor.* 15.47ff.

[13] The allegorical procession itself is compared in *Purgatorio* xxix.58-60, to a wedding procession: "Indi rendei l'aspetto a l'altre cose / che si movieno incontr'a noi sì tardi, / che foran vinte da novelle spose." ("Thence I turned my face to other things, which were moving to meet us so slowly that they would have been outrun by new brides"). Beatrice is greeted by an abbreviated quotation from *Songs*: "Veni, sponsa de Libano..." (*Purgatorio* xxx.11).

50   *Irenic Apocalypse*

vocem magnam de throno dicentem: Ecce tabernaculum Dei cum hominibus, et habitabit cum eis. Et ipsi populus eius erunt, et ipse Deus cum eis erit eorum Deus...

[And I, John, saw the holy city New Jerusalem descending from heaven and from God, dressed and decorated like a bride for her bridegroom. And I heard a great voice from the throne saying: "Behold God's dwelling-place with humanity. He will dwell with them. And they will be his people and he himself will be their God for them..."]

The angels who "rise up" to greet Beatrice's descent into time remind the pilgrim, not surprisingly, of time's end and of the church's *continuing into* paradise, flesh's continuing into spirit: "Quali i beati al novissimo bando / surgeran presti ognun di sua caverna, / la rivestita voce alleluiando,... (*Purgatorio* xxx.13-15) ("Like the blessed at the final trumpet, who will rise up straightway each from his tomb, each re-dressed voice singing alleluia,...").

In Dante's Eden, supernature is added onto nature and sacred history is added onto natural history. As the pilgrim is about to pass from Purgatory into the celestial spheres, his new spiritual status is imaged in terms of an ongoing, natural process: the annual growth of a plant "towards the stars":

> Io ritornai da la santissima onda
> rifatto sì come piante novelle
> rinovellate di novella fronda,
> puro e disposto a salire a le stelle.
>   (*Purgatorio* xxxiii.142-45)

[I returned from the holy flood, made over again like young plants renewed by new shoots; I was pure, disposed to go up to the stars.]

Dante is not an Edenic plant, created there "sanza seme" as was Adam (*Purgatorio* xxviii.69), but an ecclesial plant, grown from corrupt seed in the second garden which Beatrice manifests in Eden. The seeds of all material creatures, man included, were first in Eden, but there no seed need be corrupted in order for creation to "be fruitful and multiply."[14] The corruption attendant upon Adam's fall was passed on through his seed to all his descendants, save one; vegetable seed,

---

[14] Adam is represented as having been created as a mature plant in *Paradiso* xxvi.91-92: "O pomo che maturo / solo prodotto fosti..." ("O apple who alone were produced ripe..."). Aquinas' lengthy consideration of the problem of generation in Eden (*Summa Theol.* Ia, qq. 97-98) reflects the widely divergent opinions among the church fathers. Although he objects to the Greek tradition which entirely relegates sex to fallen nature and although he characteristically sees no lack of spiritual integrity in humanity's natural functions in Eden, he winds up his argument quoting Augustine (*De Civitate Dei* XIV.26) on the possibility of Edenic coitus "without the impairment of the genital

which Matelda recounts as having been blown from Eden to the hemisphere of land by the winds of the spheres, must now "die before it is given new life" (*Purgatorio* xxviii.103-14; *I Cor.* 15.37). But though Matelda will tell the pilgrim of his species' woes, the *difalta* he knows only too well, she unaccountably smiles and refers him to a passage in scripture:

> "Voi siete nuovi, e forse perch'io rido,"
> cominciò ella, "in questo luogo eletto
> a l'umana natura per suo nido,
> maravagliando tienvi alcun sospetto;
> ma luce rende il salmo *Delectasti*,
> che puote disnebbiar vostro intelletto..."
> (*Purgatorio* xxviii.76-81)

[You're new here, she began, and perhaps, because I smile in this place chosen for humanity's nest, you're a bit frightened in your wonderment; but the psalm *Delectasti* will give some light to defog your intellect...]

For the pilgrim to rehearse the psalm "Delectasti" in his mind is to realize that that psalm not only is the reason for Matelda's smile but also exactly defines his present position. For the poet, the psalm is the necessary link between his character's short time in the garden of Eden and the unprecedented experience he will soon have of the garden of Paradise.[15] After a general paean to the magnificence of that which God has created, the psalm notes the temporary sway of evil, only to be overcome finally by a superabundance of mercy. The psalm concludes:

> Iustus ut palma florebit;
> Sicut cedrus Libani multiplicabitur.
> Plantati in domo Domini,
> In atriis domus Dei nostri florebunt.

organs" (q. 98, art. 2). For the analogy between vegetable and human seed in Thomas, see *Summa Contra Gentiles* II.88.9, where the *virtutes* of a living thing are contained in its seed. Dante uses the same form (*virtù, virtute*) in his description of the seeding of the hemisphere of land in *Purgatorio* xxvii.103ff and in Beatrice's account of Dante's youthful "potential" in *Purgatorio* xxx.115-17.

[15] Augustine, *De Civitate Dei* XIII.21, sees the ecclesial link between Eden and Paradise as a "better" way of interpreting the meaning of Eden itself (Migne, *PL* XLI, col. 395):

> Possunt haec etiam in Ecclesia intelligi, ut ea melius accipiamus tanquam prophetica indicia praecedentia futurorum: paradisum scilicet ipsam ecclesiam...: quatuor autem paradisi flumina, quatuor Evangelia; ligna fructifera, sanctos; fructus autem eorum, opera eorum; lignum vitae, Sanctum sanctorum, utique Christum;......

> [These things may also be understood with respect to the Church in order that we may better receive them as prior prophetic signs of things to come: the garden (of Eden) is of course the Church itself...; the Garden's four rivers are the four Gospels; the fruitbearing trees are the saints; their fruit is the works of the saints; the tree of life is the Holy of Holies, Christ;]

>   Adhuc multiplicabuntur in senecta uberi
>   Et bene patientes erunt...
>
>   (*Psalms* 91.13-15)
>
> [The just man shall flourish like the palm tree;
> like the cedar of Lebanon shall he be multiplied.
> Planted in the Lord's house,
> In the courts of the house of our God, they shall flourish.
> Even to their old age they shall be fruitful and multiply:
> They shall be ripening to the full.]

Matelda smiles in Eden because the evil done there has been definitively overcome; the promise made to man there has been kept.[16] The seed of the just man will grow and flower and bear fruit if it is planted in the Lord's house, the *ecclesia*, in "this place" which is humanity's new "nest." Only this garden, provided for by the advent of the Christ in time, can begin to compensate for the unavoidable corruption of Adam's seed after the fall. Vergil's crowning of Dante as a just man ("libero, dritto e sano è tuo arbitrio" *Purgatorio* xxvii.140) and Matelda's leading him to the Lethe which corroborates that justice are cases of special providence which have cultivated the "potentiality" (*virtus*) of Dante's unique seed in order to preserve it; they are labors added to the general providence which preserves all the species. Beatrice, of course, is the most important agent of this special providence for Dante. She comes most clearly *in ecclesia* and almost immediately tells Dante of the history of his seed which, while participating in the general gratuity of God towards creatures, is a personal history and ultimately inscrutable:[17]

---

[16] In Augustine's commentary on the psalm, the value of the palm-tree is precisely in contradistinction to the temporary but doomed blooming of evil/grass: "Transit foenum, transit flos peccatorum: quid de iustis? 'Iustus ut palma florebit.' " ("The grass withers and so does the sinners' 'flower': and the just? 'The just man shall flourish like the palm-tree' "). Augustine also finds in the palm the theme of maturity so central to the end of *Purgatorio*: "...in novissimis suis... pulchra est;... finem ipsius in cacumine, ubi habet totam pulchritudinem: aspera radix videtur in terra; pulchra coma sub coelo est. Erit ergo tua pulchritudo in fine." ("...[the palm] is beautiful in its very final stage... its end is high up, where lies all its beauty: its coarse root is seen in the ground but its lovely fronds are in the sky. And so will your beauty, therefore, appear at the end"). See *Enarr. in Ps.* XCI, in Migne, *PL* XXXVI, col. 1179. Cf. Charles Singleton, *Dante Studies* II (Cambridge, Mass., 1967), 206-07, and, especially, Cassiodorus, *Expositio in Psalmis*, XCI, in *Corpus Christianorum*, series latina, vol. 98, where the psalm and palm tree are explicitly linked to the "Venite, benedicti patris mei..."

[17] The philosophical distinctions underlying the poetry are summarized by Aquinas in *Summa Theol.* Ia, q. 98, art. 1:

> We must also observe that nature's purpose appears to be different as regards corruptible and incorruptible things... Therefore, since in corruptible things none is everlasting and permanent except the species, it follows that the chief purpose of nature is the good of the species... On the other hand, incorruptible substances [angels, humans] survive, not only in the species, but also in the individual; and therefore even the individuals are included in the chief purpose of nature.

> Non pur per ovra de le rote magne,
> che drizzan ciascun seme ad alcun fine
> secondo che le stelle son compagne,
> ma per larghezza di grazie divine,
> che sì alti vapori hanno a lor piova,
> che nostre viste là non van vicine
> questi fu tal ne la sua vita nova
> virtüalmente, ch'ogne abito destro
> fatto averebbe in lui mirabil prova.
> Ma tanto più maligno e più silvestro
> si fa 'l terren col mal seme e non cólto,
> quant'elle ha piu di buon vigor terrestro.
> <div align="right">(<i>Purgatorio</i> xxx.109-120)</div>

[Not only by the work of the great wheels which direct each seed to some end according to their conjunctions with the stars, but also by the breadth of divine graces which distill to rain in such high vapors that our sight can never come near them, was this one (Dante) potentially of such a kind in his early life that every good habit would have exercised itself wonderfully in him. But the more the ground is apt to grow seed well and vigorously, the more bad and uncultivated seed will make it a wild and bad place.]

The passage emphasizes the effects of the fall on a seed which potentially (*virtüalmente*) embodies an excellent plant. What was good seed *virtüalmente* becomes "mal seme" when its potency turns to act in the moment of germination. Dante goes so far here as to provide a slightly different image from those mentioned in the parable of the sower in *Matt.* 13. Beatrice's image is of bad seed on good ground. The good ground permits the seed to grow vigorously but it will only be the more wild and noxious if grown unhusbanded (*non cólto*). For bad seed to grow on good ground and to realize its potential, it must be cultivated. This somewhat enigmatic statement on Beatrice's part continues with the mention of a series of events which are all too clear to Dante. Beatrice refers to her "sustaining" him with her "youthful eyes," to her death and Dante's abandonment of her for other

---

See *Basic Writings of Saint Thomas Aquinas*, ed. Anton C. Pegis, vol. I (New York, 1945), 930. Cf. *Summa Contra Gentiles* III.113. Augustine, commenting on the spiritual reason behind humanity's physical corruption in *De Civitate Dei* XIV.3, quotes *Aeneid* VI.730-32 which contains striking verbal parallels to Dante's text:

> Igneus est ollis vigor et coelestis origo
> Seminibus quantum non noxia corpora tardant,
> Terrenique hebetant artus moribundaque membra.

> [Of those seeds heaven is the source, and fiery
> The energy within them, did not bodies
> Hamper and thwart them, and these earthly
> Limbs and dying members dull them.]

The translation is H. Bettenson's, in his *City of God* (Baltimore: Penguin ed., 1972), p. 551.

women, for those "false images of the good," "che nulla promession rendono intera" ("which fulfill no promise"). She reminds him of her attempts to reach him "in dreams"; he had "sunk so low," she says, that only the sight of hell might save him. She directly interceded for him and recruited Vergil's aid.[18] It should now be clear to the pilgrim and to the reader that Beatrice has been hard at work cultivating this particular seed all along and is now bringing it to a point of maturity when it can begin to bear fruit: "rinovellate di novella fronda, / puro e disposto a salire a le stelle." Beatrice, then, is a gardener.

The imagery of seed and plant can enlighten us, too, about the relationship between Matelda and Beatrice.[19] Matelda need not labor at her gardening in Eden as Beatrice must in the garden of the church. "Cantando e scegliendo fior da fiore" (*Purgatorio* xxviii.41), Matelda presides over a garden of incorruptible plants which the author of the *Georgics* recognizes as being in no need of care ("...qui la terra sol da sé produce" *Purgatorio* xxvii.135). She reminds Dante of "what was" Proserpina in the perfect moment before her incorruptible springtime was lost, as definitively as was Eden at the fall.[20] Proserpina *was* a goddess of fecundity but is now, in *Purgatorio*, a spirit of potential fecundity. A passage in which Augustine mentions Proserpina is noteworthy in this context (*De Civitate Dei* IV.8, Migne, *PL* XLI, col. 118). Speaking of the endless multitudes of Roman gods and goddesses, Augustine says that at least nine of these were invoked at different moments in the process of growing a stalk of wheat. Proserpina has specific charge of the seed's germination: "Praefecerunt ergo Proserpinam frumentis germinantibus..."—the critical moment of corruption because of which, in the logic of Dante's seed metaphor, Matelda can only be thought of in past tenses; a representative of the "new creation" (*I Cor.* 5.17; *Apoc.* 21.5), a tiller of the second garden, must take over. The instance of the perfection of human seed to which Dante momentarily turns existed as a promise, a pledge. Eden was given to man, says Matelda, "per arr'a lui d'etterna pace" (*Purgatorio* xxviii.93; *arra* = anticipation, pledge, promise of payment).[21] Its existence in the "now" of the poem reminds the pilgrim that its

---

[18] *Purgatorio* xxx.121-41.
[19] For a consideration of the ambiguous nature of Matelda, see Emerson Brown, Jr., "Proserpina, Matelda, and the Pilgrim," *Dante Studies* 89 (1971), 33-48.
[20] For a direct relation of Proserpina to seeds, see the well-known etymology, Proserpina = "pro-serpendo fruges" ("sowing fruits") in Isidore of Seville, *Etymologia* VIII.60, in Migne, *PL* LXXXII, col. 320.
[21] In Isidore, *Etym.* IX.6 (Migne, *PL* LXXXII, col. 364), "arrha" is the pledge of fulfillment of "qualibet promissa re," including, most commonly, a "sponsio coniugalis." In this sense of the word, Dante may be said to be formally "engaged" in Eden; Matelda

promise is still valid and newly realizable, for he witnesses in Eden the pageant of the establishment of another garden to mediate between the one lost and the one which seemed unattainable. Matelda, likewise, exists as the promise which Beatrice brings to fruition. The innocent seed Matelda oversees will promise eternal peace now only potentially (*virtüalmente*); Eden's promise is fulfilled irenically in the church, in the necessity of struggling to cultivate corrupt seed. Beatrice will be able to tell Dante, after his confession of wrongdoing, to "sow the seed of weeping" ("pon giù il seme del piangere..." *Purgatorio* xxxi.46), in other words, to let the corrupt seed germinate and marvel at its transformation to fruitfulness. Beatrice makes the historical analogy to the burial and corruption of her own mortal body; Dante's sin, she implies, was failing to wait upon the glorious transformation of that sown seed.

> pon giù il seme del piangere e ascolta:
> sì udirai come in contraria parte
> mover dovìeti mia carne sepolta.
> (ll. 46-48)

[sow the seed of weeping and listen: so will you hear how my buried flesh should have moved you in the opposite direction.]

The imagery is clear in *Psalms* 125, which Dante has echoed:

> In convertendo Dominus captivitatem Sion,
> Facti sumus sicut consolati.
> ....
> Qui seminant in lacrymis,
> In exaltatione metent.
> Euntes ibant et flebant,
> Mittentes semina sua.
> Venientes autem venient cum exaltatione,
> Portantes manipulos suos.

[When the Lord completely turned us away from the captivity of Sion, we were as a people consoled... They who sow in tears, reap in exaltation. Going forth, they went and wept, broadcasting their seed. Coming back, they come in exaltation, carrying their sheaves.]

could be seen as a proxy, a formal "sponsio" or surety of the bride to come in *Ecclesia*; in the sense developed above, she is a "real image of the good," of Beatrice who comes as a bride. See S. Battaglia, *Grande dizionario della lingua italiana* (Torino, 1961) I.677-78. It seems possible, too, that this *arra d'etterna pace*, pointing toward Paradise, could be a Dantesque pun on the temporal political ideal of the universal Roman peace becoming for him less and less crucial. That peace was symbolized in Augustan Rome in the monumental altar or *ara pacis*. See the article "Ara Pacis" in the *Oxford Classical Dictionary*, 2nd ed. (Oxford, 1970).

Dante's dalliance with Matelda serves to clarify the problem of his personal salvation-history by making obvious both its origins and that which it lacks; it lacks the "new" *eschata* revealed by Beatrice the gardener who, proleptically, *comes rejoicing, bringing in the sheaves* (*Ps.* 125.6; see above). If Matelda exists as promise-potential-ungerminated seed, the fact that Beatrice finally comes literally to overlap her in Dante's sight[22] and to cultivate germinated seed signifies a vindication and reformation of nature itself so that it might be continuous with and render spirit. Following Matelda through Eden, then, is just the opposite of "imagini di ben seguendo false, / che nulla *promession* rendono intera" (*Purgatorio* xxx.131-32, emphasis mine). Because Eden's *promession* (*arra*) is performed and bettered in Beatrice, Dante can rightly see Matelda in a pastoral not only erotic but now irenic, as a "vera imagine di ben."

Having established and at least partially described the irenic-apocalyptic context with which Dante characterizes his text in the final cantos of *Purgatorio*, I would like to apply Dante's terms to the problem of interpretation in *Paradiso* x-xiv. It would be well, however, to outline the poet's continued reliance on the metaphor of seed and plant and to demonstrate the structural likenesses between signification and interpretation—already briefly discussed as processes involving both things (nature) and acts (spirit)—and the process of maturation from nature to spirit in the human "plant."

Dante's seed, planted "in the Lord's house," can be cultivated and trained up to the stars because, in the second garden, the fecundity of all plants depends on their being hybrids. Orthodox soteriology has always stressed the "reformation" of human nature by its being joined to the divine in one person who really suffers; in Dante's natural metaphor, the Christ-griffon grafts the cross-tree to Adam's apple (Dante's rootstock) for the conservation of all just people who, through Adam, are born of corrupt seed. "Sì si conserva il seme d'ogne giusto" (*Purgatorio* xxxii.48) ("Thus is the seed of every just person conserved"), the griffon cries out.[23] Dante's is a general refer-

---

[22] Dante walks with Matelda step by step "pari di lei" (*Purgatorio* xxix.8). She turns directly to him ("tutta a me si torse," l. 14) to announce the approach of the procession. Dante focuses on the elements of the procession as they pass the place she stands, "a rimpetto di me da l'altra sponda" (l. 89). The procession stops "quando il carro a me fu a rimpetto" (l. 151). Beatrice comes directly opposite Dante and therefore on a line of vision with Matelda's place by the riverbank.

[23] A short essay by R.E. Kaske provides documentation which shows the tree in Eden to be the Tree of Knowledge. His notes on seed are very helpful: he refers, especially (as did Joachim of Fiore in the *Liber Figurarum*), to the conserving activity of the *lignum* of Noah's ark and to Noah himself as *vir iustus*. See "Sì si conserva il seme d'ogne giusto" (*Purgatorio* xxxii.48), *Dante Studies* 89 (1971), 49-54.

ence to the mercy of the griffon who, rather than simply break off branches from the corrupting tree, has grafted himself on (ll. 43-46). Rather than the narrow political image which some see here (Grandgent's commentary, for example), the text behind Dante's must certainly be Paul's (in *Romans* 11.16-24) where the apostle is grateful for his own return to the rootstock, by Christ's graft (*insitio*) and hopes that branches temporarily broken off will be grafted back in. With respect to the chosen people of Israel, Paul's hope is eschatological insofar as it equates their grafting in with the final resurrection of the body. Dante, who was lately presented with a text which enlightened him as to his identity and the natural-supernatural process of his own maturation—"*Justus* ut palma florebit"—experiences in *Purgatorio* xxxii a foretaste of hybrid fruit to come as he witnesses the showy flowers which now appear on the tree. Overcome by the sight, he wakes and compares himself and what he has seen to the story of the Transfiguration.

> Quali a veder de' fioretti del melo
> che del suo pome li angeli fa ghiotti
> e perpetüe nozze fa nel cielo,
> Pietro e Giovanni e Iacopo condotti
> e vinti, ritornaro a la parola
> da la qual furon maggior sonni rotti,
> e videro scemata loro scuola
> così di Moïsè come d'Elia,
> e al maestro suo cangiato stola;
> tal torna'io, e vidi quella pia
> sovra me starsi che condutrice
> fu de' miei passi lungo 'l fiume pria.
> E tutto in dubbio dissi: "Ov'è Beatrice?"
> Ond'ella: "Vedi lei sotto la fronda
> nova sedere in su la radice."
> (*Purgatorio* xxxii.73-87)

[As, when led to see some of the flowers of the apple tree whose fruit makes angels gluttons and makes for a perpetual wedding-feast in heaven, Peter, James and John were first overcome and then returned to that word by which even deeper sleeps were broken and saw their group lessened by Moses, by Elias, and saw its master's garments changed; so did I return to myself and saw that pious woman standing over me who had been the guide of my steps along the river. I said, totally in doubt, "Where is Beatrice?" Whence she, "See her beneath the (tree's) new growth, sitting at its roots."]

The blooming of the hybridized tree is a successful concurrence of nature and supernature, promising a fruit (*suo pome*) which only initially can be interpreted as logically extending a simply temporal metaphor; in time, the hybrid will produce *both* Christ hanging ripe from the cross *and* the "seed of every just man" come to fruition, ripening patiently in the suffering church.[24] It is an exceedingly complicated way of representing the same basic doctrine of Christian theology which Beatrice's coming as a Christ in *Purgatorio* xxx represented. Each Christian is *alter Christus*, another Christ. But each Christian's identity "then" is experienced in part "now," insofar as apocalyptic suffering anticipates and already knows irenic fulfillment. This can be the only reason Dante chooses one of the most clearly eschatological events narrated in the synoptics as a similitude for the successful graft, the historical reformation of human nature and its possibilities. The poet gives his character the same vantage point, *talis qualis*, as Peter, James and John occupied when human flesh took on "glory" for the first time and when that transfigured flesh was accepted by God. But the moment in time which they share is the moment after the vision, when the apostles were awakened by Christ and Dante awakened by Matelda.[25] The poet's alleged point of view, in other words, cannot but remain the "now" of temporality and suffering, even in the representation of a fiction of "glory."

In the Transfiguration narratives, Christ promises both his death and his resurrection.[26] Both these physical events, as endpoints, are "fruit" in the sense we have seen Dante develop; but he chooses to dwell on anticipatory images of fleshly resurrection or, more precisely, to emphasize in his rhetoric the memory "now" of the surprising and half-realized moments of "bloom" (*fioretti*) which promised

---

[24] Dante seems to accept the tradition that the wood of Adam's tree was of the same species as the "lignum crucis." He thus describes the hybridization (*Purgatorio* xxxii.49-51): "E vòlto al temo ch'elli avea tirato, / trasselo al piè de la vedova frasca, / e quel di lei a lei lasciò legato" (...and he left bound to it that which came from it). Among the hymns of Venantius Fortunatus (sixth century), the fruit of the cross-tree is Christ himself hanging from its branches; for example, the "Crux benedicta": "Appensa est vitis inter tua brachia, de qua / dulcia sanguineo vina rubore fluunt." Cf. "Vexilla regis," str. vii. See J. Julian, *A Dictionary of Hymnology* (London, 1915), pp. 273 and 1219.

[25]
> Però transcorro a quando mi svegliai,
> e dico ch'un splendor mi squarciò 'l velo
> del sonno, e un chiamar: "Surgi: che fai?"
> (ll. 70-72)

[So I pass on to the time when I awoke, and I maintain that a brightness rent the veil of my sleep, and a calling: "Rise up: what are you doing?"]

[26] See *Matthew* 17.9, 12; *Mark* 9.8, 11; *Luke* 9.31. Although many commentators cite the passage in *Matthew* alone for *Purgatorio* xxxii, an important detail in Dante's poem is found only in *Luke* 9.32: "Petrus vero et qui cum illo erant, gravati erant somno. Et vigilantes viderunt maiestatem eius,..." ("Peter and those with him were weighed down by sleep. But keeping awake they saw his majesty,..."). Dante sees the vision of the tree and, according to his simile, is "overwhelmed"; he is overcome as well (as were the apostles) by "'l velo / del sonno."

the fruit that is eternally spiritualized flesh. It is clear that the principal anticipatory image is the Transfiguration itself. Christ's "stola," seen now as ordinary once again after its momentary radiance, anticipates the glorified flesh or "bianche stole" which Dante (in *Paradiso* xxv.95) translates out of *Apocalypse* 7.9-17. Another anticipatory image is far more subtle. The apostles returned out of their vision (in *Luke*—see f.n. 26 below—"gravati erant somno") to hear Christ's voice "...la parola / da la qual furon maggior sonni rotti" (l. 78). What greater or deeper sleeps did Christ's word break? It broke the *somnus mortis* on several occasions. But it is not unlikely that Dante is recalling in this passage, as an anticipation of the final resurrection, the specific event of the raising of Jairus' daughter which is told in *Luke* 8.49ff and in *Mark* 5.33ff, almost immediately preceding the Transfiguration story. In both these narratives, as in the Transfiguration, only Peter, James and John were admitted to the experience and are told not to reveal what they have witnessed. In both, as in the Transfiguration (in *Luke* and in the *Purgatorio*) a "sleep" is specifically broken—a greater sleep than the apostles' or Dante's, death itself. "At ille dixit: Nolite flere, non est mortua puella, sed dormit" (*Luke* 8.52) ("And he said: do not weep, the girl is not dead, she is asleep").

The poet insists upon the logic of the plant metaphor. In *Paradiso* xxv, Beatrice will show Dante the second garden's harvest, the fruits collected by the revolution of the same spheres which scattered their seed out of Eden.[27] Those who, like Beatrice, struggle as cultivators of seed, have become themselves—inasmuch as they too are "plants"—a superabundant *ubertas*; they are fruit ripe for consumption and full of nourishment.

> Oh quanta è l'ubertà che si soffolce
> in quelle arche ricchissime che fuoro
> a seminar qua giù buone bobolce!
> (*Paradiso* xxiii.130-32)

[Oh how great the superabundance which is put up in those richest larders which were, here below, such good farmers!]

Compare *Cant.* v.1: "Veniat dilectus meus in hortum suum, et comedat fructum pomorum suorum" ("My beloved comes into his garden and eats the fruit of his apples").

---

[27]
> e Bëatrice disse: "Ecco le schiere
> del triunfo di Cristo e tutto 'l frutto
> ricolto del girar de queste spere!"
> (*Paradiso* xxv.19-21)

[and Beatrice said: "Behold the hosts of Christ's victory and all the fruit harvested by the turnings of these spheres!"]

> O sodalizio eletto a la gran cena
> del benedetto Agnello, il qual vi ciba
> sì, che la vostra voglia è sempre piena,
> (*Paradiso* xxiv.1-3)

[Oh sodality, elected to the great supper of the blessed Lamb, who feeds you in such a way that your desire is always fulfilled.]

The plant metaphor, with which Dante has characterized the process of growth in the pilgrim and in every just man, ends at table (*mensa–Paradiso* xxiv.5), at the marriage-feast of the Lamb which is the hieratic center of the *Book of Revelation*. The supper of the Lamb is the finally irenic gloss on Dante's Transfiguration simile whose rhetoric, as we have seen, is primarily anticipatory. The fruit of the tree, *suo pome*, feeds the angels *spiritualiter* and (the reference should no longer seem a leap in logic) "makes an eternal wedding-feast in heaven." In the simile, the fruit is the cause of the wedding because—vis-à-vis the future of a transfigured Christ—it *is* the Paschal Lamb/Bridegroom, to be wed and consumed *spiritualiter*: "for now Christ is risen from the dead, the *first fruits* of them that sleep" (*I Cor.* 15.20, emphasis mine).[28] The passage in Paul implies what we already know, that the fruit in question is a hybrid, that it is all of death-cursed human nature which has been for the first time transfigured and given divine approval. In Dante's simile, then, the grafted tree and its new fruit, as well as the temporal, ecclesial garden from which other fruit will be gathered (where Dante-pilgrim himself is placed by his "good farmer") anticipate and experience "now" that which is to come. Both fruits—Christ the Bridegroom and his Bride the church—are wed and consumed. The similitude of glory returns to that context which the fiction, once it established it, never leaves: the church in time and

---

[28] The first Clementine Epistle to the Corinthians treats the idea at length, stressing the manner in which future glory is observable now:

> Consideremus, dilecti, quamadmodum Dominus continue nobis ostendat resurrectionem quae futura est; cujus primitias fecit Dominum Jesum Christum, suscitans eum e mortuis. Intueamur, dilecti, quae omni tempore fit, resurrectionem... Videamus fruges: seminatio grani quomodo fiat. Exiit seminator, et jecit semen in terram: jactisque seminibus, quae arida et nuda ceciderunt in terram, dissolvuntur; deinde ex ea dissolutione, magna providentiae Domini potestas resuscitat: atque ex uno, fructum pluribus auctum profert.

> [Let us consider, beloved, just how the Lord continually demonstrates for us the resurrection which is to come, the first fruits of which he made the Lord Jesus Christ, raising him from the dead. Let us observe, beloved, that there is always resurrection... We see the earth's fruits: and how the sowing of grain takes place. The sower goes out and casts the seed on the ground: the seeds having been cast, fallen bare and dry upon the ground, they decompose; thence and from that decomposition, the great force of the Lord's providence revives it: and from a single thing multiple fruits are borne.]

See Clement of Rome. *Epistola I ad Corinthios*, 24.

Beatrice on guard at its roots in good ground (*terra vera*–*Purgatorio* xxxii.94).[29]

Dante's plant imagery is, most fundamentally, an imagery of process in which the structures of nature will surely—though they seem entirely perverse—render spirit. Although the quality of any particular process of maturation can only be judged from its endpoint, that endpoint is such insofar as it is recognized as being continuous with a series of events, some common and some idiosyncratic, which have shaped it. It must be emphasized that Dante is not naïve about the ways in which natural structures are apt to go bad. Infernal imagery has a place in all three *cantiche*. In *Paradiso* xxvii, greed so floods the natural environment of the human fruit-tree (which is nourished, one must suppose, in the same figure: by good objects of desire as normal rainfall) that its fruit rots as it matures. The aberrant can become ordinary.

> Ben fiorisce ne li uomini il volere;
> ma la pioggia continüa converte
> in bozzacchioni le sosine vere.
> (ll. 124-26)

[Will flowers well in human beings; but the continuous rain turns good plums into discards.]

---

[29] When Dante wakes from his sleep he sees Matelda standing "sovra me" (l. 83). This detail and her words "Surge: che fai?" (l. 72) are calculated to lead the reader to expect the Christ who, in the Transfiguration account in *Matthew*, stands over his crouching disciples and says "Surgite." But Dante has already been trained, as a reader, by the metonymic character of the divine economy. He rightly expects Beatrice: "Ov'è Beatrice?" (l. 85). Matelda, or "quella pia" in the long and deliberately ambiguous periphrasis which identifies her, here functions as a pure metonymy for Beatrice. Beatrice, like the divine "maestro," is outwardly "changed" (l. 81). She came in the church in irenic glory; now "sola sedeasi," (l. 94), she waits with the church through its apocalyptic struggle. Many other uses of the seed-plant metaphor occur in the poem. See, among others: *Purgatorio* xxv.54 (which notes the difference between vegetable and human seed); *Paradiso* xii.71-72 (where St. Dominic is a "farmer" in Christ's "garden"); *Paradiso* xii.95-96 (where the twenty-four saints who surround Dante are "plants" sprung from the ecclesial "seed"; they are, as we shall see below, nurturing the pilgrim's own growth); *Paradiso* xix.48 (Satan "fell unripe" because he refused "to wait upon the light"); *Paradiso* xxv.35-36 ("our rays" ripen all which comes to heaven from earth); *Paradiso* xxvii.118ff and *Paradiso* xviii.27ff (Dante, in two widely separated passages, images the coincidence of nature and spirit as two trees: nature has its roots in the *primum mobile*, spirit—"che frutta sempre e mai non perde foglia"—takes life from its summit and, I can only suspect, has put down roots in the second garden; *Paradiso* xxiii.73 and *Paradiso* xxxiii.7-9 (Christ is the fruit of the womb of the *rosa mystica*, the "heat" of whose organic life—ignited *spiritualiter* without seed—germinates the seed which can produce the entire celestial rose). For Christ's being conceived without seed, see Aquinas, *Summa Theol.* Ia, q. 119, art. 2.

The poet immediately connects this plant-image of perverse desire with the problems attendant on the maturation of the structures of language—that most natural human activity which functions (to use Augustinian terms) as a representation of desire. Eloquence, for Dante, can be the effective sign of a terrifyingly "natural" human cognition gone wild and turned upon its own kind.

> Tale, balbuzïendo ancor, digiuna,
> che poi divora, con lingua sciolta
> qualunque cibo per qualunque luna;
> e tal, balbuzïendo, ama e ascolta
> la madre sua che, con loquela intera,
> disïa poi di vederla sepolta.
> (ll. 130-35)

[Some people fast while they still talk baby-talk; once their tongue is untwisted, they devour whatever food, at whatever hour. Some people, while talking baby-talk, love and heed their mother; once their speech matures, they desire to see her in her grave.]

This from the same poet who is consistently scrupulous about a rigorous application of linguistically determined philosophical and theological ideas—evidencing a confidence in language which may seem to us foolhardy but which, for Dante, is based on a confidence in nature, in the real. If it is human *nature* to make signs and to interpret them, then those ordinary processes of signification and interpretation will render a *scientia* continuous with them just as surely as fruit, ordinarily, is rendered by and is continuous with a history of bloom. But we have seen that Dante's plant imagery includes a garden of hybrids whose fruits are "new," totally unwonted in and yet continuous with the order of nature. Their eschatological character is unambiguous and Dante, at the close of the same *Paradiso* xxvii, uses the prophetic future tense to signal it: "e *vero* frutto verrà dopo 'l fiore" (l. 148, emphasis mine) ("And true fruit will come after the flower"). The conclusion might seem millenarian in a simplistic sense, especially when one takes into account the grim images of diminished human nature and human language upon which it follows; the "vero frutto" seems only to be hoped for in the future. But, as Dante answers St. James about the nature of hope in *Paradiso* xxv, "Spene... è uno attender certo / de la gloria futura..." (ll. 67-68) ("Hope... is a sure waiting upon future glory..."). The waiting *itself* is certain; the fruit to be matured in the third garden, says James, is the very same fruit which has come there from the second garden situated in the perverse and contingent "mortal world."[30] Since Dante-pilgrim explicitly cites the epistle of James as a *stillare* (distilling process) which watered his maturing fruit, "sì ch'io son pieno" (l. 77) ("such that I am full"),[31] it is well to note that the word used for "hope" there (as in the *Apocalypse*) is not *spes* or any of its cognates, but *patientia*; and the major figure for hope in the epistle is a farmer waiting patiently for rain and for the earth's precious fruit:

> Patientes igitur estote, fratres, usque ad adventum Domini. Ecce agricola expectat pretiosum fructum terrae, patienter ferens donec accipiat temporaneum et serotinum. (*James* 5.7)
>
> [Therefore be patient, brethren, until the Lord's coming. Behold, the farmer waits upon the earth's precious fruit, bearing up patiently until it receive the autumn and the spring rains.]

Those rains come "now," in time, and (just as the rain of James' epistle "filled up" Dante in his reading of it) themselves bring a fulfillment, a fruit—even if total maturation is still subject to patience, "ad adventum Domini." Dante's filled up and still maturing fruit is glossed in the epistle's opening words: "Patientia autem opus perfectum habet: ut sitis [now] perfecti et integri in nullo deficientes" (*James* 1.4) ("And patience works its total effect in you: that you may be perfect, complete, lacking in nothing"). It was especially glossed by the conclusion of the psalm "Delectasti," which Matelda proffered as a text for Dante. Not only will the palm-tree flourish in the Lord's house but it will bear, when it comes mature, and continue bearing: "Adhuc multiplicabuntur in senecta uberi / Et bene patientes erunt..." (*Ps.* 91.15). Apocalyptic *patientia*, then, is continuous with irenic *spes*; the dynamism or complementarity of these forms of maturation, and

---

[30] "Leva la testa e fa che t'assicuri:
ché ciò che vien qua sù del mortal mondo,
convien ch'ai nostri raggi si maturi."
Questo conforto del foco secondo
mi venne... (*Paradiso* xxv.34-36)

["Raise your head and reassure yourself: for anything mortal which comes up here is necessarily matured by our lightrays." This comfort came to me from the second fire...]

[31] The definition of *stillazione* in the De Voto-Oli *Dizionario della Lingua Italiana* (p. 2362) seems tailor-made to Dante's figurative use of *stillare*: "In arboricultura e selvicultura, la caduta delle gocce d'acqua piovana delle piante più alte a quelle sottostanti." According to Dante's plant metaphor, both the pilgrim and the saint are plants, and James is certainly "higher" than Dante (he is literally so in ll. 34 and 38). An even higher plant, David the psalmist, "sommo cantor del sommo duce" (l. 72) was the immediate source for the water which James provided Dante. Dante, in turn, will water others: "e in altrui vostra pioggia repluo" (l. 78).

indeed, forms of apprehension (a dynamism simultaneously ascetic and aesthetic) is expressed, even in a play of noun and participle, in Paul: "Spe gaudentes: in tribulatione patientes…" (*Rom.* 12.12) ("By hope rejoicing: in struggle bearing up"). For Dante, "vero frutto" will come after the flower "now" as well as "then," as surely as the revelation of the future of flesh was available to the three apostles, and as surely as the blooming of the hybrid tree—for which the Transfiguration is a figure—is available to the pilgrim. Dante's irenic confidence in language extends—the conclusion is inescapable—to his own fictions which claim a context in which they can be surely available to fill up other ripening fruits: "e in altrui vostra pioggia repluo" (l. 78, see f.n. 31) ("and I rain your rain over again upon others"). It seems, as I have said before now, absolutely outrageous; but that is the fiction. The words present their structures to the reader as they more and more explicitly single the reader out the way, says Dante, the Word singled out Peter, James and John[32] and the way Beatrice—in the narrative—is singling out and cultivating the pilgrim. The text makes its particular demands on the reader because, quite simply, it claims to convey particular truths. The *Commedia* is didactic in the strictest sense. A seemingly endless debate over Dante's claims vis-à-vis the Bible has served, generally, to confuse the issue. Dante imitates the Bible and the ways in which it conveys its truths; but his claim is to pass on truths idiosyncratically, according to the unique, personal manner of his representing himself as having been called and read by the Bible, by Beatrice as text, and, to a lesser extent, by myriad other texts. The *Commedia* does not claim the same status as the historically fixed *biblia sacra*. It does claim, however, textual status as a kind of apology or written kerygma, in which the *fiction* is that the reader will allow himself to be cultivated by the text only if he can be convinced that the public "confession," as *exemplum*, represents a unique *experientia* of conversion and vision.[33]

---

[32] In *Paradiso* xxv.29-33, Beatrice addresses James with a *captatio benevolentiae* which praises his singling out and recalls to the reader the fact that Dante-pilgrim has made himself privy, in his *imaginativa*, to two occasions of the apostle's special revelation. They are, as we have seen, the Transfiguration and the raising of the daughter of Jairus. When James asks what is hoped for, Dante's answer—the resurrection of the body—is something of which, in the poem, they both have known "un attender certo." (It was revealed particularly clearly in the *Apocalypse*: "e 'l tuo fratello assai vie più digesta, / là dove tratta de le bianche stole, / questa revelazion ci manifesta." (ll. 94-96) ("and your brother much more explicitly, where he treats of the white raiment, manifests this revelation for us").) According to Origen, Peter, James and John, by virtue of their being singled out at the same two occasions mentioned by Dante, were the first Christian gnostics. See his *Commentary on the Gospel of Matthew*, t. 1, ed. R. Girod (*Sources Chrétiennes*), 68-69.

[33] For the distinction *experientia–exemplum*, see *Par.* i.70-72.

The address to the reader in *Paradiso* ii is important in this regard. Dante says, in effect, "Many are called but few are chosen." The "many," "O voi... / desiderosi d'ascoltar" (ll. 1-2) ("Oh you... desirous of hearing"), are well-intentioned but seriously flawed as readers. They lack a history of being disciplined by the entire range of the interpretative process as Dante and the Middle Ages understood it: interpretation both *materialiter* and *spiritualiter*. More specifically, they are nostalgic readers, who respond only in terms of structures they have already recognized. Theirs is the common (and extremely important) human experience of a *scientia* of things, without the ultimately idiosyncratic *sapientia* which results from a history of being disciplined as well by attempts to interpret the mysterious. From an epistemological point of view, we might represent Dante's hermeneutic (as we have earlier in this chapter) in the difference between the univocal and immensely useful structure $3^2 = 9$ and the identical structure available to be diversely interpreted, $[(3^2 = 9)$ means... $]$, the "use" of which is not immediately apparent and which threatens to become overly idiomatic. Both structures require disciplines by which they are understood: the former, disciplines of the generation and recognition of structures based on principles of identity and analogy; the latter, disciplines based in the former kind of knowledge but including as well the transformation of given structures into "idiotic" (or idiosyncratic) objects of knowledge. Both epistemological modes are examples, given what we have seen of Dante's plant imagery, of nature rendering spirit, of seed (ordinarily) growing to flower, and to fruit. But Dante's "vero frutto," in which the context for reformed nature's maturing and producing is ideally ecclesial (in a wider sense, communal), is saved by that context from the danger of incomprehensibility inherent in its idiosyncratic nature. The danger is that the fruit may not nourish. Dante's care for the reader, the ethical dimension of his text, means, as we have seen, creating a context where personal fictions demand adherence to their terms so that the diverse interpretations which result might, at the least, have a common ground.

In Dante's image of his narrative as a sea-voyage in *Paradiso* ii, then, the "many" are told to take refuge in the already recognizable: "tornate a riveder li vostri liti: / non vi mettete in pelago..." (ll. 4-5) ("go back to see your own shores: don't put out to sea"); their equipment is simply insufficient to the voyage: "...voi che siete in *piccioletta* barca" (l. 1, emphasis mine) ("O you who are in a tiny boat"). The "mysteria" to be signified and interpreted are too new: "L'acqua ch'io prendo già mai non si corse" (l. 7) ("The waters I am taking have never been sailed"). But those most apt to be nourished by the text, the "few," are imaged as having accepted a lengthy and particular kind of interpretative discipline; they have matured in an irenic-apocalyptic context where "vero frutto" is available both "now" and "then" and where fulfillment is both simultaneous with and reveals lack.

> Voi altri pochi che drizzaste il collo
> per tempo al pan de li angeli, del quale
> vivesi qui ma non sen vien satollo,
> metter potete ben per l'alto sale
> vostro navigio, servando mio solco
> dinanzi a l'acqua che ritorna equale.
> Que' gloriosi che passaro al Colco
> non s'ammiraron come voi farete,
> quando Iasón vider fatto bifolco.
> (ll. 10-18)

[O you others, the few, who have stretched your necks long since towards the bread of angels, on which people live but of which they are never satisfied on earth, you can surely sail your vessel on the salt sea, keeping to my wake, ahead of the water that returns to resemble the rest. Those heroes who crossed over to Colchis were not as amazed, when they saw Jason turned farmer, as you will be.]

The reader is not in the same boat as the author. But the reader who has regularly had to confront and to interpret a signifier whose meaning depends upon its structure (*materialiter*) but is not (*spiritualiter*) exhausted by that structure—which is the wildly illogical *pan de li angeli*—has for himself a means (*navigio*) adequate to the poem's enterprise. But the text singles out these disciplined readers most strikingly in the new and unique mystery it imposes on them. Language in all its ambiguity and weakness (vis-à-vis the vast, undifferentiated sea) goes so far as to proffer itself as authoritative with respect to a prior experience which it has interpreted irenically. It demands that the terms in which it poses the problem be strictly adhered to (*materialiter*) because it is confident that they will be continuous with and render meaning (*spiritualiter*) as surely as natural bread becomes the bread of angels for those who have struggled to understand such things. In the phrase which claims such authority, "servando mio solco," Dante's anxiety for the fate of the reader is apocalyptic. He echoes John's admonition to the reader in *Apoc.* 1.1, repeating the verb *servare*: "Beatus qui legit et audit verba prophetiae huius: et servat ea, quae in ea scripta sunt: tempus enim prope est." The future of the well-trained reader will be amazement at an unwonted transformation effected by the textual enterprise. As the Argonauts were amazed at Jason turned into a farmer, "fatto bifolco," so the reader will marvel, one must conclude, in the same figure. Dante-pilgrim's "sulcation" (*solco*) will not only signify, for the reader in his wake, but also (the Latin *sulcare* has the double meaning) plow and inseminate the fertile ground where a new warrior race can spring up: that poly-semous otherness which Dante, in the letter to Can Grande, calls the allegorical sense.[34]

We have been discussing Dante's natural model of seed and plant as an image of the maturation process involved in each human act of interpretation or signification. The similitude is not uniquely Dantesque. Christ's exegesis of his own parable of the sower in *Matthew* 13.18ff reaches similar conclusions: "Qui verum in terram bonam seminatus est hic est qui audit verbum et intellegit et fructum affert, et facit aliud quidem centesimum, aliud autem sexagesimum aliud vero trigesimum" (v. 23) ("But he who has received seed on good ground, it is he who hears the word, understands it and bears fruit and yields one a hundredfold, one perhaps sixtyfold, another thirtyfold'"). All acts of interpretation and signification in which the letter gives way to the spirit involve growth or maturation. We have seen at length the ways in which these acts are, in one sense, dependent on the received letter or text. But they are also, or simultaneously, independent of any text (*materialiter*) insofar as maturing takes place uniquely: the similarly seeded plants in the parable all grow but they have different yields; their end, *ubertas*, is sure but diverse. As Paul explains in *I Cor.* 3.6-9 to a readership which was fighting over whether to receive him or Apollos as authoritative "text": "Ego plantavi, Apollo rigavit: sed Deus incrementum dedit. Itaque neque qui plantat est aliud, neque qui rigat: sed qui incrementum dat, Deus... Dei enim sumus adiutores: Dei agricultura estis..." ("I planted, Apollo watered, but it is God who makes growth. So that neither he who plants nor he who waters is anyone important; but he who gives growth, God, [is crucial]... We are, then, God's helpers; you are God's field of crops..."). In Dante's text, divine *agricultura* is the pilgrim's maturation, with the help of many farmers, from seed to "true" fruit. Fruit, of course, is the product of a mature plant which contains its corruptible seed within it. Here, and only here, I think, the natural metaphor diverges from the spiritual reality toward which it claims to point. Its very divergence, as metaphor, signals an eschatological viewpoint which the poet, boldly and literally, *embodies* in his fiction. For Dante's insistence that the pilgrim was in the flesh from hell to heaven is his

---

[34] See Paget Toynbee, ed. *Dantis Alagherii Epistolae*, 2nd ed. (Oxford, 1966), p. 173. In the passive "fatto bifolco" Dante turns the Jason story to his own ends, making the sowing which is the text dependent upon a prior semiotic act. It is a version of Dante, "fatto scriba" in *Par.* x.27. *Par.* ii.1-18 may even be a complex paraphrase of *Hebr.* 5.11-18.

fiction's most authentically apocalyptic element. The pilgrim, in a "now" which the text views in retrospect, sees, in his body, that the saints' paradisiacal fulfillment still lacks their bodies. By journeying in the body and coming back, Dante is assured proleptically (in the ecclesial sense: ritually) that his own nature has a future "then" which is different from but not discontinuous with its present. He is assured that his corruptible body/seed, inasmuch as it "sees" the *mysteria*, is on the way to producing something which its present structure (and nature itself) simply will not yield in any logical sense: an incorruptible body/seed. He is assured, analogously, that the acts of signification and interpretation, doomed to work with "a hand that shakes" (*Paradiso* xiii.78), inasmuch as they "read" *spiritualiter*, are on the way to producing the transformation of their unyielding structures: filling in the gap (however the new aesthetics of a new spiritual body might "perceive" it!) between the signifier and the signified. In the fourteenth book of the *De Trinitate*, Augustine (commenting on *I Cor.* 13.12 and 15.52) joins together all the notions—seed and plant, body and maturation, time and its faulty but "mysterious" mediations—which we have been tracing through the *Commedia*.

> In ipso namque ictu oculi ante iudicium resurget in virtute, in incorruptione, in gloria corpus spirituale, quod nunc seminatur in infermitate, corruptione, contumelia corpus animale... nunc autem proficit per speculum in aenigmitate.
>
> [For in the twinkling of an eye, before the judgment, that will rise in power, incorruption and glory as a spiritual body, which is now sown in weakness, corruption and dishonour as a natural body... it is making progress towards it now through a mirror in an obscure manner.][35]

Maturation, for Dante, is very much a matter of learning to read well. This is primarily because his work among his fellows—his ethical responsibility, as he so often characterizes it—is to be a poet. A great many episodes in the *Inferno* and, especially, in the *Purgatorio* may be understood as representations of the problems connected with the interpretative act.[36] But insofar as he is also a theologian, an interpreter of divine things—every Christian's calling in Paul—Dante is concerned, preëminently in the *Paradiso*, with the theology of the hermeneutic process. That theology, as it is expressed poetically in *Paradiso* x-xiv, is, I propose, most properly a pneumatology: connected with the theory of the Spirit's activity in the world of created

---

[35] *De Trinitate* XIV, 19, in Migne, *PL* XLII, col. 1056.
[36] For a recent study, see the dissertation (Yale University, 1976) of Susan J. Noakes, *The Reader's Work*.

things. To fully understand Dante's spiritual hermeneutic in its context, the constant tradition of *intelligentia spiritualis* in both the Christian West and East, would be an undertaking far beyond the bounds of this chapter and would call for a detailed application to Dante of the riches available to us in, for example, H. de Lubac's massive *Exégèse médiévale*. I will work here, then, with a restricted group of texts in an attempt to show that irenic apocalypse, one ideal definition of the total human "economy" in Christianity, characterizes as well Dante's ideas about the theory and practice of interpretation.

De Lubac has traced the development, in Christian thought, from hellenic *noûs* (mens) to the term *pneûma* (spiritus).[37] Both, it should be noticed from the outset, are "spiritual" faculties; they are, to put it succinctly, that which makes the species human. But *noûs* is subject to the fall; it can be consciously perverse. *Pneûma*, though its energy may be distorted by the "fallen" manner in which it is appropriated, is a constant presence of or participation in truth. With respect to the acts of interpretation and signification, it is a grace proper to the noetic-linguistic character of human nature; "mysteriously," it breaks open the closed, self-referential systems by which men ordinarily know, transcending while still prescinding from all linguistic, cultural or ideological horizons of knowledge. In a discussion of this *pneûma*, Augustine quotes, as example, the noetic-linguistic event narrated in *Acts* 10.44-46:

> Adhuc loquente Petro verba haec cecidit Spiritus sanctus super omnes qui audiebant verbum. Et obstupuerunt ex circumcisione fideles qui venerant cum Petro: quia et in nationes gratia Spiritus sancti effusa est. Audiebant enim illos loquentes linguis, et magnificantes Deum.
>
> [While Peter was speaking these words, the Holy Spirit fell upon all who heard the words. And all the faithful of the circumcision who came with Peter were amazed because the gift of the Holy Spirit was spread to the gentiles as well. For they heard them speaking in (other) tongues, and praising God.]

Although Peter's intention or the precise content of that which was communicated by his kerygma are not at all discernible here, the point is that real communication has definitely taken place: among those of many languages, among circumcised and uncircumcised, among the initiate and uninitiate. Augustine comments, echoing *John* 3.8, "the spirit breathes where it will." The minimal control which

---

[37] *Histoire et esprit* (Paris, 1950). There are, of course, exceptions, notably in Scotus Eriugena and his followers for whom the distinction is implausible. See M.-D. Chenu, "Spiritus: le vocabulaire de l'âme au XIIe siècle," *Revue des Sciences Philosophiques et Théologiques* 41 (1957), 213.

humans exercise over this spirit can be either daemonic or eudaemonic—either ignoring it (language as sheer information) or discerning and serving it (language as proffered to be diversely interpreted).[38] Dante, for one, carefully defined his individual poetic style along the general lines of an *intelligentia spiritualis*.

> ...I' mi son un che, quando
> Amor mi spira, noto, e a quel modo
> ch'e' ditta dentro, vo significando.
> (*Purgatorio* xxiv.52-54)

[As for me, I am one who, when Love breathes in me, I take note, and according to the way he dictates within, I go on signifying.]

Dante's poem is filled with rhetorical disclaimers of total control over his signifiers, but he claims here that the signifying activity itself (again the participle, *significando*, is a clue) is pneumatic. He says "a *quel modo*" only insofar as he says he discerns and is at the service of (at a given interpretative moment) an in-spiration unique to him. That kind of inspiration and proffer involve the words on the page, which Dante knows can only signify "*quodam*modo" at best; the reader is invited to serve the occasion of that flawed letter, to work toward an interpreting activity which is spiritual.

Any Christian hermeneutic, writes de Lubac, includes "la nouveauté de l'Esprit."[39] Knowing in a spiritual way is described, from Origen to Joachim of Flora (to cite an important, if somewhat heterodox, lineage) and from Augustine to Gregory to Bernard, as a heavenly banquet or eternal feeding which is tasted now, ironically, by means of the whole of interpretative activity proper to human nature.[40] Whether it be the book of the starry heavens or the book of the scriptures that is read, real nourishment can occur because a noetic understanding of the letter's structures can be joined to a pneumatic

---

[38] See Augustine's *De Trinitate* XV, 35-36, in Migne, *PL* XLII, cols. 1085-86.

[39] *Exégèse médiévale, op. cit.*, pt. I, 1, p. 358. See *Rom.* 7.6, "...ut serviamus in novitate spiritus, et non in vetustate litterae."

[40] See H. de Lubac, *Exégèse médiévale* (Paris, 1959-64), pt. I, 1: pp. 355-60 and pt. II, 1: pp. 437ff. For the most complete discussion of the idea in Joachim, see his *Expositio...in Apocalipsim* (Venezia, 1527), "Liber Introductorius." Joachim provides a further irenic image of interpretation in the "Prologus" of the same work. It is the irenic-apocalyptic marriage of Rebecca and Isaac. Isaac is only worthy of his bride (and of the marriage's implications: the salvific line) after a long period of painful servitude. So the reader is only worthy of the interpretation after a long struggle which involves first serving the letter and then putting off its literal sense (as biologically and psychically attached to him as are the old structures of kinship which marriage puts off) for the mysterious, spiritual sense "...pro sponso et patria quorum gloria nescit" ("...for a spouse and a homeland the glory of which he knows not").

sense of those same structures, while never obliterating "now" the experience of loss and struggle which the letter always communicates. "Now" and "then" join in a tension which is itself the content of an interpretation known in the activity of receiving any phenomenon at a given moment. And this last, in Christian terms and by analogy, is a Trinitarian statement. A "given moment," in other words, can be a propitious moment because a given moment was made propitious (a *kairos*: see *Ephes.* 1.10) in the real joining of eternity and temporality in the Incarnate Logos who materially manifests (as signifier) the Father (as signified) —with whom the Logos is spiritually one—in their Spirit (as act of signification). Cantos x to xiv of the *Paradiso* concern above all else the ways in which the intratrinitarian life can be extratrinitarially apprehended and appropriated.

In the opening lines of Canto x, Dante stresses this Trinitarian context for any text (as artifact) and for any interpretation or idea. Triune creation, the expression *ad extra* of the two "processions" in the Godhead which Dante calls *come figlia* and *come spira* (l. 51), subtends not only the order of physical existants but also the noetic-linguistic structures and acts which perceive and communicate them. The external Trinity informs "quanto per mente e per loco si gira" (l. 4): from the most complex thought, potentially revealing a unity, to the simplest seed, potentially revealing a complexity.[41] John Freccero has written "in sì aperta e 'n sì distesa lingua," that Dante's direction of the reader's glance to the point of celestial concord between the sun's two movements ("dove l'un moto e l'altro si percuote," l. 9), in the context of two concordant circles of spirits, must be read as a glance at the perfect *concordia* of the two Trinitarian processions because of which there is describable in the created order analogous *discordia concors*.[42] Implicit, however, in each analogy Dante provides in these cantos—the double-geared clock, the doubly-struck vat of water, the double millstone which is the saints' contradance, their antiphonal hagiography of Francis and Dominic and the spring equinox itself—is another Trinitarian analogy: that *discordia concors* which is the signifier's aspiration towards the signified.

Dante's second address to the reader in Canto x is explicit about the irenic apocalyptic character of both interpretation and signification.

> Or ti riman, lettor, sovra 'l tuo banco,
> dietro pensando a ciò che si preliba,

---

[41] See the Trinitarian creation passage in *Paradiso* xiii.52-66.
[42] "Paradiso x: the Dance of the Stars," *Dante Studies* 86 (1968), 85-111. The dance of twelve stellar spirits in those cantos, says Freccero, though it has many other sources as well, is explicitly apocalyptic. Its Old Testament type is found in *Daniel* 12.3.

72 *Irenic Apocalypse*

> s'esser vuoi lieto assai prima che stanco.
> Messo t'ho innanzi; omai per te ti ciba;
> ché a sé torce tutta la mia cura
> quella materia ond'io son fatto scriba.
> (ll. 22-27)

[Now stay at your desk, reader, thinking over that which you now foretaste, if you wish to be pleased long before you are tired out. I've set it in front of you; do your eating for yourself from now on. For that subject-matter of which I have been made the scribe bends my complete concern to itself.]

The foretaste which is the reader's act of reading (*"pensando* a ciò che si preliba"*)* is expressed as apocalyptic struggle (*stanco*) in the overriding context of irenic understanding (*lieto*). The single or isolated meal of the proffered text "tastes" the same—from the point of view of Dante's epistemology—as the taste of the divine presence when it is perceived anywhere in the order of creation: "...ch'esser non puote / sanza gustar di lui chi ciò rimira" (ll. 5-6) ("...for there can be no not tasting Him [God] for the person who reflects on that [any part of created reality]"). That taste, then, is always both sweet and bitter, as it was in *Apocalypse*. Any act of understanding—a tension between irenic and apocalyptic elements—can only permit one of these two to drop out under the pain of inevitable *discordia* or misinterpretation. What we all know all too well as the common event of misinterpretation is nonetheless a serious event. Such discord is so serious for Dante that he makes it analogous to a hypothetical loss of the creature's entire possibility (*potenza*) to be informed by the principles (*virtù*) of divinely ordained concord—were the cosmic tension between equator and ecliptic (intentionally "twisted" off-center) to be altered.[43] Lack of understanding is not necessarily scandalous but it is, at least part of the time, avoidable. In inventing the irenic concordances of Cantos x-xiv, Dante would seem to be proffering a text which is at pains to make it possible for the reader to live up to his or her potential *as reader*. It is in providing repeated textual concords and cautions that Dante dares to imitate most exactly the way God "writes" in the heavens.

The example of misinterpretation which St. Bonaventure provides Dante is a tragic and public misappropriation of a text. In the controversy between the spiritual Franciscans led by Ubertino da Casale and the conventuals led by Matteo d'Acquasparta, Bonaventure prophesies:

> Ben dico, chi cercasse a foglio a foglio
> nostro volume, ancor troveria carta

---

[43] See *Paradiso* x.16-18, immediately preceding the address to the reader.

> u' leggerebbe "I' mi son quel ch'i' soglio,"
> ma non fia da Casal né d'Acquasparta,
> là onde vegnon tali a la scrittura,
> ch'uno la fugge e l'altro la coarta.
> (*Paradiso* xii.121-26)

[I say plainly that he who might look through our book page by page would still find a page where he would read "As for me, I am what I always was"; but it will be neither from Casale nor Acquasparta, whence come those who have such an attitude to the written text (Rule) that one flees it while another contorts it.]

The spirituals overemphasize the irenic side of interpretation and manage, therefore, to "flee" the text as problem; the conventuals, in their concern with the letter alone, violently "restrict" and contort the text to their own end. Misreading of the Franciscan "scrittura" on both sides entails a perversion of the irenic apocalyptic structure of tension in interpretation so that the text's future is itself in crisis because a textual body of orthodox criticism vis-à-vis that text ("nostro volume") is so slow in being built up. To be a faithful critic of a given text—to say "I' mi son quel ch'i' soglio"—is, in terms of Dantesque metaphor, to be dependably a source of nourishment in *another's* hands. Thus, the misreaders are the "tares" whose tradition of misreading ("la mala coltura") makes them unfit to be ground into flour and made available as bread.

> e tosto si vedrà de la ricolta
> de la mala coltura, quando il loglio
> si lagnerà che l'arca li sia tolta.
> (*Paradiso* xii.118-20)

[soon some of the harvest out of the bad cultivation will be seen, when the tares will complain that the bin is taken away from them.]

We can expect that Dante, whom we have seen already as the object of Beatrice's constant *buona coltura*, will image his interpretative acts as producing flour. He does in Canto xiii, where a violent threshing out of problems is necessary as the double millstone of saints ("la santa mola," *Paradiso* xii.3—all of them interpreters in their lives) is engaged in the process of grinding out interpretative flour. St. Thomas speaks:

> e disse "Quando l'una paglia è trita,
> quando la sua semenza è già riposta,
> a batter l'altra dolce amor m'invita."
> (ll. 34-36)

[and he said "When one sheaf is threshed, when its seed is already put up, sweet love invites me to pound the other."]

As Dante experiences specific doubts being resolved, about the character of Solomon and the decadence of the Order of Preachers, Thomas provides a synesthetic image of the process itself.

> Or apri li occhi a quel ch'io ti rispondo,
> e vedräi il tuo credere e 'l mio dire
> nel vero farsi come centro in tondo.
> (ll. 49-51)

[Now open your eyes to that which I answer you, and you will see your act of belief and my act of speech centering in on the truth like the center of a circle.]

Dante is asked to "look at" a resolution, by means of language and logic, of two seemingly contradictory opinions; he is asked to visualize the irenic "solution" of a problem and to realize that such a place is where he already is: at the center of the circle. In the interpretative circle, Dante realizes that his own understanding (along with Thomas' speech) is part of the problem's complexity, its expressed periphery; this realization is simultaneous with his finding out, "seeing" the truth *for* himself at the center. Dante will shift the point of view of the center-circumference image again, to Beatrice as center, in order to convince the reader that the *coincidentia oppositorum* of exchanged words results in irenic understanding in the fiction. Thomas' speech from the periphery and Beatrice's from the center elicit the simile of a round container of water struck from the "outside" and from the "inside."

> Dal centro al cerchio, e sì dal cerchio al centro
> movesi l'acqua in un ritondo vaso,
> secondo ch'è percosso fuori o dentro.
> (*Paradiso* xiv.1-3)

[From the center to the circumference and from the circumference to the center water is moved in a rotund vessel accordingly as it is struck without or within.]

In this case, two complex terminals exchange words so that the linguistic event might render something new and substantial for another mind. The "rotondo vaso" is the *vas coniunctionis* of human nature (as early as Lactantius) which reduces complex perception to unified understanding because it is made up of both body and spirit; it is, in a more "modern" usage, the alchemical vessel or *vas coniunctionis* in which diverse and complex elements render a new substance.[44] The image exemplifies an epistemological principle which is restated in its

---

[44] See Lactantius, *Divine Institutes* 2.12.11 in Migne, *PL* VI, col. 321. For the reference in medieval alchemy, see Maria Louise von Franz, ed., *Aurora Consurgens* (a document attributed to Thomas Aquinas on the problem of opposites in chemistry) (New York, 1966).

ideal form in the Trinitarian hymn sung by the *spiriti* as they grind out this particular interpretation. "Quell'uno e due e tre che sempre vive / e regna sempre in tre e 'n due e 'n uno, / non circunscritto e tutto circunscrive," (*Paradiso* xiv.28-30) ("That one and two and three who always lives, who reigns always in three and in two and in one, not circumscribed it circumscribes all"), celebrates in linear fashion (the only way language can) the Trinity's circular life or "perichoresis"—the foundation of all knowledge—in which unity and complexity, center and circumference, are one. It celebrates as well the Trinity's "reign" *ad extra*, for created reality, which Dante renders linguistically by juxtaposing naming ("tre") and describing or characterizing ("in tre"). The song, sung around Dante as prelude to the problem's solution, is indoctrination, dogmatic education in the best sense of the words; all value, aesthetic value included, is judged according to its literal verisimilitude, which is to say, its similitude to the Trinity which is the structural principle of all existants in Christianity.[45] It is important to note, too, that "three" is the turning point of the lyric. The third person is the unifying act among the three Persons in Trinitarian theology; it is the Spirit and its activity which must be praised, in linear fashion, *before* the one "God" can be mentioned in the traditional closing of the *oratio romana* from which Dante took his controlling verbs "vive" and "regna": "per dominum nostrum Iesum Christum filium tuum qui tecum vivit et regnat in *unitate* Spiritus Sancti, Deus..."

Dante-pilgrim's new-found knowledge is that the saints themselves, even in their proximity to Trinitarian perfection, still perceive "now" very much in terms of a *lack*, an apocalyptic element in their irenic lives. They, of course, lack their bodies. Though they convey the truth to the pilgrim without a doubt, they are flawed as signifiers.

---

[45] That the play of proportion (*analogia*) does not always result in harmony was clear in the ancient world. It should be clear enough to us as readers that the play of verbal analogies does not always result in communication. But it does in cantos x-xiv which explicitly appropriate the Holy Spirit as the principle of *analogia*, creating the harmony of the spheres, the dance, the "concordi numi" (*Paradiso* xii.31). The Spirit's unifying activity is attested to constantly in the church fathers. I would cite here only a passage from Clement of Alexandria which makes many of the same points as Dante's:

> And this pure song which supports the universe and makes a concord of all its beings, after having been spread abroad from the center to the extremities and from the extremities back to the center, has ruled the "ensemble"... [The Logos creates the song, but the singing act which effects the concord of the two motions is the Holy Spirit itself] he ruled the ensemble with the Holy Spirit... he makes use of this infinite-voiced instrument [polyphōnou] to celebrate God, and sings himself—in accord with the human instrument.

Protreptikos I.5, 1-3, in *Sources Chrétiennes*, ed. C. Mondésert (Paris, 1949); translation mine.

The poet's activity shares the tension proper to the reader's. Only in the mode of both painful and selfless service to the matter of his text can the writer legitimately offer the text to be interpreted by another: "che a sé torce tutta *la mia cura* / quella materia ond'io *son fatto* scriba" (ll. 26-27). An example of such selflessness in the fiction of the journey is provided in Canto x by Beatrice who (just as Dante-poet has directed the reader to the heavens and to his book simultaneously) directs the pilgrim to that "materia" which is crucial for him: to the God ("il sol degli angeli") whose art or representation of itself can be interpreted by the human mind. In giving thanks for the text-at-hand, for a complex signifier (il sol "sensibil" and, by extension, the entire cosmos) intended for a complex mind which knows by differentiating, Dante-pilgrim's attempt at "unified" understanding momentarily "eclipses" Beatrice as a source of light.[46] His experience is irenic as is her selfless response to it:

> Non le dispiacque, ma sì se ne rise,
> che lo splendor de li occhi suoi ridenti
> mia mente unita in più cose divise.
> (ll. 61-63)

[It did not displease her; rather she so smiled at it that the splendor of her smiling eyes divided my unified intellect into further objects (of intellection).]

Since the journey directed by Beatrice is for a man still in the flesh, her light returns as the diachronic presence to which a synchronic movement necessarily gives way. The pilgrim's peaceful confrontation with the proffered "materia"—his prayer—produces a renewed complexity or division of the terms of the problem as he sees not one or two but twelve "ardenti soli" (l. 76) dancing in a circle around him. Dante claims that the concord of their voices and movements is so perfect that it may only be appreciated "then" in heaven, where the diachronic gives way completely to the synchronic: "...colà dove gioir s'insempra" (l. 148) ("...there where rejoicing eternalizes itself"). But in the simile he adduces to express it—the double-geared clock ringing matins in church—divine harmony is known "now" in the irenic apocalyptic situation of liturgy.

> tin tin sonando con sì dolce nota,
> ch'l ben disposto spirto d'amor turge.
> (ll. 143-44)

[ringing 'tin tin' with so sweet a note that the well-disposed soul swells with love.]

---

[46] For Dante's notion of the "complex" mind, see *Paradiso* x.82-87, in which the unified splendor of a differentiated Trinity is "multiplicato in te" or available to the complex, tri-partite human soul as it is described in Aristotle's *De Anima*.

To be "well disposed" in ritual is to know that, although the spirit's "swelling" is momentary, the spirit swells immeasurably, beyond number, beyond analysis. In the liturgy, the adept's "service" is an interpretative act which reveals in the temporal moment what Gabriel Marcel calls its "principle of inexhaustibility" which allows it to overcome, for a short time, its evident structures and end-directedness.[47]

The constant "cura" of the twelve and then twenty-four "spiriti sapienti" is that Dante learn to interpret his vision well. Thomas Aquinas' clarification of the seemingly discordant *quaestiones* in his spoken text, the one-to-one structural parallel between the hagiographies in Cantos xi and xii (in exegetical terms, a *concordia ad numeros*), all the learning devices, in sum, which the poet brings to bear on his reader "sovra il... banco," are brought to bear through the pilgrim's experience at the center of a double and then triple circle which, given what we have already seen, might properly be called a heuristic circle. The rules and tools of interpretation are provided there so that the pilgrim might find his way to any limited *significatio*. Such finding is, in turn, always a personal way *back* to his own unlimited source: "...per quella scala / u' sanza risalir nessun discende" (*Paradiso* x.86-87) ("...by that stairway where no one comes down without going up again"). To put succinctly what will require a lengthier explanation below, the third corona or circle "of the Holy Spirit" appears (though subliminally) because the Spirit—both in its intratrinitarian and extratrinitarian life—is the "persona ductrix at Patrem." In time, its specific "mission" is to enflame the complex mind—each mind and each kind of complexity—and to return it through its noetic-linguistic operations (on which the first two circles center) to an experience of unity.[48] Such an outline is valid both for what medieval hermeneutics means by interpreting a metaphor (an "intelligentia *spiritualis*") and for what medieval theology means by knowing God ("sapientia"). The two acts are different but not radically different.

[47] Gabriel Marcel, *Being and Having* (Harper Torchbooks, New York, 1965), pp. 102-03. In Dante's simile, the end-directedness of eros opens up to agapè by means of the Christian reading of the bride in the *Song of Songs* as the church: "...la sposa di Dio surge / a mattinar lo sposo perché l'ami" (ll. 140-41) ("...God's bride arises to sing a morning song to her spouse, that he may make love to her").

[48] Two texts are primary for this reading of the third corona and for the explanation to follow. They are Thomas Aquinas' *Scriptum Super Sententiis Magistri Petri Lombardi* (Paris, 1929-47 and 1956) and, a masterful commentary on Thomas' commentary, Francesco Marinelli, *Personalismo Trinitario nella storia della salvezza* (Roma, 1969). See bibliography for complete references. Many points of terminology—including the *Persona ductrix...*—are made more easily graspable in J.A. Lopez-Casuso's long review of Marinelli's work: "Sobre una nueva valoración del personalismo trinitario tomista," *Estudios Trinitarios* 7, no. 1 (1973), 79-109 and especially p. 95.

> Ed ecco intorno, di chiarezza pari,
> nascere un lustro sopra quel che v'era
> per guisa d'orizzonte che rischiari.
> E sì come al salir di prima sera
> comincian per lo ciel nove parvenze,
> sì che la vista pare e non par vera,
> parvemi lì novelle sussistenze
> cominciare a vedere, e fare un giro
> di fuor da l'altre due circunferenze.
> Oh vero sfavillar del Sancto Spiro!
> come si fece sùbito e candente
> a li occhi miei che, vinti, nol soffriro!
> *(Paradiso* xiv.67-78)

[And behold roundabout, of equal brightness, a light was born upon the one which was there, like an horizon's brightening. And like at the early evening sky's march upwards new appearances begin in the heavens, such that the sight both seems and does not seem real, it seemed to me there that new substances began to appear and to circle about beyond the other two circumferences. Oh true sparkling of the Holy Spirit! How suddenly and shining it became to my eyes which, overcome, could not stand it!]

The way back, in theology, is by means of the Spirit. In the letter to Can Grande della Scala, Dante quotes the *Apocalypse* in order to assert that the only fitting terminal point for his poem, as the representation of a journey back, is theology's terminal point: a representation of God itself, the "Alpha and O."[49] But the poem is unlike theology most of all in the sense that, rather than beginning directly from God, it deliberately begins *in medias*, "nel mezzo del cammin..." in a situation of alienation from the natural, which is to say, the spiritual "motio" or "impulsio" back to God.[50] Part of the burden of this chapter has been to show how well the final cantos of the *Purgatorio* translate into poetry two dicta in Christian theology: that grace builds on individual nature and that the eschaton begins "now" with grace. The appearance of a third circle of lights in *Paradiso* xiv, I would suggest, is a momentary glance at the spiritual implications of doing or representing anything in the *present* irenic apocalyptic or eschatological situation. The poet's problem of representing God (or anything else) fictionally is analogous to the problem, in the fiction, of the pilgrim's *really* returning to God. As we have already seen to a certain extent, both are pneumatic activities.

[49] *Epist.* 10.473ff; see *Apoc.* 1.8, 22-23.
[50] Thomas Aquinas, *Summa Theol.* Ia, 1, q. 36, a. 1 and q. 37, a. 4: "Spiritus, quo nomine quedam vitalis motio et impulsio designatur... ad aliquid faciendum" ("Spirit, by which name is signified a certain vital movement and impulse... toward the accomplishment of any act").

Aquinas, in his commentary on Peter Lombard's *Sentences*, characterizes all spiritual and physical reality as in some sense moving in a circle. This circular movement has a double aspect: *exitus* (a going out) and *reditus* (a coming back). We have already noted that in the intratrinitarian life, the third Person is the principle of that unified circular motion among the three Persons which Greek theology terms perichoresis. Its being unifies the two acts which are Trinitarian life: generation of the Son by the Father and spiration of the Spirit by the Father and the Son. Represented in a linear fashion—as in Dante's 123321 model—these two "processions" are a Trinity in which the third Person completes a circle back to the Father. In extratrinitarian life, circular motion is flawed even though it aspires to perfect circularity. All pneumatic concords of the movements *exitus* and *reditus* are truly *discordia concors* insofar as they exist in time and are subject to lack. In Dante's fiction in the heavens, then, the first two coronae of spirits moving in opposite circular motion point, we have seen as well, to the two divine processions. But their activity as signifiers is flawed because the way back, the *reditus*, is yet to be completed in time. This is why the spirits yearn for the new means of perceiving which will be theirs when they are "rifatti," "tutta quanta" ("whole"; *Paradiso* xiv.17, 45) at their bodies' resurrection. This is why the third corona, although imaged in quite specific terms, is incomplete or just barely visible. In Dante it "seems" to be seen, just as, for Hilary of Poitiers, "...ita quod ex te per eum sanctus spiritus tuus est, etsi sensu quidem non percipiam, sed tamen teneo conscientia..." ("...that the Holy Spirit is yours from you [the Father] through him [the Son], though in truth I may not perceive it sensually, I nevertheless am conscious of it..."). The principle of analogy between creator and creature still remains. As Thomas puts it, "...ita processus temporalis creaturarum ab aeterno processu personarum."[51] ("...so the temporal procession of creatures is from the eternal procession of Persons"). The circular movement of the creature back to its origin ("apokatastasis" in Greek theology) must in some sense be analogous to the unifying movement of two processions among three Persons (perichoresis). The unifying activity of the Spirit, what one scholar of Thomas' commentary calls

---

[51] *Scriptum super sent.*, *op. cit.*, prologus lib. I. For intellectual background to the notions of perfect and imperfect circularity, especially as they apply to the literal movement of the pilgrim in the fiction, see John Freccero, "Dante's Pilgrim in a Gyre," *PMLA* 76 (1961), 168-81. For the quotation from Hilary's *De Trinitate*, 12.56, see J. Doignon, "L'Esprit souffle où il veut...," *Revue des Sciences Philosophiques et Théologiques* 62 (1978), 350-57. Notice Hilary's reliance here upon the *per filium*- rather than upon the *filioque*-formula.

"un terzo aspetto della circulatio," must therefore act *ad extra*, in and for the creature. This third aspect of circular motion is the foundation in time of the attitude I have called irenic apocalypse; it is the very possibility of an eschatological orientation leading, *modo circulare*, to a *coniunctio ad Deum* or *adhaesio fini*. It is given freely and superabundantly to nature on the way back (*redeundi*), and is ordered, in particular, to the complex human mind which must move (by means of linearity and language) to circularity if it is to mature. Such is the pilgrim's mind and his journey as a maturing plant, coming into the inheritance which Matelda (as *arra, promession*) represented in Eden.[52]

Though there cannot be a third *processus* within the Trinity, there are innumerable *processiones* or *missiones* for humanity which perfect its eschatological orientation after the initial experience of grace.[53] The spreading abroad of new and diverse graces is the "missio visibilis spiritus sancti ad extra." In both Western and Eastern pneumatological writing, rhetorical distinctions between the notion of the Spirit's grace and grace's being divided or spread abroad are most common. The typical rhetorical pairings would be:[54]

unus	harmonia	promissus	unitas	promotor
dividens	distribuens	mittens	multiplicans	movens

Dante signals the *missio Spiritus Sancti ad extra* in *Paradiso* xiv in the figure of fire which recalls the advent of that mission at Pentecost. The poet says "...si fece subito..."—a direct translation of "factus est repente" in the Pentecost narrative in *Acts* 2.2; what comes is not the *favilla* of a single grace, but the immeasurable spreading abroad of the Spirit's grace, *sfavillar*, a rhetorical turn very much in the tradition of writing on the Spirit's continuing activity in the world. Another

---

[52] Francesco Marinelli, *Personalismo trinitario nella storia della salvezza* (Rapporti fra la SSma Trinità e le opere ad extra nello scriptum super sententiis di S. Tommaso) (Roma, 1969), p. 46ff. See *Scriptum super Sent.*, III.13, 1,1: "Perfectio autem ad quam disponit gratia est coniunctio ad Deum; et haec est multiplex: scilicet in aenigmatibus et per speciem." It seems to me that much light would be shed on the exceedingly complicated metaphor of upside-down and rightside-up trees in *Paradiso* xxvii, were we to apply to it the notions of *exitus* and *reditus* which are here applied to other nature-metaphors in Dante.

[53] See Thomas' "De Potentia" IX.9 in the *Quaestiones Disputatae* (Paris, 1925): "...sed sequitur ulterius processio in esteriorem naturam."

[54] For an anthology of representative Greek and Latin texts, see Sebastianus Tromp, ed., *De Spiritu Sancto anima corporis mystici* (Pontificia Universitas Gregoriana, Textus et Documenta, series theologica, no. 1, 7, Roma, 1932). The *unus-dividens* rhetoric is most notably Pauline; see, for example, *I Cor.* 12.11. In note 45 above, Clement's *Protreptikos* has it that the Spirit is not the song itself but the "infinite-voiced instrument" producing it.

conspicuous use of "sfavillar" in the *Paradiso* is quite the same, structurally, as *Paradiso* xiv. The poet's vision of massed signifiers becoming contextualized for the pilgrim in *Paradiso* xviii.70ff, is called "lo sfavillar de l'amor che li era" (l. 71) ("the sparkling of love that was there"). An act of signification, spelling out a message in the heavens, it involves two contrary motions named "prima" ("first") and "poi" ("then") (ll. 79-80) exactly as the motions of the two coronae are imaged and named in *Paradiso* xiii.18. The participles ("cantando" and "diventando"), almost ikons in the text at this point, clearly signify the act's taking place.[55] The "discordia concors" of a complex intention achieved, the innumerable spirits behind the letters experience an irenic moment of completed (if imperfect) circularity: "un poco s'arrestavano e taciensi" (l. 81) ("they rested somewhat and quieted themselves"). Both at Pentecost and in the pilgrim's "now" in the heavens, the Spirit's most important gifts are linguistic— "interpretatio sermonum."[56] Spiritual understanding has been the goal in these cantos all along. The third corona validates, makes satisfactory, the tension in interpretation which was already experienced and which, in time, must remain. Earlier in this chapter, we dealt with the idea of *pneûma* as an abiding spiritual character of the human soul. A name applied to this character throughout the patristic and medieval periods happens to be a synonym with *favilla*: "*scintilla animae*." Dante uses both words for the same meaning of "spark" and, given the complex idea of *sfavillar* in *Paradiso* xiv, must intend for the word to bear the implications of the spreading abroad of *scintillae*. Those implications, put briefly, are exactly what we might expect. In neoplatonic texts, *scintillae* are always on the way back, *redeundi*, or up from their unnatural movement down as star-born sparks. In gnostic texts, the scintilla is the Spirit and the principle of concord. In Origen and Jerome, *scintillae* create the *intelligentia spiritualis* which the pil-

---

[55] A note on participles. They are the grammatical sign in the tradition of Christian rhetoric of the unseizable character of the Spirit's activity; I have had to use and interpret many in this book. The most elaborate recognition of this function I know of is in Athanasius. In the *Oratio III contra Arianos*, 24 (in Migne, *PG* XXVI, col. 373), he says: "By the *participation* of the Holy Spirit, we are knit into the Deity." We are finally and always contextualized, in other words, by this pneumatic participation which in Greek (*metochē*) is also the grammatical term for participle. Then there is Isidore of Seville's definition of the grammatical term (*Etym.* I, 11 in Migne, *PL* LXXXII, col. 88) which a clever exegete would have little trouble in turning into Trinitarian grammar: "Participium dictum, quod nominis et verbi capiat partes, quasi particapium. A nomine enim vindicat sibi genera et casus; a verbo tempora, et significationes; ab utroque numerum et figuram."
[56] Gregory the Great, *Moralia in Job* 2.53 in Migne, *PL* LXXV, cols. 598-600.

grim is being taught to seek on his journey back.⁵⁷ Thomas calls it the soul's best part and says specifically, "haec virtus transcendit rationabilem."⁵⁸ In Dante, the *sfavillar* is momentary and the mind cannot hold onto it ("...quelle vedute... che non seguir la mente" (ll. 80-81). Thomas, in the same passage, calls it a "dawn" (*albedo*) in the mind which cannot be extinguished by the *tenebrae* of sin or even of mistakes in reasoning. Dante's *sfavillar* is both a dawning ("per guisa d'orizzonte che rischiari," l. 69) and the presence of lights which shine even at evening ("...al salir di prima sera / comincian per lo ciel nove parvenze" ll. 70-71).⁵⁹ Bonaventure sees it as *syndhaeresis*, the principle of conscience or discernment of spirits; Thomas agrees but qualifies the voluntarist notion by saying that the *scintillae* do not discern "freely" but "according to rules."⁶⁰ The *scintillae animae* or *sfavillar del Sancto Spiro* are the foundation of the process of discernment, the hermeneutic process, in medieval criticism and particularly in the cantos of literary interpretation *spiritualiter* in the *Paradiso*.

In Canto xiv, the third corona is "di chiarezza pari" (l. 67) because it is the visible act of concordance of the first two coronae as fictive analogues to the coequal Trinity.⁶¹ But it is subliminal—"...la vista par e non par vera" (l. 72) —finally because it is only an analogue. Though the terms are perhaps too word-centered to be entirely valid theologically, I think it useful to look again at the Trinitarian model with respect to language. In the Trinity, the signifier (Logos) in its signifying activity (Pneûma) *is* THE signified (Father); in language the word (logos) in its signifying activity (the "spirit" of the letter) points to or provides the occasion for A signified. Its way back is unclear and qualified; the way back in the Trinity is "to the same," "reditus in idem."⁶² In New Testament terms, "No one comes to the Father [as

---

⁵⁷ For an article which traces the entire idea of *scintillae* in detail, see Michel Tardieu, "Psychaios Spinther: Histoire d'une métaphore dans la tradition platonicienne jusqu'à Eckhart," *Revue des Etudes Augustiniennes* 21, 3 (1975), 225-55; individual references to the several notions of *scintillae* mentioned here are provided in the article in abundance.

⁵⁸ *Scriptum super Sent.* IV.39, 3, 1.

⁵⁹ Medieval alchemical doctrine distinguishes individual luminosity (*scintilla*) from an infinite expansion of luminosity in the mature, harmonious soul (*scintillae*—or Dante's *sfavillar*) which is, in its turn, imaged as the starry heavens and is one with them in contemplation. The mature, ripe soul is a luminous *aurora* which does not cede to darkness but to starry lights shining in the darkness and promising a new dawn. See M.L. von Franz, *op. cit.*, pp. 171-72.

⁶⁰ *Scriptum super Sent.* II.24, 3.

⁶¹ The Spirit proceeds from the Father and the Son "utrique coaequalis et ad Trinitatem pertinens," in *Scriptum super Sent.* I.1, 2.

⁶² Marinelli, *op. cit.*, p. 46. For a Trinitarian epistemological model in Dante, see *Paradiso* xxxiii.124-26.

signified] except through me [as signifier]" (*John* 14.6) must certainly be glossed with "No one can say, Lord Jesus, unless in the Holy Spirit [the spirit of the letter]" (*I Cor.* 12.3). John Chrysostom's gloss on the problem sees it as specifically hermeneutic.[63] He indicates the possibility of a hermeneutic model for *Gal.* 4.6-7:

> The proof that you are sons [logoi] is that God has sent [*exitus*] the Spirit of His Son [Pneuma logou] into your hearts crying [participle denotes act of signification]: Abba, Father [*reditus*, signified]; it is this that makes you a son [logos], not a slave [locked into the letter's material structure]. And if God has made you son, then he has made you heir.

The final phrase involves—if we allow ourselves to follow the structural logic—what I called earlier in this chapter Dante's irenic confidence in language. Human language, in the Christian tradition, is waiting upon its inheritance of signification.

---

[63] "De S. Pentacostae," *Hom.* I, 4, in Migne, *PG* I, col. 458.

4   Petrarch: De Legendo Deo

Readers of the *De Vita Solitaria* have long been convinced that it embodied, in the middle of the *trecento*, a radically different approach to one of the most important forms of religious life in the Middle Ages. Zeitlin's early characterization of the treatise as epicurean, "an ideal purely personal and private,"[1] is, however, as oversimple with respect to Petrarch's rhetoric as is F. Serpagli's recent insistence that it is "spiritual" and "contemplative" in an entirely traditional sense.[2] P.O. Kristeller, addressing himself less to the text than to its ideas, says that Petrarch "...transformed the monastic ideal of solitude into a secular and literary ideal..."[3] Similarly, Giovanni Gentile sees Petrarch as actively refusing to represent his solitude in the traditional fashion, as a vehicle for man's "nullification" into God.[4] Both these latter conclusions are helpful; but they must be read with certain cautions. If Kristeller uses "secular" to mean "worldly" or the opposite of spiritual, as seems to be the case, then we must modify his viewpoint by interpreting Petrarch's text as thoroughly spiritual in that it seeks the

---

[1] Francesco Petrarca, *The Life of Solitude*, translated with introduction and notes by J. Zeitlin (University of Illinois, 1924), p. 56. Zeitlin notes an "aesthetic fastidiousness unbecoming in a person of religious pretensions" (p. 60) which begs the question of just what may be said to constitute "religious" vision and, indeed, a "Christian" religious vision.

[2] Francesco Serpagli, *Prolegomeni al "De Vita Solitaria" di Francesco Petrarca* (Parma, 1966), pp. 25, 31. Thorough scholarship, to which this chapter is often indebted, never prevents Serpagli from taking Petrarch at his word. Typical of Serpagli's overall view is the following: "Questo carattere spirituale e principalissimo che disvela la grande religiosità dell'animo petrarchesco, appare dimostrato e dalla natura della solitudine dichiarata dall'autore, dagli effetti soprannaturali da essa promanenti, da esemplificazioni storiche addotte, nonché dall'aperta confessione del Petrarca stesso" (p. 25).

[3] *Eight Philosophers of the Italian Renaissance* (Stanford, 1964), p. 14.

[4] See *Storia della filosofia italiana*, vol. I, a cura di E. Garin (Firenze, 1969), pp. 138-40.

perfection of the human will so that the *solitarius* might achieve that perspective in which he can recognize himself as both creature and image of God.[5] While Petrarch definitely does not immerse or "nullify" himself into the divine essence, the rhetoric of the *De Vita* would go beyond a literary mode of self-affirmation and describe the momentary experience of another type of "nullification" which critics seem not to have recognized. In these moments, Petrarch pictures himself as an ecstatic, *de litteris*. I hope to demonstrate that the text specifically uses, makes its own, the irenic-apocalyptic language of monastic spirituality. Though its undeniably heterodox stance with respect to this "religio" reveals the theoretical possibility of a "secular," classicizing reading, the text not only says that it is an ascetic work but contains the lineaments of a new ascesis. The reader either has or has not been hoodwinked; he, literally, cannot know. The critic's role is not to decide for him but to describe the problem in terms of the ways this text intends to be confusing.

Perhaps the surest approach to both the rhetoric and context of Petrarch's "spirituality" is to contrast it with an authoritative text of the older ascetic tradition of which the *De Vita* seeks to be a part. One treatise on solitude is just so authoritative in the twelfth century and afterwards: the *Epistola ad Fratres de Monte-Dei* or *Epistola Aurea* of Guillaume de St.-Thierry. Written about 1145 at the Cistercian monastery of Signy, the letter was quickly attributed to St. Bernard of Clairvaux and its fame spread with that of his other works. It was continuingly favored by the Carthusians even though their founding fathers had written at length on the same subject. It became required reading for hermits, cenobites, and even the mendicants, whose active life made the retreat to solitude all the more crucial; such, at least, was the rationale of both Sts. Bonaventure and Anthony of Padua in recommending the *Epistola* to their order.[6] One study on the constant influence of twelfth-century devotional writing in the fourteenth and fifteenth centuries makes special mention of the popularity of the *Epistola*, citing thirty-four manuscripts which have come down to us from Petrarch's century alone.[7]

---

[5] The other possible reading of "secular"—lay as opposed to clerical—would not make very much sense. Kristeller is certainly not unaware of the sizeable phenomenon of lay-hermits in the Middle Ages (see Jean Becquet, "L'Eremitisme clérical et laic dans L'Ouest de la France," in *Miscellanea del Centro di Studi Medioevali* IV (1962), pp. 186-89; and Petrarch, after all, did receive minor orders.

[6] See M.-M. Davy, *Un Traité de la vie solitaire: Epistola ad Fratres de Monte-Dei* (Etudes de Philosophie Médiévale: 29) (Paris, 1940), pt. II, pp. 40-54.

[7] Giles Constable, "The Popularity of Twelfth-Century Spiritual Writers in the Later Middle Ages," in *Renaissance Studies in Honor of Hans Baron*, eds. A. Molho and J. Tedeschi (Dekalb, Illinois, 1971), pp. 5-28.

From the outset, the *Epistola* is unmistakably a treatise on mystical theology from the particular point of view of monastic solitude. Guillaume greets the Carthusians of Mont-Dieu with the words "sabbatum delicatum," "a sabbath of delights." In one symbolic phrase which recalls the eschatological character of the Christian community in *Hebrews* 4.9-10, *Apoc.* 1.10 and St. Bernard's theme of "dulcia sabbata"—created both to "redeem the time" through action and to "give oneself over to God" at rest—Guillaume places his reader's labors in the atemporal day of rest in which John had placed the *Apocalypse*.[8] Thus the monk will experience, in a more concentrated way, that sabbatical tension between "then" and "now" which is common to all Christians. The sabbath of delights must return to time, to an evening and nightfall which recall the monk to struggle, vigil, terror at the loss of light and hope for its return.[9] The irenic salutation is offered, then, in the context of a time, place and vocation which monastic rhetoric has always seen as apocalyptic: the cell or hermitage as battle-ground (according to Peter Damian) for a life-or-death encounter with the whore of Babylon.[10] The earliest appearance of Christian monasticism involved irenic retreat to a solitude which nurtured another generation of "bloodless" martyrs whose witness was as eschatologically directed as was the witness of *Apocalypse*'s intended readership. In a letter on the new monastic phenomenon, St. Jerome apostrophizes: "O desertum Christi floribus vernans. O solitudo in qua illi nascuntur lapides, de quibus in Apocalypsi civitas magna regis extruitur..." ("O desert blooming with Christ-flowers. O solitude where the stones are hid with which the King's great city is

---

[8] *Hebrews* 4.9-10: "Itaque relinquitur sabbatismus populi Dei. Qui enim ingressus est in requiem eius, etiam ipse requievit ab operibus suis, sicut a suis Deus." ("There remains therefore a sabbath-rest for God's people. For whoever enters into his rest, he too rests from his own labors, just as God did from his."). For *vacare Deo*, see Bernard's *Sermones in Cantica XII, PL* CLXXXIV, col. 60. However *vacare Deo* may be translated, it should be understood as containing the notion of "lack" which it has in classical Latin and which the rhetoric of contemplation retains from Seneca through Jerome and the twelfth century. Hence, *vacare Deo* means both possession and incomplete possession, both attainment of a goal, and abstention from the inquietude of trying to attain the unattainable (see Jean Leclercq, OSB, *Otia Monastica*, "Studia Anselmiana" II [Rome, 1963], chapter III). The experience of lack in fullness, says Guillaume, is made bearable by *patientia* which is, as we have seen in a previous chapter, an apocalyptic term (*Epistola* 112). For other readings of the "sabbatum delicatum," see M.-M. Davy, *op. cit.*, pt. II, p. 5, f.n. 2.

[9] In Augustine's reading of the *Genesis* story, God's day of rest from his creating labors has no evening and, hence, expresses no finitude or lack (*De Civitate Dei* XX.7; see Jean Leclercq, *Otia Monastica*, p. 46). It is the sabbath of which each sabbath in time is an incomplete type.

[10] Peter Damian, *Laus Vitae Eremitae, PL* CXLV.

built in Apocalypse..."). As Guillaume himself puts it: "Post passionem vero Domini, calente adhuc in cordibus fidelium effusi eius sanguinis recenti memoria... deserta repleta sunt"[11] ("After the Lord's death, by the recent memory of his spilled blood still burning in the hearts of the faithful... the deserts got crowded"). The *Epistola* addresses those who had intentionally returned to the pure, eremetical monasticism of the desert fathers; the character of their struggle would be particularly irenic.

> Altissima enim est professio vestra. Celos transit, par angelis est, angelicae similis puritati... Aliorum est Deum servire; vestrum est adherere. Aliorum est Deum credere, scire, amare et revereri; vestrum est sapere, intelligere, cognoscere, frui... (11, pp. 73-74)... querere Deum Iacob, non communi omnium more, sed querere ipsam faciem Dei... hoc est cognitionem eius, querere faciem ad faciem... (16, p. 77)[12]

> [Yours, therefore, is the highest of (religious) professions. It penetrates to heaven itself, it is on a par with the life of angels, with angelic purity... Let others serve God; yours is to embrace him. Let others believe in God, know, love, and revere him; yours is to taste him, to understand, to know intimately, to enjoy... (your profession) is to seek after the God of Jacob, not in the common way of all men, but to seek his very face... to know God intimately means to seek a face-to-face knowledge...]

Since these Carthusians were to be some of the few who attained the fourth *gradus* described in the *De Diligendo Deo*, Guillaume felt free, in the passage above, to share Bernard's language concerning that state. The soul in the fourth *gradus* "totus pergat in Deum, et *adhaerens* Deo unus cum eo spiritus fiat"[13] ("may totally move towards God, and *embracing* God may become one spirit with him").

Guillaume's tract is divided into two basic sections, named "speculum" and "enigma"; the Pauline metaphors are here made to correspond with Bernard's or, as some have argued, a generally Cistercian view of the mystic's life as leading from vision mediated by meditation mainly on scripture (*speculum*) to ecstatic God-centeredness (*enigma*) and a unitive vision in which, though incompletely (hence "enigmatically"), love understands God as God understands itself.[14] To leave the world

---

[11] Jerome, *Epistola ad Nepotianum*, PL XXII, col. 527. For the Guillaume text, see Migne's edition of the *Epistola*, PL CLXXXIV, col. 310.
[12] All references to the sections and page numbers of the *Epistola* will refer to pt. I of M.-M. Davy's edition, cited above. All translations, unless otherwise noted, are my own.
[13] PL LXXXII, col. 595c (italics mine).
[14] For a detailed explanation of *amor-intellectus* in Guillaume and its relationship to Cistercian thought, see Patrick Ryan, OCSO, "The Witness of William of St.-Thierry to the Spirit and Aims of the Early Cistercians," in *The Cistercian Spirit: a Symposium*, ed. M. Basil Pennington, OCSO (Shannon, Ireland, 1970), pp. 224-53 and especially pp. 244-49.

and enter into solitude is to renounce obsession with the self and to leave room for the experience of the other which is God. In the world, a human being was "solus," bereft of any real friendship; alone in the cell, the hermit is "solitarius," for whom the increasing intimacy of the other gradually subdues selfullness. The descriptions of the *unio mystica* which, as we might expect, conclude the *Epistola,* isolate those extraordinary illuminations of a life which is ordinarily one of ascetic exercises, physical labor and "dark" (non-sensual) contemplation. These passages repeatedly use the passive voice and insist on the momentariness of the experience; the rhetoric is full of qualifying words which stress the inadequacy of human language to the substance of the vision.

> Electo enim et dilecto Dei, *aliquando* vicissim lumen *quoddam* vultus Dei *ostenditur...* ut per hoc quod *quasi in transcursu vel transpuncto* videre *permittitur...* hereditatem plenae visionis Dei... gratia perstringit sensum amantis, et eripit ipsum sibi, et rapit in diem qui est a tumultu rerum ad gaudia silentii, et pro modulo suo, ad *momentum,* ad *punctum* id ipsum ostendens ei videndum sicuti est... (110, pp. 147-48)... quia *factus est* unus spiritus cum Deo, spiritualis est. (116, p. 153; italics mine)

> [Sometimes, something of the light of God's face is shown by him to his elect and beloved... in such a way that when (the soul) is permitted to see as if in passing and in a split second... (it burns to possess) the inheritance of the complete vision of God... grace captures the senses of the lover, draws him to itself, and ravishes him to that day [the "sabbatum delicatum," certainly] which is far from the tumult of created things, to the joys of silence; and there, according to the soul's capacity, God gives himself to be seen as he is—in a moment, in the fraction of an instant... for the soul has been made one spirit with God, and it is therefore called "spiritual"...]

In one sense, the mystical life "is given"—the subject remaining predominantly passive; in another sense, however, the mystical life can be said to have been learned. Immediately after describing something of the experience of mystical union, Guillaume continues:

> Ubi cum didicerit quid intersit inter mundum et immundum, redditur sibi, et remittitur ad mundandum cor ad visionem, ad aptandum animum ad similitudinem: ut, si aliquando rursum admittatur, sit purior ad videndum adhuc, et stabilior ad fruendum. (111, p. 148)

> [Whence, having learned to recognize what a gap exists between the clean and the unclean, (the soul) is returned to itself, is sent back in order to clean the heart to better enable it to see, to accustom the soul to its similitude (with God): so that, if sometime again it is re-admitted to the vision, it might be purer so to see and more stable so to enjoy.]

By "learning" the uniqueness of divine illumination or, better, by remembering the sweetness it brings and the spiritual gap which it fills ("quid intersit..."), the hermit practices a daily ascesis which more and more perfects his "similitudo" with the divine nature and makes him more capable of bearing a vision of which he is increasingly aware. *Memoria*, for Guillaume, is the repository of those spiritual thoughts which are the residue of the mystical experience and which excite the soul to wait upon further graces ("si aliquando rursum admittatur..."). Once the grace has been received, in other words, it can be recognized as having had a divinely-planned history in the personal life of the believer and a particular disposition to his unique personality ("pro modulo suo"). It can be awaited with more realistic hope because the believer becomes "spiritualis" in concrete and personal terms; his "spirituality" (including his language about his experience) is both nurtured by and nurtures the tension between presence and lack. The *Epistola* carefully notes the difference between the two but also the fact that they somehow work in tandem: "...et tamen ut dicamus, ut cogitemus, *amore eius* vel *amore amoris eius* provocamur et trahimur" (119, p. 156) ("...and all the while both with respect to our words and our thoughts, we are incited and drawn out by his love, or by the love of his love").

Although the ideal situation of the solitary is to "vacare... Deo" (19 and 20, pp. 78-79), this kind of sabbath-rest can only be known through the functions of time and matter which force people to perceive differences; sabbath-rest necessitates workdays or, just as proper to monastic rhetoric, schooldays. To enter the hermitage is to put off old wisdom and become a childlike idiot in the school of love, always aware that the "schola caritatis" is eventually the "schola contemplativa" because, as Guillaume says, "caritas contemplat."[15] "Stulti facti propter Deum, per stultum Dei, quod sapientius est omnibus hominibus, Christo duce, humilem APPREHENDITE DISCIPLINAM ascendendi in celum" (8, p. 71) ("Made dunces for God, ascending to heaven, led by Christ, learn the humble discipline like God's dunce who is wiser than all men"). The "stultus," at first, requires the mediation of scripture, art and meditation on the images of holiness (73, p. 122); he must memorize them and rehearse them in his heart. Manual and intellectual labor are valuable insofar as they help conquer the temptation to simply let time pass or let the mind's eye wander where it will, a situation in which "vacare Deo" turns into "accidia." This vice is particularly treacherous because it mimics the delights of the sabbath-rest; the difference between the two is qualitative and often turns around the key words *otium* and *quies* and the extent to which

---

[15] See M.-M. Davy, *Théologie et mystique de G. de St.-Thierry* (Paris, 1954), pp. 302-10.

these, as rhetoric, do or do not convince the reader of their eschatological signification. Since these ambiguous terms are so central to Petrarch's no less ambiguous re-reading of the ascetic tradition as well, it would be helpful to look at them more closely.[16]

In classical Latin, *quies* is associated with *sopor* and *somnus* and often follows upon eating or drinking; *vigiliae* is its opposite. While Celsus sees after-dinner *quies* as therapeutic in a physical sense, Seneca is the first to make a generalized *quies* into a virtue to be cultivated. His is already the oxymoric rhetoric of perfect repose: "Inter se ista miscenda sunt, et quiescendi agendum et agendi quiescendum est," ("These things are intermingled, both activity in repose and repose in activity,")[17]; Christians will interpret this according to a spirituality based on the action of grace. *Quies* will be re-read eschatologically. In the Vulgate Old Testament the word often refers to a final resting after the desert wanderings; it is, explains Jean Leclercq, the Promised Land which becomes the Christian liturgical "requiem aeternam" via the Jewish apocalyptic of IV Esdras.[18] Augustine will apply the basic Senecan oxymoron to the state of the blessed in the heavenly Jerusalem: "Eius [sanctis] erit perpetuo vigilans quies et actio non segniter, sed indefatigabiliter otiosa"[19] ("There will be for the saints eternally a waking rest, an activity not lazily but tirelessly relaxed"). Again, with regard to the constant praise of the saints: "Hoc erit otiosum negotium, hoc opus vacantium, haec actio quietorum, haec cura securorum" ("This will be a relaxing business, the job of those at rest, the activity of those who are calm, the bother of those who are untroubled").[20] The former quotation exemplifies Augustine's occasional uncertainty about the reading of *otiosa*; while the notion of a "vigilans" *quies* seems not to be a problem, *actio*... "otiosa" obviously is, requiring the adverbial modifiers: "...not lazily, but tirelessly." A qualifiedly positive reading of *otium* characterizes the late monastic rhetoric which Guillaume and Petrarch share. The burden of its

---

[16] I am guided here, for the most part, by the magnificent labors of Dom Jean Leclercq in his *Otia Monastica*, cited above, as well as in *L'Amour des lettres et le désir de Dieu* (Paris, 1957) and *Recueil des études sur S. Bernard et ses écrits*, 3 vols. (Rome, 1962).

[17] L. Annaei Senecae, *Ad Lucilium Epistulae Morales*, ed. L.D. Reynolds (Oxford, 1965), I.3.

[18] *Otia Monastica*, p. 22.

[19] See *Otia Monastica*, p. 23, f.n. 18.

[20] (*In Psalmis*, 110.1), see *Otia Monastica*, p. 40, f.n. 30. The idea of Christian repose is always eschatologically directed. Leclercq comments: "Cette référence à l'eschatologie est essentielle à la doctrine chrétienne au sujet du repos comme à propos de tout, et c'est elle qui permet de concilier, d'une façon paradoxale, certaines antinomies inhérentes à un langage qui avait été forgé en dehors de la Révélation" (*ibid.*, p. 24).

irenic signification lies in the intentions behind the choice and interpretation of simple modifiers. The false-twin or false-mimicking aspect of *otium* which occasions Augustine's cautious rhetoric becomes attached not only to *otium* standing alone and unqualified but also to the word *accidia*.[21]

Guillaume mentions that the writing of his *Epistola* overcame his own temptations to *accidia* (6, p. 69). At least on one level, then, he values his writing as no more or less important than chopping wood or copying a manuscript. Either reading or writing, seen as ends in themselves and not as springboards for fixing the mind on God, are idolatrous. Both must be intentional actions, leading to that calm work which is irenic in character: "Studia hec... quietam desiderant cordis in labore corporis... et pacem in exterioribus pressuris..." (91) ("These studies... need the heart's repose during the body's labor... they require peace amidst external pressures..."). But both reading and writing risk a false, illusory, substanceless fulfillment, imaged by Guillaume in the pretty flower: "Hec studia... [*in bono*] scrutantur virtutes non tam flores quam radices, non ut luceant sed ut sint: non ut sciantur sed ut hebeantur" (*Ep.* 91) ("These studies are to examine the roots of virtues, rather than their flowers, so that such virtues may really exist rather than simply shine: so that they may not be simply known but possessed"). "Litteratoria" are not only inferior to "spiritualia," they also belong to an entirely different order of being—so that letters cannot, by their nature and apart from the reader's intention, bring forth the spirit. Guillaume explicitly condemns a kind of *accidia* in which pleasurable images, including the literary, take a disproportionate hold on the affective life of the hermit. He seems to define, *avant la lettre*, the style of the *De Vita Solitaria* and, in condemning it, to speak in the same style as does Petrarch's fictional accuser in the *Secretum*.

> ...ipsae [cogitationes]... sunt vanae illae et otiosae, neutro intellectui per cogitantis intentionem se applicantes, non repente perimentes sed sensim et paulatim corrumpentes, occupantes tempus, necessaria impedientes, et animum inficientes: non tam cogitationes, quam ex veris vel imaginariis recordationibus simulacra quaedam cogitationum, seu ipsae recordationes ultro et multipliciter de memoria scaturientes. In quibus passio quaedam voluntatis potius esse videtur, quam actio... (*Ep.* 101)

---

[21] Leclercq points out that the neologism *otiositas* (used *in malo* in the *Rule* of St. Benedict) also absorbed some of the pejorative implications of a now sublimated *otium* (*ibid.*, p. 41).

[...these are those vain and idle thoughts applied, as to the thinker's intention, in a lukewarm fashion: they do not kill quickly but corrupt slowly and gradually, filling time, stopping necessary things from getting done, infecting the soul. They are not thoughts but, whether from true or imagined memories of thoughts, sort of mimicking masks of real thoughts, or the very recollections surging up in great multiplicity and spontaneously from the memory. Passivity rather than an activity of the will is observed in such thoughts.]

But before attempting to contrast Guillaume's ascesis with the spiritual sensibility of Petrarch, I think it would be helpful to interpolate here some words concerning methodology. There is no doubt that the rhetorical analysis of a theological text cannot help but leave a good amount of theology scientifically unexamined. I have spoken only tangentially of the complicated role of the will in the *Epistola*. I will have little more to say of that science which is fundamental to much of the *De Vita*: textual criticism and an encyclopedic knowledge of Latin literature. But both these works were written at a time in which the word was preeminently a sign, a "spoor" ("vestigium" as St. Bonaventure put it) to be followed through a text, implying a technique not unlike the renewed attention to semiotics in our own day. Such signs could either be equal to or opposite from other signs; they could imply the "presence" of other signs to the moments of the reader's time which they fill. As I have tried to show, the expressions *sabbatum delicatum* and *vacare Deo* are, and were understood to be, so isotopic that the astute monastic reader, who has taken the Bible and perhaps even St. Bernard to heart, can recognize the deeply contemplative nature of Guillaume's tract from the start. The paucity of definitions of terms would indicate that the relationship between the words *intelligere–servire* and *credere–adhaerere*, for example, is already emblematic of two very complex terminals of human energy, of two different ways of understanding the same crucial act of faith. Guillaume intends the reader to identify with the latter emblem and progressively to fill out the picture with other key signs provided in the text. The single sign "adhaerere" *comes to* mean, or *comes to* include, "otium," "vacare," "stultitia," "frui," "unio." Simply to say it is metonymic for these other signs would be to de-emphasize *process*, an element particularly stressed in medieval hermeneutics.

Jean Leclercq is very careful to associate the rhetorical, grammatical analysis of monastic texts with the commonly practised medieval discipline of memorizing the significations of word-signs. Leclercq applies to "monastic culture" as a whole Guillaume's implication in the *Epistola* that remembering God and remembering the spiritual (as opposed to sensual) images of a literary text can be analogous processes and the latter, therefore, salutary.²² We cannot overestimate, surely, the intentionality of devotional writers in this context. Bernard's "et in corde magis quam in omni codice" ("better in the heart than in any handbook") *intends* to make the reader remember the rhetorical juxtaposition of *corde–codice* and their significations of spirituality–worldliness, perfect–imperfect, God's Word–man's word. Both Guillaume and Petrarch are just as rhetorical in their treatments of the spiritual life. Towards the close of the *Epistola*, Guillaume writes:

> Via Dei, quae non tam rationis est profectus, quam iam in sapientia perfectionis affectus. Hec enim quia sapiunt sapienti, sapiens est; quia factus unus spiritus cum Deo, spiritualis est. Et hec in hac vita hominis perfectio est. (116, p. 153)
>
> [And this is God's life, not so much a progress of reason as a love of perfection continuingly ("iam") present in wisdom. He who tastes these things is called "wise"; he is called "spiritual" because he has been made one spirit with God. Such is humanity's perfection in this life.]

This summation of the contemplative life is almost a mnemonic; its lapidary rhetoric is so much at the service of theology that an exposition of the theology alone, from the point of view of a literary critic, would almost seem to obscure the text. The way to meaning here is a rhetorical one. The eyes or ears of the reader are arrested by the opposition of *rationis profectus* to *perfectionis affectus*; the almost transtemporal *iam* indicates that the way to God is at every moment accessible in love, that, for one who rests in God, the trajectory is already completed, that one must live as if there were no trajectory at all.²³ The *vita Dei* which opens the passage and *vita hominis* which closes it (and here, grammatical logic is subordinate to the logic of eyes and ears) are brought daringly together by a word-play which points to the exemplary unity of sensual, intellectual and spiritual in the mystic's life (*sapiunt sapienti, sapiens est—spiritualis est; sapio* means both "to taste" and "to understand").

One final example will serve to illustrate a kind of sign-memory common to monastic literature and central to Petrarch's "devotional" rhetoric: biblical or liturgical allusion. Guillaume writes of true vir-

---

²² *L'Amour des lettres et le désir de Dieu* (Paris, 1957), p. 73.

> Elle explique le phénomène, si important, de la réminiscence, autrement dit le rappel spontané des citations et d'allusions qui s'évoquent les unes les autres, sans aucun effort, pour le seul fait de la similitude des mots; chaque mot fait agrafe, pour ainsi dire: il en accroche un ou plusieurs autres, qui s'enchaînent et constituent la trame de l'exposé.

²³ For a study which touches upon this sense of *iam*, see Lowry Nelson, Jr., "The Rhetoric of Ineffability," *Comparative Literature* 8 (1956), 323-36.

tue's being found in a simple life: "Proprie enim est simplicitas perfecta ad Deum conversa voluntas, unam petens a Domino, hanc requirens, non ambiens multiplicari in saeculo" ("Simplicity is, properly, a will perfectly turned toward God, asking one thing from the Lord, seeking this alone, and not going about the business of busyness in the world").[24] We have seen the negative word *multiplicari* and its cognates (*multipliciter*) before . They signify the constant human inclination towards dispersal of spiritual energies,[25] the necessary "multiplicity" of wandering thoughts and of language itself when compared with thoughts mindful of God. But the passage is not simply a general religious counsel; it speaks very specifically to the situation of the *solitarius* in his cell. It does so because the phrase *unam petens... hanc requirens* will recall to the reader, who knows much of the psalter by heart, *Psalms* 26.4-5, lines which tell him who he is by describing what the opposite of *multiplicari* might be: "Unam petii a Domino, hanc requiram / ut inhabitem in domo Domini omnibus diebus vitae meae, ut videam voluptatem Domini, et visitem templum eius. / Quoniam abscondit me in tabernaculo suo..." ("There is one thing I ask of the Lord, this I seek: that I may dwell in the Lord's house all the days of my life, that I may see the Lord's beauty and visit his temple. For he has hidden me in his tabernacle...").

There is no convincing proof that Petrarch ever read the *Epistola ad Fratres de Monte-Dei*. Writing his *De Vita Solitaria* at Vaucluse between 1346 and 1366, Petrarch, one might imagine, must have come in contact with such a well-known antecedent to his own tract. Yet even in his short biography of St. Bernard as solitary, in the second part of the text (drawn largely from Guillaume's *Vita Prima S. Bernardi*), a Bernardine treatise on solitude is never mentioned. What Petrarch does say, most emphatically, is that his book will be a completely original effort: "In hoc autem tractatu magna ex parte solius experientie ducatum habui..." (I, p. 298) ("In this treatise then for the most part I have been led by my own experience").[26] Hans Baron has shown how much Petrarch's religious experience was hinged to *lit-*

---

[24] See the Migne edition, *PL* CLXXXIV, col. 507.
[25] This language is used by Theodore Berkeley, OCSO, in his translation of the above passage, in William of St.-Thierry, *The Golden Epistle*, Cistercian Fathers Series no. 12 (Spencer, Massachusetts, 1971), p. 28.
[26] Quotations from the *De Vita Solitaria* and *Secretum* refer to page numbers in Francesco Petrarca, *Prose*, a cura di G. Martellotti, E. Carrara, *et al.* (La letteratura italiana: storia e testi no. 7, Milano, 1955).

teratoria.²⁷ But which "letters" and in what way? The frequent use of classical references does not of itself make a text classical or secular in character; the moral exhortation in Guillaume's text, on the surface, is just as Senecan as the humanist Petrarch's.²⁸ The spiritual biographies which occupy virtually all of Book II of the Petrarch are certainly classicizing, modelled on Suetonius, but much less original, for that, than is Book I. The Christian sources for Book II are the various compendia of *vitae patrum* whose combination of straight biography and tale-telling epiphanies Petrarch beautifies with his Latin style. It is the Christian sources for Book I, however, the theoretical treatises on solitude and contemplation like the *Epistola* to which Petrarch makes no overt reference. Yet the precise originality of the *De Vita Solitaria*, I would contend, (and the reason Book II is of little interest for our present purposes), is its deliberate confusion of *litteratoria* and *spiritualia* in Book I. The signification of these and other common word-signs in the tradition of the *Epistola* are revised by Petrarch to include new meanings, new possibilities. That is the method of the *De Vita*. Its purpose, preeminently in the Book I which narrates part of that most crucial spiritual biography omitted in Book II—the life of Petrarch himself—is to attempt an irenic response to the specific problems of how to live one's life with which the author was confronted in another work, the *Secretum*. In this text, written just before the *De Vita*, Petrarch constructs a fictive "Augustine" who directs what seems to be a mostly unmitigated language of violent apocalypse against a fictive "Francesco" who refuses to abandon the irenic position which, in his mind, makes a synthesis of the literary and spiritual lives possible.²⁹

---

²⁷ For example, in "The Evolution of Petrarch's Thought: Reflections on the State of Petrarch Studies," *Bibliothèque d'Humanisme et de Renaissance* 24, no. 1 (1962), pp. 7-41 and in "Petrarch and the Humanist Discovery of Man's Nature," in *Florilegium Historiale* (essays presented to W.K. Fergusson), eds. J.G. Rowe and W.H. Stockdale (Toronto, 1971).

²⁸ See J.-M. Déchanet, "*Seneca Noster*. Des Lettres à Lucilius à la Lettre aux Frères du Mont-Dieu," in *Mélanges Joseph de Ghellinck, S.J., Museum Lessianum,* section historique no. 14 (Gembloux, 1951), pp. 753-66. The article discusses the continuous reverence on the part of late medieval letters for the "almost" Christian Seneca. The principal points of Senecan thought referred to in the *Epistola* are the divine origin of the human soul and its natural alacrity to adhere to its origin; proper assessment of the reality of physical life without living *propter corpus*; poverty, stability, solitude and repose as virtues; the need for a human model and guide.

²⁹ Just as Augustine's voice, in the *Secretum*, could represent a violent apocalypse opposed to Francesco's movement towards the irenic, so Petrarch could similarly characterize St. Jerome's attitude towards profane letters in a passage from *Fam.* XXII.10: "Neque ideo tamen quia hos praetulerim, illos abicio, quod se fecisse Ieronimus scribere potiusquam sequenti stilo approbare visus est michi, ego utrosque simul amare posse videor..." Petrarch, Jerome notwithstanding, sees value in both styles.

The dialogue of the *Secretum* is broadly humorous; and the violent, one-willed language of the patriarch is often the butt of the joke. Given what we know of Petrarch's reverence for both the classical learning and Christian wisdom of the real St. Augustine, it is perhaps most amusing of all to observe the way in which Francesco's Augustine plays the Pelagian to Petrarch's cherished original. Seen in retrospect, the jokes begin with the first sentence. The opening of the dialogue portrays a somnolent Francesco as already somewhat conscious of a moment, the supposed implications of which Augustine never manages to get him to "see" in the dialogue. Augustine's constant refrain is: *memento mori!* The text's opening sentence finds Francesco doing just that:

> Attonito michi quidem et sepissime cogitanti qualiter in' hanc vitam intrassem, qualiter ve forem egressurus, contigit nuper ut non, sicut egros animos solet, somnus opprimeret, sed anxium atque pervigilem, mulier quedam inenarrabilis etatis et luminis... adiise videretur. (Prohemium, p. 22)

[While I was senseless, meditating, as I often do, on how I came into this life and how I was to leave it, it happened, not long ago, (I was not vanquished by sleep, as is usually the case with infirm souls, but rather anxious, quite awake) that a certain woman of indescribable age and splendour... was seen to appear.]

Francesco's vision insists upon itself as literary construct in much the same way as does the famous *Familiares* IV.1 (the ascent of Mt. Ventoux), and with much the same problem in mind. Moral value depends upon intention. In the realm of the literary, intention involves operations which are ultimately aesthetic in nature—questions of "style," both writing style and reading style. How one sees, one's point of view, is a determinant of what one does: in the case of the literary, it determines the moral action of either creating or interpreting images. The debate in the *Secretum* is really over which style to adopt, insofar as writing and reading carry moral responsibility. Francesco argues for an open-ended, personal and ambiguous literary style (*indoles*) which becomes an open-ended, personal and ambiguous piety (*religio*) by virtue of the fact that the entire dialogue is characterized with the devotional title *secretum meum*. The secret in the title and in the opening address to the book (Prohemium, p. 26) refers to the "secret" of *Isaiah* 24.16 which medieval exegetes read most often as the unique and inviolable, yet problematic, style of the soul's relationship with God. "Secretum meum mihi. Secretum meum mihi. Vae mihi! Praevaricantes praevaricati sunt, et praevaricatione transgressorum praevaricati sunt" ("My secret is mine. My secret is mine. Woe is me! The perjurors have perjured themselves, perjured in the intrigue of their own transgressions"). The prophet clings to his secret in the midst of one of the *Isaiah* apocalypses in which the horrific end of the world is predicted. As an attitude toward that end-point, it sets itself against a rhetoric of deceit which puts the validity of something so complex and personal as the prophet's secret into question. It is with the *Isaiah* secret that the *Epistola Aurea* explicitly ends ("*secretum meum michi...*") and, as we have seen, elaborates a personalist notion of contemplation. In the sermons *In Cantica*, Bernard of Clairvaux sees this secret as ultimately undefinable and built upon the individual soul's personal gifts and point of view or place (in the sense of vocation). In Rupert of Deutz, the secret is a personal history of apocalyptic tribulation, because the believer knows that revelation, perceiving the truth, will always be sweet in the mouth and bitter in the stomach, mimetic, in other words, of John's revelation.[30] In *Isaiah*, in the late medieval monastic writers, and in the *Secretum* itself, the secret is perceived and kept irenically, in the midst of general doubt and fear, and of specific threat to its value as revelatory. To say as much is not to say that the drama of the *Secretum* does not convey a profound sense of disquietude in the character of Francesco. My point is, rather, that the author, while dramatizing such lack of certainty, has Francesco and Augustine take consistently opposing rhetorical stances on just what to do about the problem. Augustine's rhetoric is merely apocalyptic, Francesco's more like irenic apocalypse. Thus, Augustine is made to condemn the ambiguity inherent in both Francesco's solitude at Vaucluse and in his continued love for Laura. "Everybody," says Augustine, "interprets benignly that which he thinks of as his own" (Lib. III, p. 142).[31] Though he says he takes this serious condemnation to heart, Francesco refuses to give up his personal style— his personal sense of the bittersweet—in a way which must recall the reader to the seriousness of the struggle inherent in Isaiah's secret and in what medieval exegesis made of it. The fictional persona, though openly pained by his own ambiguity, announces the validity of both an aesthetic and an ascetic style which the author, as the reader reads, is accomplishing in the rhetoric of the text.

Augustine, in Petrarch's hand, both here and at the top of Mt. Ventoux, would have it that true ascesis involves first turning inward

---

[30] Bernard of Clairvaux, *Sermones in Cantica*, XXIII.9-10, in Migne, *PL* CLXXXIII, col. 884: "...but he has chosen us and established us in a certain place and each of us remains where he has put us. A woman penitent found her place at Jesus' feet... Thomas received this secret grace in the Saviour's side... Peter in the bosom of the Father and Paul in the third heaven". See also Rupert of Deutz, *De Operibus Spiritus Sancti* (tome II), IV.13, in *Sources Chrétiennes* 165, 1685C.

[31] "...unus quisque suarum rerum est benignus interpres..."

to find God and thence to find its creatures; Francesco would turn inward to find man and thence to God. Every mention of *memento mori* on Augustine's part elicits a statement of human emotion and complexity from Francesco, rather than the willed action of conversion which Augustine associates with the fig tree of *Confessions* VIII.[32] Francesco maintains that his reading of the *Confessions* produces hope, but hope mixed with a paralyzing fear; his contrary emotions with respect to a religious problem are epitomized for him not in Augustine's book but in the Virgilian *metuunt cupiuntque dolent gaudentque* (they both fear and desire, both suffer and rejoice) (*Aen.* VI.733; Lib. I, p. 64). Augustine accuses Francesco of not knowing the truth when he sees it; the discernment of truth, for Francesco, is tied to its various contextualizations in the history of his life, contexts which are invariably literary. Petrarchan self-irony explicitly points to the problem of style, as I have stated it, when Francesco is unable to recognize the arbitress Veritas (Truth itself) until she reminds him that he had already described her, beautifully, in one of his books. Memory of *spiritualia* will not be detached from the literary process and even depends upon it, as Petrarch underlines the beguiling attractiveness of his own fictions: "...in Africa nostra *curiosa* quadam *elegantia* descripsisti... mirabili *artificio* ac *poeticis* ut proprie dicam manibus... erexisti" (Prohemium, p. 22, italics mine) ("...you described me [Veritas] in our *Africa* with a certain beguiling elegance... you structured [a splendid dwelling-place] with admirable artifice and, so to say, with a poet's hands"). In *Secretum* II, a crucial, rhetorical reevaluation is made by which the monastic vice of *accidia* is translated not as unproductive laziness, but as "suffering mixed with pleasure," as melancholy.[33] In Francesco's affirmation of a phenomenology of doubt, creatureliness and complexity, *accidia* becomes a more positive and peculiarly literary form of meditation on his own nature. The "spiritual" life toward which the perfectible will moves is not a being-lost in God, a God-centeredness. It is, rather, a constant assignment of value to the ambiguities of personal thoughts and emotions which enables the soul, at least from its own point of view (the view which Augustine, of course, has explicitly called into question), to better understand itself in the presence of incomprehensible divine mystery. As a result of such revisions in meaning as these,

---

[32] Lib. I, pp. 40, 42. See John Freccero, "The Fig Tree and the Laurel: Petrarch's Poetics," *Diacritics* (Spring, 1975), 34-40. Freccero uncovers the special relationship between fig and laurel in the *Secretum* and directs the type toward a study of the *Canzoniere*.

[33] See P.O. Kristeller, *op. cit.*, p. 15 and f.n. 18 and 19.

the erotic topography of the *Canzoniere* will be paralleled by another fiction: a devotional topography which seeks, in the *De Vita Solitaria*, to vindicate the Petrarchan style from the crisis of the *Secretum*. In the final exchanges, Francesco certainly promises to reform his life but, he says, he must first put some order into his thoughts and literary projects. Though he recognizes them as "deviations" from the piety and style Augustine has urged upon him, he must work through them.

There is no irenic, atemporal *sabbatum* in *De Vita Solitaria* which could be called a resting in God alone. There is, however, a resting in the work of literature, imaged in the irenic rhetoric of the *sabbatum* and, therefore, represented as devotion or piety. The words *vacare*, *otium* and *frui* are constantly employed, but they appear emptied of any strictly mystical signification and refer to their author's very human need for leisure and the freedom to do what *he* pleases. Petrarch's dedication to Philip, bishop of Cavaillon, is concerned with the practical fear that his friend may be engulfed by the political turmoils of the papal curia at Avignon. Philip should come to Vaucluse, says Petrarch, and adopt the solitary life in which he would "...vivere ut velis, ire quo velis, stare ubi velis..." ("...live as you please, go where you please, stay where you please..."). Juxtaposed against the fear of his own desire for worldly activity and for the great poet's fame (two of Augustine's accusations in the *Secretum*), Petrarch provides a system of rhetorical memory devices to set the world off from his solitude: "...hanc vitam leto otio, illam tristi negotio incumbere," "solitudo angelica"—"tumultus tartareus" (pp. 298 and 300). The *De Vita* characterizes itself with the same generic term as had a multitude of medieval devotional tracts, including the *Epistola Aurea*: it is a *speculum*. But this *speculum solitudinis* is not a way of seeing the hermit's journey to God which, in Guillaume, goes beyond the mirror image toward unmediated vision. Petrarch says: "...velut in speculo, totum animi mei habitum, totam frontem serene tranquilleque mentis aspicias" (p. 294) ("...you will see, as in a mirror, the entire aspect of my soul and the complete countenance of my tranquil and serene mind").[34] The mirror never leaves Petrarch himself. Yet Petrarch meant his *speculum* as seriously as did Guillaume; the *De Vita*, because of its rhetoric, can be read neither as philosophical nor private, but

---

[34] Even in the long biographical section in which famous solitaries are proposed as additional *specula* for the reader's edification, the narration tells us less of the character of their mystical experiences than of the ways in which they had to battle the encroaching world both to become and to remain solitaries. Petrarch would have the reader believe that their battle was also his.

only as a didactic, devotional writing in which the character of the devotion has drastically changed.

An excellent example of such a change is Petrarch's exposition of the differences between the daily life of the *occupatus* and that of the *solitarius* (the *De Vita*'s version of *solus* and *solitarius* in the *Epistola*). No scholar, as far as I can tell, has recognized the rhetorical complexity of the passage, its purpose and its significance for what amounts to part of a humanist *devotio*.[35] In the *Epistola Aurea*, the solitary is described as rising in the middle of the night to pray the office of matines; as is the case with lauds, the diurnal hours, vespers and compline, the offices are simply mentioned. They are means to a greater end of opening up the hermit's spirit to God and to a higher and more abiding prayer of the heart. In the *De Vita*, the canonical hours are never mentioned by name but instead are the basis of an extended rhetorical conceit where beautiful words become ends in themselves and where the revelation of God's presence is simultaneous with and depends upon the literary exercise. With a purposeful vagueness, Petrarch indicates the offices by weaving their incipits and phrases from the body of the office into his text. In the following excerpts, the ordinary text of relevant prayers are provided on the left of the page. Rather than attempt a translation of the Petrarch, which would be almost useless here, I have used asterisks to indicate word-play with the names of the hours themselves; the verbal parallels are italicized.

MATINES

"Domine, labia mea aperies; et os meum annuntiabit laudem tuam."

"Deus, in adiutorium meum intende; Domine, ad adiuvandum me festina."

Surgit solitarius atque otiosus, felix, modica quiete recreatus, somnoque brevi non facto sed expleto, et interdum pernoctantis philomene cantibus experrectus, thoroque vixdum leniter excussus, pulsisque torporibus quietis horis* psallere* incipiens, *ianitorem labiorum* suorum ut egressuris inde matutinis* *laudibus** *aperiat* devotus exposcit, et cordis sui *dominum in adiutorium suum* vocat, nihilque iam viribus suis fidens et imminentium conscius metuensque discriminum

---

[35] F. Serpagli's study, *op. cit.*, pp. 59ff, holds that Petrarch's immediate inspiration for the passage is Augustine's *De Moribus Ecclesiae Catholicae* and provides substantial proofs. Though he does note a few of the liturgical borrowings, especially the Ambrosian hymns (p. 44), Serpagli does little more than comment on the elegance of the writing and says nothing about why it might appear as it does in the text. An insightful, one-line remark remains undeveloped by its own author. On the Ambrosian hymnody, says Serpagli, "il Petrarca foggia l'estetica del suo eroe" (p. 73).

ut *festinet* obsecrat:... Et sepe interea... securi timoris ac trepide spei plenus memorque preteriti ac futuri providens, leto dolore et felicibus lacrimis abundat... protinus ad honeste cuiuspiam iocundeque lectionis studium convertitur.

HYMN FROM LAUDS[36]

"Praeco diei iam sonat
Jubarque solis evocat."

HYMN FROM PRIME[37]

"Linguam refraenens
  temperet
Ne litis horror insonet:
Visum fovendo contegat,
Ne vanitates hauriat.
Sint pura cordis intima,
Absistat et vecordia:
Carnis terat superbiam
Potus cibique parcitas."

Iste ubi primum floreum sedile salubremque nactus collem constitit, *iubare* iam *solis* exorto, in diurnas* Dei laudes* pio letus ore prorumpens... innocentiam in primis*, *linguae frenum litis* nescium, *visus tegmen vanitatis* obiectum, *puritatem cordis, vecordie absentiam* et domitricem *carnis abstinentiam deprecatur.*[38]

HYMN FROM TIERCE*[39]

"Nunc Sancte nobis
  Spiritus
Unum Patri cum Filio,
Dignare promptus ingeri
Nostro refusus pectori.
Os, lingua, mens, sensus,
  vigor
Confessionem personent:
Flammescat igne caritas
Accendat ardor proximos..."

Nec multo post, tertius* in laudibus, tertiam in *Trinitate* personam veneratur et *Sancti Spiritus* poscit adventum, *linguam* quoque et *mentem confessione personantem* salutifera, et *caritatem* celico *igne flammantem* ac *proximos accensuram*.... Inde autem pedetentim sua relegens vestigia, scandente iam in altum et qui *mane* novum illustraverat *meridiem accendente* solis radio, nil potius quam *flammas litium... calorem noxium auferri* flagitat.

HYMN FROM SEXT[40]

"...splendore mane illuminas
Et ignibus meridiem:

---

[36] This is the Ambrosian "Aeterne rerum Conditor," vs. 2. Liturgical texts may be consulted in the Roman *Antiphonale... pro diurnis horis*, a Solesmensibus monachis editum (Tornaci, 1949).
[37] "Jam lucis orto sidere," vss. 2-3.
[38] *Abstinentiam*, not a direct parallel, stands for *potus cibique parcitas. Deprecatur* is italicized as Petrarch's concluding verb because the verb which opens (vs. 1) the exposition of the prime-hymn is *precamur. Trinitate* is synecdochal.
[39] "Nunc Sancte nobis Spiritus," vss. 1-2.
[40] "Rector potens, verax Deus," vss. 1-2.

Extinque flammas litium
Aufer calorem noxium..."

Denique quod unum poeta satyricus sine periculo posci docet, in corpore sano mentem sanam orat. Quis horum [the "occupatus" or the "solitarius"], oro, hactenus horas suas expendit honestius?[41]

....

COMPLINE

"Fratres: Sobrii estote et vigilate: quia adversarius vester diabolus, tamquam leo rugiens, circuit, quaerens quem devoret: cui resistite fortes in fide. Tu autem, Domine, miserere nobis."

"Te lucis ante terminum
Rerum Creator poscimus
Ut solita clementia
Sis praesul et custodia.
Procul recedant somnia,
Et noctium phantasmata:
Hostemque nostrum comprime,
Ne polluantur corpora..."

"In manus tuas, Domine, commendo spiritum meum..."

"Visita, quaesumus, Domine, habitationem istam, et omnes insidias ini-

Iste vel apricum fontem, vel herbosam ripam, vel equoreum litus adit, gaudens diem illum sine dedecore transivisse, et *lucis ante terminum* adversus secuture noctis pericula dolosque et *insidias*. ac *rabiem*[42] leonino more *rugientis adversarii, vigilem sobrietatem* atque orationis et *fidei clipeum*,[43] *adversus somnia pollutionemque* et *nocturna fantasmata*, excubare sibi *solitam clementiam* sui *creatoris* implorat; atque *in manus ejus commendato spiritu* et *angelis suis* ad *habitaculi* proprii *custodiam* invocatis, se se in suam domum recipit... Ad summam, totis ille diebus vivos spoliat, *hic pro defunctis orat*;[44] ille matrum ac virginum pudicitiam attentat, *hic Virginem Matrem* officiosissime* *veneratur.*[45] Denique ille martyres facit, hic celebrat; ille sanctos persequitur, hic honorat (pp. 301-04; 314).[46]

---

[41] Martellotti points out the lovely paranomasia, *horum – oro – horas* (f.n. 4, p. 304). Petrarch prays for "mens sana in corpore sano," the prayer of the satyric poet Juvenal and certainly not that of a Christian ascetic or mystic.

[42] *Rabiem* stands for *quaerens quem devoret*.

[43] Petrarch tightens *cui resistite fortes in fide* into his own *fidei clipeum*.

[44] Petrarch refers to the prayer for the dead, *Fidelium animae*...

[45] One of several different hymns to the Virgin is included in each recitation of compline.

[46] The prayer *Divinum auxilium*... is offered for all the faithful, the "saints" in the sense of the *Apocalypse*. This reading of "saints" as referring to the still living and embattled is strengthened by the negative references to the evil man who "makes martyrs" and "persecutes the saints" in the present tense.

mici ab ea longe repelle:
Angeli tui sancti habitent
in ea, qui nos in pace custodiant..."

"Divinum auxilium maneat semper nobiscum: et
cum fratribus nostris absentibus."

"Fidelium animae per misericordiam Dei requiescant in pace."

The point is, I think, sufficiently made. The structure of the monastic day is recreated in such a way that God is continually praised in the context of sleeping, eating, reading, writing and watching the beauty of nature; the Petrarchan way of life is, *or is made to look like*, a mode of authenticity proper to Christian asceticism: irenic apocalypse. In his descriptions of his solitude, the simultaneity of strife (A) and peace (B), the structure fundamental to irenic apocalypse, is underlined rhetorically. His solitude is:

...(A) campus pugnantium, (B) arcuis triunphantium, (A) biblioteca legentium, (B) cella meditantium, (A) penetrale [templo] orantium, (B) mons contemplantium, et quid dicam, nisi simul omnia?

Similarly, the rhetorical figure of oxymoron accommodates Petrarch's revised sense of the *accidia* which now best characterizes human nature (*securi timoris, trepide spei, leto dolore, felicibus lacrimis*) and naturally overflows into literary endeavor ("protinus ad ... lectionis studium convertitur"). The conceit here is that the figure of oxymoron, which all of Petrarch's rhetorical emblems of his own weakness share, can point to a reality which is spiritually authentic as does, for example, the oxymoron *felix culpa* in the Christian tradition which Petrarch is manipulating.

Charles Trinkaus points out that Petrarch almost never mentions the *remedia* of the ecclesiastical sacraments.[47] But what are his "sacraments"? The proto-sacrament, given what we have discussed above, is the Incarnation. It is crucial in the *De Vita* not so much because it saves Petrarch from sin as because it definitively clarifies his nature to himself as godlike and saveable. Because God became man, all serious thought about human nature can be, gratuitously, salutary. Such thoughts and their translation into literary figures are Petrarch's

---

[47] *In Our Image and Likeness* (London, 1970), vol. I, p. 17.

other sacramentals. He presents his fictions, in the *De Vita*, as having been grace-bearing for himself; as such, he offers them to the reader. The accent of this devotion is distinctly meditative rather than contemplative: it deals with the spiritualization of the ordinary flow of human thoughts rather than emptiness from thought or a fullness of unitive vision. Yet it is significant that Petrarch proposes his kind of *remedia* (in the *De Ocio Religiosorum* written simultaneously with the *De Vita*) to the Carthusians at Montrieux who were, so to speak, the professional contemplatives, if not mystics, of their time. St. Benedict, on the other hand, had described hermits as struggling to keep away from thoughts rather than nurturing their "sweet sadness": "...securi iam sine consolatione alterius, sola manu vel brachio contra vitia carnis vel cogitationum, Deo auxiliante, pugnare sufficiunt" ("...without any other form of consolation and with God's help, they are steadfast in struggling against the vices of the flesh or of thoughts").[48] St. Romuald, founder of the Camoldolese, had spoken of just how careful a hermit should be to allow thoughts into his cell: "Sede in cella cautus ad cogitationes, quasi bonus piscator ad pisces."[49] Petrarch's writing for the Carthusians seems to suggest that older and newer lines of piety had already crossed in his lifetime. They had so much crossed by the end of the fifteenth century that Canon Jean Mombaer de Bruxelles mentions in his *Rosetum* (1494), a mnemonic text on meditation widely diffused among the canons and brothers of the *devotio moderna*, two works which will be most edifying for novices entering upon the monastic life. They are: the *Epistola ad Fratres de Monte-Dei* of St. Bernard (Guillaume de St.-Thierry) and the *De Vita Solitaria* of Francesco Petrarca. What we have described at length as Petrarch's spiritualization of his own style and exemplified in the passage parodying the divine office, Mombaer and the modern devotionists read as an early predecessor of their own tracts which emphasized systematic meditation and such elaborate techniques as the *orologium spirituale* (spiritual clock). The divine office parody is an *orologium*, however idiosyncratically; Mombaer took it as an obviously authoritative example of a genre which came to include comparisons of the day's hours to moments in Christ's life, the seven ages of man or the history of salvation from Adam to Judgment.[50] However we may

---

[48] *Regula Monachorum* I.5.
[49] Quoted in Ezio Franceschini, "La figura dell'eremita nella letteratura latina medioevale." *Miscellanea del Centro di Studi Medioevali* IV (1962), p. 561.
[50] See Emile Bertaud, "Horloges spirituelles," in *Dictionnaire de spiritualité* VII (fasc. 46-47), col. 745-63. For Mombaer's debt to the monastic tradition and to the *Epistola* in particular, see Pierre Debognie, *Jean Mombaer de Bruxelles: Ses écrits et ses réformes* (Lou-

characterize the complexity of intention behind Petrarch's text, it must be seen as an important event in a gradual shift in piety which eventually permitted the modern, humanist *devotio* to embrace what we have seen as two very different approaches to the solitary life.

Both Petrarch and Guillaume borrow from Seneca the notion that the cell is a kind of hospital where vices are cured. Both say that the cell can also be a prison and a hell. For Guillaume it is so when it is bereft of God; for Petrarch (via Seneca), though he would never deny the necessity of God's presence, "...solitudo *sine litteris* exilium est, carcer, eculeus" (*De Vita*, p. 330) ("...solitude without reading and writing is an exile, a prison, a torture"). The life of letters has become primary, the key to self-knowledge which is, ultimately, knowledge of God. The *Epistola* insists that the hermit never fear his solitude because God is present; Petrarch is unafraid because of his own tranquil presence of mind, "...nec metuit solus esse, dum secum est" ("...nor did he fear to be alone when he is alone with himself"),—in which the thought of God seems not too different from literary self-reflection. The *De Vita*, not surprisingly, even overtly refers to the ways in which it appropriates the precise rhetoric of mysticism. It comments upon the fourfold scales of perfection to be found in Plotinus and in the *Somnium Scipionis* of Cicero, and upon a tri-partite "way" similar to Guillaume's. Yet Petrarch refuses to locate himself in any of these stages. He cannot understand the possibility of ecstasy without some sort of mediation; the ecstasy which he has known is a product of the struggle of contrary passions and not of their domination. But the narrative style of such an ecstatic experience should be quite familiar to us:

> ...versari passim et colloqui cum omnibus, qui fuerunt gloriosi viri; atque ita presentes malorum omnium opifices oblivisci, nonumquam et te ipsum, et supra se elevatum animum inferre rebus ethereis, meditari quid illic agitur, et meditatione desiderium inflammare... et ardentium quasi verborum faculas calidis admovere precordiis. Qui, quod inexperti non intelligunt... solitarie vite fructus est.[51]

---

vain, 1928), especially pp. 134-37, and M. Viller, "Le *Speculum Monachorum* et la 'Dévotion moderne'," in *Revue d'Ascètique et de Mystique* 3 (1922), 47ff. Cf. M.-M. Davy, *Un traité...* vol. II, pp. 48-53. Another book from the modern devotion, Erasmus' *De Contemptu Mundi* (1521), might well be seen as a direct descendant of the *De Vita Solitaria*. An analysis of the Erasmus, especially relevant to the ideas of this chapter, is in R.R. Post, "The Windesheimers after 1485: Confrontation with the Reformation and Humanism," in *The Reformation in Medieval Perspective*, ed. Steven E. Ozment (Chicago, 1971), pp. 157-84.

[51] *De Vita*, p. 356.

> [...to slow one's step here and there and to enter into colloquy with all those who were illustrious men; and in such a wise to forget the authors of all evils, and sometimes even to forget oneself and to move the soul, thus elevated, beyond itself towards heavenly things; to meditate then on that heavenly state, and by that meditation to inflame one's desire... and to take to one's heart, already in flames, the flames, so to speak, of burning words. This—and he who has not tasted [is not an 'expert'] will not understand—is the fruit of the solitary life.]

The rhetoric is that of the mystical ascent with its divine colloquy, its apocalyptic contempt for the world and self-forgetfulness, its irenic ecstasis, its pious meditation leading to desire and finally to sensual union. But the union here is one with "words"—"verborum faculas"; the colloquy is with the almost divinized Greeks and Romans who founded human culture and letters. At one point, Petrarch stops himself from appropriating too much. Narrating his own experience of solitude and tranquillity which makes a year seem like one joyful day—in contrast to the rich urbanite for whom one day is an endless tedium—Petrarch begins with the same words Paul used in *II Corinthians* to describe his being rapt to the third heaven, a *locus classicus* of the mystical life. "Scio hominem...," says Petrarch; but then, "non dicam ut Paulus sed hominem in corpore verum..." ("...I know a man... I'm not speaking in the manner of Paul—but a true man in the body").[52] The allusion to Paul has not been censured but carefully interrupted by the Petrarchan style. He would convince the reader that though he is not a mystic, though his experience is only analogous to Paul's, it is an experience which can collapse the struggle of time into one irenic moment—in this body and by means of a literary ascesis. A year before his death, Petrarch writes: "...opto ut legentem aut scribentem, vel si Christo placuerit orantem, vel plorantem mors inveniat" ("...I choose that death may find me either reading or writing, or praying if Christ so wish, or weeping").[53] Reading and writing are on a par with and not in progress towards the irenic activity of prayer; they are preferred to prayer, at least rhetorically, to make the point that both can be seen as very much the same thing.

[52] *De Vita*, p. 398. This means to recall and contrast with the Pauline "sive in corpore nescio, sive extra corpus nescio" ("whether in or out of the body, I know not").
[53] *Seniles* XVII.2. In his opening paragraph on the purposes of the *De Vita* (p. 296), Petrarch similarly uses a *sive . . . sive* clause to level the differences among the soul's search for God, for itself, for "honest studies," for a good friend.

5 Daily Bread: The "Horrible Mysteries" of Rabelais

> The importance of the novelist's art in its highest form is that it shows us that the insignificant, strictly speaking, cannot and does not exist.
>
> Gabriel Marcel, *Being and Having*

The bread to which the Gospels refer is first and foremost just that: bread. Like the wine with which Rabelais and his tradition couple it, bread does not exist in nature; it is confected, and therefore more or less good, the sum of its constituent parts reformed by humanity's seemingly constant yet terrifyingly fragile labor and art. We ask for it in an imperative mood because we so fully understand how necessary it is: "Give us this day our daily bread." As long as it is "daily," ordinary, readily available, we can hope and even demand that its efficient nourishment be made, or be found to be, even more fulfilling. Starvation, to extend the paradigm, is finally the lack of the ordinary strength either to hope or to utter the language which says: "It is, right now, imperative that I have..." Fill in the blank. The polymorphosis of language is used by its speakers to get at all specific, conceivable desires. And bread, the commonest of foods and, therefore, of words (be it confected of wheat, rice, maize, cassava, what-have-you: uttered in whatever language) becomes a metonymy for all good food and by extension for all desire fulfilled. If nothing, "strictly speaking," can be insignificant, then all linguistic structures, from those which are systematic (Marcel's "strictly" refers back to his supposition of a metaphysics) to those which are alleatory, surely signify. The unintentional hyperbole of critics who have often characterized the more curious structures of Rabelaisian narrative as "signifying nothing" reveals the real fear they share with the author they read: that human language may be ephemeral, ineffective, ever apt to be completely mistook. Yet this critical hyperbole, a function of a particular anxiety with respect to language, occludes what Rabelais' stories make clear: that language (and its limitations) is as readily available and as ordinarily satisfying as is bread or wine.

Everyday language, then, like bread, is an historical answer to an historical problem. Built upon the human experience of an absence/presence duality in all acts of knowing, the language of fictions especially embraces this epistemological problem with a high degree of intentionality. But because their assertion of a presence *ipso facto* reveals an absence, the value of acts of signification as true or adequate is called into question and often denigrated. Jean Paris, in his monograph on Rabelais, rightfully suspects any writing which does not acknowledge its own ambiguity. Rabelais, of course, revels in ambiguity. But Paris goes further: "...c'est que le signifiant cesse ici de participer du signifié, qu'entre eux le lien est désormais tranché, qui jusqu'alors les unissait en Dieu..."[1] The terms of the statement are too vague ("le lien," "en Dieu") to permit it to signal the great revolution in the history of ideas which Paris has in mind; it becomes evident that, while he sees Rabelaisian language as debunking *certain* medieval theories of the way signification works, he ignores the implications for those same fictions of the fact that it does, normally, work. Ambiguity, language as self-referential system, are neither humanist nor existentialist discoveries, even though it is valid to say that sixteenth-, seventeenth- and twentieth-century writing has these as very conspicuous common denominators. But to suggest that acts of signification (which I take to be primarily relationships between signifiers and signifieds in the conceptual order, in the "language game") are totally "cut off" from the given, natural order because *absolutely ambiguous* or *closed* systems, is peculiarly modern and not at all Rabelaisian.

I hope to demonstrate that Rabelais conceives of acts of signification and interpretation as eschatologically oriented, victims of apocalyptic diminution and, just as crucially, occasions of irenic fulfillment. Language in Rabelais simultaneously claims as its own enough innocence to remain open to various interpretations or occasions of meaning, and enough guile to criticize the pretensions of systems and institutions to definitive interpretation. M.A. Screech's thesis about Rabelais as "evangelical" is strongly supported by this reading which proposes that apocalyptic is an important part of the fiction's aesthetic/ascesis;

---

[1] *Rabelais au futur* (Paris, 1970), p. 126.

and Screech's thesis is equally supported by a reading which finds Rabelaisian semiotics and hermeneutics lineal descendants of the earliest Christian theory about Paris' "lien" or "union": that they are (as this study has indicated at several points) pneumatic. To put it another way: it does violence to Rabelais' very stress upon ambiguity, to his grotesque (in Bahktin's sense) manipulation of linguistic structures, to conclude that the author does not believe there to be an agent (human or divine) which, while functioning in terms of morphology and syntax themselves, can guarantee the manifestation of absolute truth in a human history conceived of as finite. Even more simply, two assumptions which often go uncriticized cause readers to miss the mark about the status of signs in Rabelais: first, that the time in which the language game is played is infinite (an assumption which still underpins the praxis of most modern science) and, second, that the only agency affecting history in a purposeful manner is human. Rabelais' fictions accept neither of these assumptions.

In his finely balanced article on "Cratylisme et Pantagruelisme,"[2] F. Rigolot notes the evangelical import of Rabelais' recognizing the limitations of language while using all of its possibilities in order to occasion meaning. Language is alienated, fortuitous, for St. Paul— "sounding brass and tinkling cymbal" (*I Cor.* 13)—only when it is without love, or, without Pantagruelism. (I think it best here to imitate Rabelais' own stylistic preference for analogy rather than for definitions which look airtight.) Rigolot quotes the statement about Pantagruelism given in the Prologue to the *Quart Livre* as an example of the fact that, in Rabelais, the fortuitous can be gratuitous. This "phrase-emblème" (Rigolot) typifies Rabelais' irenic-apocalyptic stance as well: Pantagruelism, "c'est certaine gayeté d'esprit conficte en mepris des choses fortuites" ("it's a certain joyfulness of spirit confected despite the chanciness of things"). Such gaiety is possible first of all because bread and wine and conversational language are so readily at hand: "Je suys, moiennant un peu de Pantagruelisme..., sain et degourt; prest à boire, si voulez" ("I am, using the mediation of a little Pantagruelism... healthy and fit, ready to drink, if you'ld like"). Such disdain for the threats which "outrageous fortune" makes against these ordinary artifacts is a result of the fictional characters' realization, *in the process of using them*, of their extraordinary possibilities for satisfying human nature "now," before time runs out. Rabelais makes the point in the same Prologue with rhetorical formulae (including the present

---

[2] "Cratylisme et Pantagruelisme: Rabelais et le statut du signe," *Etudes Rabelaisiennes* 13 (1976), 115-32.

participle to indicate *process*) which should by now be familiar to us. Reading the Pantagrueline adventures will lead to fulfillment,³ but the readers are advised against any temptation to seize such fulfillment, just as *Apocalypse* had advised its readership: "attendez encores un peu avecques demi once de patience" ("Wait yet a little more, with half an ounce of patience") and "Soubhaitez doncques mediocrité: elle vous adviendra; et encores mieulx, deument ce pendent labourans et travaillans" (*Q.L.*, Prologue) ("Therefore, wish for moderate things: it [fulfillment] will come to you, and more as well, provided you are working and struggling all the while").

"La vie très horrifique du Grand Gargantua": a title which announces a text to come without any attempt at clarifying the adjective which promises to make this fictional "life" different from all others; it will be "horrific." The reader's initial reaction can only be a literalist one. It is characteristic of authentic apocalyptic that the irenic side of the horrible must be discovered by the reader or hearer of the text, as that text discloses it in its unique fashion. Thus, the initial moment of such a disclosure also appears on a title page but, as we have already seen, looks forward to the Fourth Book for what sounds more like a definitive gloss; the text is a "livre plein de pantagruelisme." The dedicatory *dizaine* which precedes the narrative proper says right off that in this book the ideal is not a goal toward which it could (in the abstract) or would point its readers. But such a denial of a complete hold on signification, a denial of a closed-ended narrative intent, is immediately qualified by an irenic, open-ended exception to the general case.

> Vray est qu'icy peu de perfection
> Vous apprendrez, si non en cas de rire.

[It is true that you'll learn little about perfection here, except when laughing.]

The connotations of "perfection," in other words, are debunked by a more accurate analysis of the natural history of the species. "Reading the book," "le lisant," the reader will be learning through laughter in part because the author, "voyant," has been noticing, along with Aristotle in the *De Partibus Animalium*, that laughter is unique to human psychosomatic complexity; it is *ad proprietatem rei*. Humans, quite simply and quite often, laugh, and their laughter permits them to know pain and fulfillment simultaneously.

---

[3] Alcofrybas' translation of the gigantesque geneology is available to his readers only "...en Pantagruelisant, c'est à dire beuvans à gré et lisans les gestes horrificques de Pantagruel" (*Gar*. I) ("Pantagruelizing, that is to say, drinking freely and reading the dread deeds of Pantagruel").

> Voyant le deuil qui vous mine et consomme:
> Mieulx est de ris que de larmes escripre,
> Pour ce que rire est le propre de l'homme.
>
> [Seeing the pain which rots and consumes you:
> It's better to write of laughs than of tears,
> For laughing is proper to humanity.]

Rabelais compares the learning process or interpreting process which he urges upon his readers to the *patientia* of a dog studying his bone, a patience based upon real hope.[4] The passage in the Prologue to *Gargantua* which makes the comparison between bone and text begins unexpectedly with a question, "Crochetastes vous oncques bouteilles?" followed by a just as unexpected exclamation, "Caisgne!". Any formal similitude is subordinated to a statement of the problem in the simple terms which are its ultimate terms: "have you ever cracked open any bottles?": have you violently entered into peaceful fulfillment?; similitude is subordinated as well to a single word which turns exclamatory humor into vatic utterance, simultaneously ambiguous and revelatory. "Bitch!" is the real point, the only point to be made. The reader either does or does not laugh, either does or does not see himself called to be a philosophical beast or a canine Lady Philosophy whose daily activity of drinking, or reading, can "...rompre l'os et sugcer la sustantificque mouelle" ("...break open the bone and suck out the substantial marrow"). Rabelais' choice of words suggests that the wider, irenic context of human activity must be understood to be part and parcel of that activity's apocalyptic, daily struggle with finite time. The "marrow" is readily available; but to understand the crisis, the necessity of getting at it now, of being nourished now and in this way, is to understand that marrow as "sustantificque." Rabelais, the Erasmian humanist, read his Gospels in Greek as well as in Latin. In the Greek text, the bread asked for in the Lord's prayer is "epioúsion," or, as the Vulgate for *Matt.* 6.11 puts it, "supersubstantialem."[5] The Rabelaisian "sustantificque" recalls a theme which we have seen

---

[4] "Studying" his bone seems the best way to render the idea of dog as "sage," given J. Bichon's gloss on the word as, finally, a hunting term. The dog's sagacity keeps to the smell of the bone/prey and does not let it go. See *Etudes Rabelaisiennes* 8 (1969), 87-90. Of equal importance is Bichon's gloss on "oeconomicque" as the private sphere of human affairs, in *Etudes Rabelaisiennes* 7 (1967), 107-17.

[5] I am grateful to Professor Gerald P. Fitzgerald of Boston University for reminding me of this notable difference in Latin renderings of the Greek Gospels. The Greek usage seems to mean either "necessary" or "more than sufficient." The Vulgate for *Luke* 11.3 has "quotidianum," the familiar Latin form maintained in the Tridentine and Roman Mass.

as common to Christian apocalyptic: the superabundant can be tasted "now," subjected as it is to the limitations of time and flesh. In his treatises *De Sacramentis* and *De Mysteriis*, Ambrose of Milan makes it clear that the fact that the altar bread is plain, everyday bread is part and parcel of the "mysterium" of its confection (*conficere*) into Christ's flesh. The human confectioner's art is subtended by God's art; the systems of human language subtended by the true Verbum: such that simply surviving over diachronic time, eating every day, is, simultaneously, an experience of superabundant presence. "Quotidie si accipis, quotidie tibi hodie est" ("If you receive everyday, then everyday is today for you").[6] The bread we need, therefore, is both "cotidianum" and "supersubstantialem." Similarly, the philosophical marrow which reader sucks from text is in no wise an end in itself or even any specific conceptual content. Any experience of hope fulfilled must be repeated again and again with respect to the finite series of revelatory ambiguities which is the reader's life and the life of this narrative.

> ...rempre l'os et sugcer la sustantifícque mouelle-... avecques espoir certain d'être faictz escors et preux à ladicte lecture; car en icelle bien aultre goust trouverez et doctrine plus absconce, laquelle vous revelera de très haultz sacremens et mysteres horrifícques, tant en ce que concerne notre religion que aussi l'estat politicq et vie oeconomicque. (*Gar.*, Prologe)
>
> [...break open the bone and suck out the substantial marrow— ...with certain hope of being made adept and courageous in the aforementioned act of reading; for in it you will find quite another taste and a more hidden teaching, which will reveal to you very high sacraments and horrific mysteries, concerning our religion as well as the political estate and private living.]

A certain kind of reading, in other words, will unfailingly prepare a reader for the occasion of meaning; the "deeper meaning" occasioned is recognizable first of all because it "tastes" differently, unlike anything else in the order of interpreting signs. The "aultre goust" resembles most of all, I submit, the "bitter" taste which accompanies the sweet in John's digestion of a revelatory book given him in *Apoc.* 10.9; Rabelais' future tenses all refer to the status of "ladicte lecture" when it will have been digested enough for the stomach to be embittered by

---

[6] Ambrose, *De Sacramentis* V, 26. This Ambrosian treatise is the best source I know for the idea of the ordinary creature's potential to be "mysterium." Both with respect to ordinary words and everyday bread, Ambrose makes it clear that it is the interpreter's job to perceive extraordinary possibilities. "Venisti ad altare, adtendisti sacramenta posita super altare et ipsam quidem miratus es creaturam; tamen creatura sollemnis et nota" (IV, 3.8) ("You have come to the altar, you turn your attention to the signs placed upon the altar, and what do you see but the creature itself! indeed, a creature one is used to and easily recognizes"). See Botte's critical edition in *Sources Chrétiennes*, no. 25 bis (Paris, 1961).

what was encountered as sweet at the beginning of the process. Both Rabelais' books and the Book of *Revelation* identify themselves as bittersweet texts which claim to incarnate, like food confected, eaten and digested, the best ways in which the "horrific mysteries" of utmost importance to them both may be destructured. Problems of devotion to God and of devotion to humanity in both the private and public sectors are engaged by both authors and proffered to readers in divers fictions which narrate (or in an older, mimetic sense, "reveal") their bittersweet quality. The Rabelaisian sign "horrificque" enjoins, therefore, the necessity for a semiotics of the irenic and apocalyptic, of the bittersweet, with respect to this text.

Apocalyptic giants often drink blood.[7] The fact that Rabelaisian giants drink irenic wine mitigates but does not completely remove their frightening aspect. In them and in the language which describes them, all that is possibly human is taken to the supernumerary. The two extra months Gargantua spends in his mother Gargamelle's womb produces a body which is, in the fictions, both measurable and immeasurable, like and unlike that of other human beings. Though always laughable, the gigantesque heroes and brimming-over prose-style are a serious conflation of the apocalyptic fictions of "then" and "now." They experimentally add together the knowable structure and the unstructurable, the 144,000 securely sealed and the more ambivalent throngs "which no man could number" (*Apoc.* 7.9) and force the human reader to decide how much he or she can recognize and therefore interpret the grotesque "sum": to decide, for example, how Rabelais' page-long rhetorical accumulations can be simultaneously absurd and revelatory. The fiction about giants, in other words, embodies "now" and, problematically, something of the fulfillment which is expected "then." The text's author, it should be pointed out, does not entirely remove himself from what may seem so clearly a reader's problem. Alcofrybas, the author's voice in the fiction, hopes to be filled up in the present time with "goods" he recognizes as desirable (they are, in hindsight, very Pantagruelian): "...d'estre roy et riche... affin de faire grand chere, pas ne travailler, poinct ne me soucier, et bien enrichir mes amys et tous gens de bien et de sçavoir" (*Gar.* I) ("...to be King, rich... so as to have a great time, not work, never worry myself, and to make my friends rich along with all good and

---

[7] Giants are related to Judaeo-Christian apocalypticism via, among other texts, the *Ethiopian* (Apocalypse of) *Enoch* where they are the offspring of fallen angels and human mothers. See also the pseudo-Clementine *Homilies* 8.9 and *Apoc.* 17.1-6. A number of other sources are cited in W. Bousset, "Zur Dämonologie der Späteren Antike," *Archiv für Religionswissenschaft* 18 (1915), 134-72.

wise folks"). But his evident lack is truly filled only when the present moment is set in its proper and barely imaginable eschatological context: "Mais en ce je me reconforte que en l'aultre monde je le seray, voyre plus grand que de present ne l'auseroye soubhaitter" (*Gar.* I) ("But I comfort myself in this, that in the other world I shall be [great and rich] even more than in the present I would dare to hope"). And the same authorial voice concludes that his readers may be similarly enriched by means of an hermeneutics which is aware of its own eschatological dimensions. If drinking and reading are made to be analogous activities in the *Prologe*, then the author speaks quite plainly when he says, drawing a conclusion from his own situation, "Vous en telle ou meilleure pensée reconfortez vostre malheur, et beuvez fraiz, si faire se peut" (*Gar.* I) ("And you, comfort your unhappiness with such a thought, or a better thought, and drink well if you can manage to").

Indications of comfort in the midst of troubles come from the most unlikely sources, even from language in which most intratextual coherence has been lost. The "Fanfreluches antidotées," unearthed in the fiction by a humanist's reverence for antiquity, present—simply present, among the nonsense language which mostly comprises them—two stanzas which make some sense only because they evoke in the reader's mind the aesthetics of *Apocalypse*, if not specific elements of the biblical text as well. Stanzas 12 and 13 of the half-eaten poem (whose ability to signify in time has been, in other words, seriously threatened *because* of time) describe the union of past, present and future in an irenic moment: "C'est an passé, cil qui est regnera / Paisiblement avec ces bons amis" ("When the year's over, he who is will reign peacefully with his good friends"); it is a penultimate moment, coextensive with a time in which violence is enchained: "Jusques à tant que Mars ayt les empas" (*Gar.* II) ("Until the time when Mars is put in chains"). In terms of the Book of *Revelation*, He who was, who is and who is to come, he who brings peace, will reign with his saints for as long as the dragon is enchained.[8] "Then," continue the "Fanfreluches," catching up with all of time in an enigmatic narrative which Alcofrybas transcribes as a necessary part of his own narrative,

---

[8] "Gratia vobis et pax ab eo, qui est et qui erat, et qui venturus est..." (1.4; cf. 4.9); "...et animas decollatorum propter testimonium Iesu... regnaverunt cum Christo mille annis" (20.4); "Et vidi angelum... et catenam magnam in manu sua. Et apprehendit draconem... et ligavit eum per annos mille..." (20.1) ("Grace and peace to you from him, who is, who was and who is to come..."; "...and the souls of those beheaded for a witness to Jesus... reigned with Christ a thousand years"; "And I saw an angel... and a great chain in its hand. And it got hold of the dragon... and tied him down for a thousand years...").

"one will come." The poem's refusal to use a name is as much the rhetoric of the sacred as it is a commonplace of the deliberately ambiguous sixteenth-century almanacs. It invites its readers both to enjoy a funny parody and to understand by acting: "Levez vos cueurs, tendez à ce repas" ("Lift up your hearts, get to this meal"), uniting the supper of the Lamb "then" (*Apoc.* 19.9) with its irenic recreation "now" in the eucharistic liturgy ("levez vos cueurs" = "sursum corda"). The reason for such celebration is a death which will never have to occur again: "...car tel est trespassé / Qui pour tout bien ne retourneroit pas..." ("...for such a one has died who wouldn't for the world come back again..."); the line both makes us laugh and reminds us of *Apocalypse*, in which the saints are invited to the meal of a living Lamb which was slain (5.6).[9] So the ancient artifact which is the "Fanfreluches" is part of Rabelais' fiction and includes irenic apocalyptic language. But the author makes no attempt to guard against the false millenialist, integralist, triumphalist interpretation to which such language has always been subject. Indeed, the problem is best glossed by the long episode of King Picrochole's war which follows it in the narrative and seems quite unrelated to it.

The first sentence of chapter XXV of Book I, which introduces the story of the Picrocholine Wars, reveals Rabelais' fiction of a local, even domestic quarrel set off between shepherds and bakers as being much more than an object-lesson about the arbitrary cruelty and selfishness of human violence. This war is a war over the vintage; what is threatened is ripeness and all its possibilities. "En cestuy temps, qui fut la saison des vendanges, au commencement de l'automne, les bergiers de la contrée estoient à garder les vines et empescher que les estourneaux ne mangeassent les raisins" (*Gar.* XXV) ("At that time, which was the time for the vintage, early autumn, the shepherds of those parts were standing guard over the vines to prevent the starlings from eating the grapes"). In making it clear that ripeness can be either saved or lost "now," Rabelais makes the Chinon vintage just as crucial, in its own way, as is the harvest in biblical apocalyptic. As Christ

---

[9] Finding comfort depends entirely upon one's perspective, as does interpreting so inane a text as the "Fanfreluches." Rabelais makes the point when discussing the many parts of Gargantua's wardrobe. The giant's gown is made of a blue velvet, we are told; when observed "par juste perspective," however, the gown reveals the unexpected, the wonderful, the totally new. "...Yssoit une couleur innommée, telle que voyez es coulz des tourtourelles, qui resjouissoit merveilleusement les yeulx des spectateurs" (*Gar.* VIII) ("...there came forth from it an unnamed color, such as you see on the necks of doves, which wonderfully pleased the eyes of the onlookers"). The color which cannot be named is, of course, *iris*cence—the irenic, covenantal rainbow of *Genesis* 9.13 and *Apocalypse* 4.3.

glosses his own parable in *Matthew* 13.39, "Messis vero, consummatio saeculi est" ("The harvest, then, is the end of the world"). The local war is preceded by warnings from Picrochole's first victims, "...que Dieu les en puniroit de brief" ("...that God would punish them for it soon"); times are already bad; there is plague but, says Rabelais, not even plague could stop the ravaging army (*Gar.* XXVI-XXVII). The good king Grandgouzier's shepherds are portrayed as innocents; one of them, Forgier, had approached the bakers "en toute simplesse" (*Gar.* XXV) and was struck. The Picrocholine battlecry "We'll teach you to eat cake!" makes them a particular kind of threat to the Chinon harvest and to the abbey-vineyard at Seuilly: their violence is a brutal, bloodthirsty "twin" of the possibilities for good eating and drinking which are in turn represented by Frère Jean's alarm to the monks, "What are we going to drink?!" It is also a debased "twin" of the destruction of the vintage in *Apocalypse*. There, after warnings to repent, after a punishment of wars and plagues, the angels trample the world's ripeness into "the wine of God's wrath."[10] This amounts to a victory for those who, in the face of persecution, "never allowed a lie to pass their lips" (like Forgier), who "follow the Lamb wherever He goes" (like Grandgouzier's good shepherds), who themselves are the remnant of ripeness saved by a Messianic reaper: "Hi empti sunt ex hominibus primitiae Deo, et Agno..." (*Apoc.* 14.4-5) ("These have been brought back from among men, first fruits for God and for the Lamb..."). The eschatological context of Rabelais' narrative, therefore, puts Grandgouzier's Kingdom close enough to the end to realize the full implications of its enemy's violence; it realizes this, lest we forget Rabelaisian parody, at least as much as it readies itself against all those ravaging starlings! Good drinking and eating must be saved, as must a remnant of those individuals who are ripening to be "primitiae," first-fruits, gifts. One of these is Frère Jean who reaps, separating out the possibilities of good and bad life, with his Messianic "sharp scythe," the great cross (*Apoc.* 14.14). Frère Jean simultaneously struggles and is at ease; he is fearless and, therefore, can forswear all armour for his "froc horrificque" (*Gar.* XLIII). Rabelaisian punning tells us through him that (in human history at least) there can be no *service divin* without the *service du vin* (*Gar.* XXVII). Frère Jean's wildly funny harangue to his fellow monks, who are too

---

[10] *Apoc.* 14.18, "Mitte falcem tuam acutam, et vindemia botros vineae terrae: quoniam maturae sunt uvae eius" ("Put forth your sharp scythe and harvest the fruit-clusters of the earth's vines: for its grapes are ripe"). Northrop Frye, *Fearful Symmetry* (Boston, 1962), p. 290, recognizes the irenic as well as the violent nature of the winepress: "The gathering in of life to prevent its death may be a symbol of the apocalypse."

busy about the business of monkery to perceive the real crisis, represents a collation on Rabelais' part of some of the most well known rhetoric of apocalyptic from the Old Testament. We laugh. But we also realize that Frère Jean's is the prophetic voice preparing his people for the end. Collating parts of *Joel* 1.5-16 with Rabelais will make the point.

Expergiscimini, ebrii: et flete Et ululate, omnes qui bibitis vinum in dulcedine,	Escoutez,... vous aultres qui aymez le bon vin... sy me suibrez!
Quoniam periit ab ore vestro.	Que fera cest hyvrogne icy?... car vous mesmes, M. le Prieur, aymez boyre du meilleur. Sy faict tout homme de bien...
Gens enim ascendit super terram meam, Fortis et innumerabilis:	sy ceulx tastent du pyot qui n'auront secouru la vigne...
Posuit vineam meam in desertum, ...	[S']ilz ne sont en nostre cloz...
Periit sacrificium et libatio de domo Domini; Luxerunt sacerdotes ministri Domini.	tous ceux de l'armée qui estoient entrez dans le clous; jusques au nombre de 13,622, sans les femmes et petits enfants...
Depopulata est regio, ...	Affin de guaster toute la vendange...
Confusum est vinum	Troubler ainsi le service divin! Mais... le service du vin...
Accingite vos, et plangite, sacerdotes. Ululate ministri altaris;	qu'ilz arriverent à Seuillé, et detrousserent hommes et femmes... le service du vin... qu'il ne soit troublé...
...vocate coetum Congregate senes...	A toutes adventures feirent sonner *ad capitulum capitulantes...*
Et clamate ad Dominum A, a, a, diei! Quia prope est dies Domini, ...	lesquelz voyant chanter *Ini, nim, pe, ne, ne, ne, ne, ne...* Mais ces responds que chantez ycy ne sont, par Dieu!, poinct de saison. (*Gar.* XXVII)[11]

---

[11] The other *locus classicus* is *Ps.* 80, "Qui regis Israel, intende" where the crisis of God's vineyard is described:

> Posuisti nos in contradictionem vicinis nostris,
> Et inimici nostri subsannaverunt nos.
> ....
> Ut quid destruxisti maceriam [vineam] eius,
> Et vindemiant eam omnes qui praetergrediuntur viam?
> ...respice de coelo

In short, the monks' responsories are out of season because their liturgy is too untroubled; they fail to see the present eschatological crisis which is, in Joel's words, "right in front of their eyes."[12] Frère Jean's anxiety is for *libatio* and *sacrificium*, in that order. Rabelais, characteristically, makes the point most daringly by subordinating all strictly theological discourse to the logic and hilarity of his narrative process. "Escoutez, Messieurs, vous aultres *qui aimez le vin: le corps Dieu*, sy me suibvez!" (italics mine) ("Listen up, Sirs, you all who love wine: by the body of God, if you'ld only follow me!"). The structure,... *le vin: le corps Dieu...*, not only is a narrative process whereby the reader finds out Frère Jean as a boozer and laughs at his sacrilegious oath; the structure also signifies another process which goes from ordinary wine to extraordinary Body. It is because the signifier is incomplete that the reader is forced to fill in its terms as one necessary movement to the signified: (le pain) *le vin: le corps Dieu* (le sang Dieu). To put it another way, a narrative process induces an hermeneutic process which points to a eucharistic process which theology calls a *mysterium*. Nothing in Rabelais' "mystères horrificques" forecloses the possibility of the reader's seeing the three as logically analogous processes.

King Picrochole is the butt of Rabelaisian humor. He is quite mad. But his madness, when it toys with the scheme of universal conquest proposed by his lieutenants, serves as the occasion for an explicit example of what has been termed in this study the "false twin" aspect of the irenic genre: claiming or seizing a repose which is in no sense prepared for or possessed and which represents itself as being beyond struggle. Two pages of narration of Picrochole's hypothetical conquests of Mediterranean and Atlantic Europe (including Greenland!), Eastern Europe, Scandinavia, Russia and the trans-Caucasus, the African litoral, the Levant and Arabian peninsula, end with the question of an old, prudent soldier: "Quelle sera la fin de tant de travaulx et traverses?" ("What will be the end of so many labors and campaigns?"). The king's answer, couched in tenses which logically admit

Et vide, et visita vineam istam;
Et perfice eam quam plantavit dextera tua.
Ps. 80.7, 13, 15-16

[You have placed us among the quarrels of our neighbors, and our enemies have derided us... For what reason have you destroyed the vine, that anyone walking along the road may harvest it?... Look down from your heaven and see, and visit this vine; and perfect that which your right hand planted.]

[12] *Joel* 1.16, "Numquid non coram oculis vestris alimenta perierunt / De domo Dei nostri, laetitia et exultatio?" ("Has not the food been lost right in front of our eyes, and joy and exaltation left the house of our God?").

that there have not yet been any "travaulx" at all, but do not "really" admit it: "Ce sera (dist Picrochole) que, nous retournez, repouserons à nos aises" (*Gar.* XXXV) ("It will be that we return home and relax at our ease"). Picrochole's ignominious end is as falsely apocalyptic as his misreading of the war was falsely irenic. Then, he elided all real struggle in order to have, to possess verbally, the kingdoms he would surely conquer. Finally, defeated, he reads a witch's prophecy of fantastic birds literally and waits, "as angry as ever," for a fleshed-out millenium. Rabelais chides Picrochole in expressly apocalyptic terms: "...esperant certainement, selon la prophetie de la vieille, estre à leur venue reintegré à son royaulme" (*Gar.* XLIX) ("...surely hoping, according to the old woman's prophecy, to be restored, at their coming, to his Kingdom").

Thélème is described as a place but is finally a process. Its foundation is occasioned by Frère Jean's refusal, as reward for his valor, of any already extant monastic institution. His refusal is in terms of a conundrum:

> Car comment (disoit il) pourray je gouverner aultruy, qui moy mesmes gouverner ne sçaurois? Si vous semble que je vous aye faict et que puisse à l'advenir faire service agreable, oultroyez moy de fonder une abbaye à mon devis. (*Gar.* LII)
>
> [Because how (said he) could I govern others who wouldn't know how to govern myself? If it seems to you that I've done and in the future may be able to do any welcome service, allow me to found an abbey in my own way.]

Frère Jean accepts the work of a foundation for others according to his own insight while admitting that his personal "foundation" is still terribly shaky. The place which the anaphora of the inscription over the great gate refer to as "cy" is a "place where" the process of self-governance and communal living may ideally occur. The words on the gate are most often signs of contradiction, of differentiation; they not only keep out those who cannot fit in but also tell the inhabitants that they are special, chosen out, "gens... bien nez" (*Gar.* LVII) ("well-born"). The phrase is ambiguous, as is much of the narrative; Thélème seems, on the one hand, a secular, humanist utopia (and so is it usually read); on the other, it is surely, for all its specific anticlericalism, a *typus ecclesiae*, in which the seemingly elitist "gens... bien nez" would have to refer to an evangelical, spiritual birth. The number of proof-texts which may be adduced for one or the other reading warns the reader against a univocal interpretation, as does the problem in hermeneutics evident in the diverse readings of Frère Jean and Gargantua which close the episode and the book. Thélème is a model for the ideal human community which specifically differentiates itself from the received models, both secular and religious, by excluding some of the traditionally privileged classes of both: lawyers, judges, members of religious orders. But it is important to note that, because the language of apocalyptic remains radical enough, in Rabelais' eyes, *vis-à-vis* the institutions it set itself against, the modern author can embrace it as the model for his own, "engaged" rhetoric of exclusion. Rabelais, like the author of *Apocalypse*, is careful, first of all, to be explicit about who may enter and who may not. Those who may not are, generally, "hypocrites," against whom most of Jesus' eschatological language is directed; Rabelais stresses the linguistic connection by listing "scribes et pharisiens" among the excluded (*Gar.* LIV). Rabelais excludes the satanic "economy" which accompanies all evil in human society: "Tirez ailleurs pour vendre vos abus" ("Get off elsewhere to sell your abuses"). The two economies, as we have seen, are a principle theme of *Apocalypse* because the saints are excluded from the world's buying and selling (13.17). Excluded as well are "Mangeurs du populaire," a common Old Testament name for the wicked.[13] The problem with lawyers, judges and clerics is that, unlike Frère Jean, they presume to be able to govern others, to interpret correctly. Their unrecognized or uncriticized internal imbalances will always affect the social organism. In *Apocalypse* and in New Testament apocalyptic, while the rewards of the saints are in process, the wicked already "have their reward" (*Matt.* 6.2). In Rabelais' *inscription*, the lawyers and judges already have their beloved "Proces et debatz" which are, from their point of view, their "salaire." But this reward, from the point of view of Thélèmite apocalyptic, is their "patibulaire," fully an instrument of torture and the debased twin of the gospel "gibbet" which saves the people. As for the chosen:

> Cy est le lieu où sont les revenuz
> Bien advenuz; affin que entretenuz
> Grands et menuz, tous soyez à milliers.
> (*Gar.* LIV)

[Here's the place where revenue is most welcome; so that both great and small may be entertained, be they in the thousands.]

The funny pun on "revenuz" reveals the eschatological orientation of Thélème, conceived of as an historical entity with a beginning and an end. Whether the word refer to "money given back" (for something's having been given) or to "those who come back" (having, in some

---

[13] E.g., *Ps.* 13.4, "Nonne cognoscent omnes qui operantur iniquitatem, / Qui devorant plebem meam sicut escam panis?" ("Do they not know, all these who do evil, that they are eating up my people as if they were ordinary bread?").

sense, left), it is a sign that Thélème is the place where the circle of the process of time, of human life and "goods" in time, moves surely, with the least interference, to its closure. For "les revenuz" to be "most welcome here" is for this place to be most profoundly *typus ecclesiae*. Though all creation in Christian theology is, *ipso facto*, on its way back to the Creator from which it came, the *ecclesia* is always the paradigm of the place where the movement *redditus*, though imperfect and enduring time, can most easily approximate the perfect circularity of the divine source of its *exitus* into time. Rabelais' ideal human economy (whether it manage the material circulation of those goods which help accomplish human desire or the spiritual circulation which is the will's life, the moral life itself)[14] imitates the divine economy, insofar as the latter is experienced both as source and end to which humanity "comes back." Locus of a "foy profonde," guardian of "la parole saincte," home of those who proclaim "le sainct Evangile," Thélème is a version of the *ecclesia*; and it is this as well because it can only be perceived as still struggling, full of ambiguity. Most ambiguous of all is its rule: "Fay ce que vouldras" (*Gar.* LVII) ("Do what you want"). The reader's interpretative problem is, presumably, a greater one than that of the Thélèmite. Though the fiction gives us reason to presume that living in "this place" will clarify the kind of willing its rule enjoins, the reader of the fiction either will or will not know that Rabelais has truncated the Augustinian dictum "Ama et fac quod vis..." ("Love and do what you want..."). The reader, in other words, is deliberately left too far outside the community which the fiction asks him to interpret. It is nonsense, on the face of it, to accept the proposition that "doing what you will" could ever produce the civic concord the author goes on to detail. The Thélèmites, paradoxically evangelical and rich, seem to understand how their rule works; but the reader's rules of textual interpretation fail to make much sense out of the fiction's paradoxes. We do know, however, that even as Rabelais associates the irenic language of *Apocalypse* with the abbey

---

[14] It is the case for most late medieval philosophy that, in the human psychosomatic complex, "to will" is to integrate acts of going out and coming back. The *anima intellectiva* integrates the movements of the soul's other faculties and their corresponding physical organs. This is the case in all normal action: walking from here to there, "at will." A corresponding psychosomatic disintegration or "confusion" might cause one to faint: "passing out" as opposed to "coming back to." See Dante, *Inferno* v-vi: "Io venni men..." / "Al tornar de la mente, che si chiuse / dinanzi a la pieta d'i due cognati, / che di trestizia tutto mi confuse..." ("I passed out...; ...when my mind came back, which closed itself off when faced with the pitifulness of the two relations, [a pitifulness] which confounded me with sadness..."). For a more philosophical gloss, see Bonaventure, *Itinerarium* II.4-7.

and its inhabitants, our violent struggle with texts is shared by the Thélèmites' struggle with their own text.

The "Enigme en prophetie" of Mellin de St.-Gelais which Rabelais has found in the abbey's foundations describes, simultaneously, the world's pain and its possibilities for good. Addressed to those who are waiting for "bon heur," it repeats the eschatological "Levez vos cueurs" already announced in the "Fanfrelouches" which opened Book I. The rhetoric of violent apocalypse, with its floods, earthquake, loss of light and heat, is followed by a "temps bon et propice" and by a meal in which "les esleuz joyeusement refaits / soient de tous biens et de manne celeste, / et d'abondant par recompense honeste / Enrichez soient; les aultres en la fin / soient denuez..." (*Gar.* LVIII) ("the elect may be reformed by all that is good, by heavenly manna, and enriched abundantly in honest recompense; the others, at the end, will be denuded..."). This very close borrowing from the text of *Apocalypse* must be understood irenically.[15] It may be well to repeat a statement I made in the opening chapter of this study which bears directly on the parodic "Enigme":

> The paradigm for any post-New Testament prophecy, in a Christian sense, is that the irenic context of *Apocalypse* has turned its own violent, eschatological prophecies into a narrative of the victory's being won "now"... All true Christian prophecy must be irenic as *Apocalypse* is irenic; which is to say it must be ecclesially oriented prophecy for those who are still struggling and imperfect.[16]

The exhumed text closes with a praise of *patientia*: "O qu'est à reverer / Cil qui en fin pourra perseverer!" ("Oh he is to be revered who will be able to persevere in the end!"). But Rabelais is careful to concretize this abstract ideal the way it must be to avoid the false peace of a too easy millenium. Gargantua recognizes the distance between the text's promise and the problematical present to which it returns him as he reads it. "La lecture de cestuy monument parachevée, Gargantua souspira profondement..." ("Having accomplished the reading of this monument, Gargantua sighed deeply..."). As one who understands the apocalyptic text as both violent and irenic, he is both

---

[15] In *Apoc.* 2.17, the gift to the church at Pergamon is a "manna absconditum." In contrast to those who in the end will be "denuez," Laodicea is promised "et non appareat confusio nuditatis tuae" (3.18) ("the confusion of your nakedness may not be apparent"). Although none of the cognates of "abundantia" may appear in the Vulgate text, it is a major idea in apocalyptic. See chapters 1 and 2 of this study. The gate at Thélème refers obliquely to the innumerability of the elect: "Grands et menuz, tous soyez à milliers."

[16] See chapter 1, p. 19.

saddened and hopeful after his reading of it and concludes by adopting the text's own aesthetic, which is that of the genre I've called irenic apocalypse, as his own.

> ...et dist es assistans: "Ce n'est de maintenant que les gens reduictz à la creance Evangelicque sont persecutez; mais bien heureux est celluy qui ne sera scandalizé et qui tousjours tendra au but..." (*Gar.* LVIII)
>
> [...and says to his retinue: "It's not only now that those brought to the Gospel-faith are persecuted; but very happy is he who will not be scandalized and who ever moves toward the endpoint..."]

Not so Frère Jean. The still problematical nature of Thélème, its lack, is nowhere clearer that in its founder's exegesis of the "Enigme." Though Frère Jean imitates the founder of the New Jerusalem in creating an institution wholly different from its conceivable precedents, "Ecce nova facio omnia" (*Apoc.* 21.5) ("Behold I make all things new"), his totally new human experiment is as apt as is he to misinterpret its own text, its own ideal history. The exegesis itself is Rabelais' humanist parody of the excesses of biblical interpretation from the older *glossatores* to the tactics, *en prophetie*, of a Joachim of Flora.[17] Jean's reading, like the Joachite *concordia ad numeros*, must see each discreet textual element as a clear symbol for something else. What is for Gargantua, then, a poetic adumbration of a spiritual struggle becomes for Jean the revelation of a physical tennis game. The back and forth volley is just plain funny. It is as well a happy misreading inasmuch as it is a powerful image of the problem of action in time: humanity's problem, the abbey's problem, the reader's problem. But Jean is carried away by his wish to escape the problematical—the game itself—so much so that his language reflects a real struggle only minimally; his interpretation passes, as quickly and painlessly as possible, to a joyful solution of the text. "Après le jeu, on se refraischit devant un clair feu, et change l'on de chemise, et voluntiers bancquete l'on, mais plus joyeusement ceulx qui ont guaingné. Et grand chere!" (*Gar.* LVIII) ("After the game, one refreshes oneself in front of a clear fire, one changes one's shirt, one feasts gladly—but even more joyfully those who won! Cheers!"). Millenialism is the risk of all idealist institutions and a millenial literalism the risk in textual interpretation both for us and for Frère Jean. Neither risk invalidates the project. Rabelais

---

[17] For Joachim's style, see the "Liber Introductorius" to his *Expositio in Apocalypsin* (Venice, 1527). Frère Jean's *reductio* is therefore a caution against the danger of angelism in Thélème. It is a risk Rabelais understands and is apparently willing to take, especially when his *typus ecclesiae* seems to be undistinguished from the Heavenly Jerusalem in *Apocalypse* in that it is without a temple.

leaves his reader with two possible attitudes toward such projects: Jean's falsely-irenic, crepuscular fulfillment on the one hand and, on the other, a horrific, gargantuan sigh.

In the "Prologue" to *Pantagruel*, the author introduces himself as one who presents a narrative which ought not be simply a neutral pastime. The repose it induces ("pour y vacquer entierement...") is capable of being enjoyed irenically; if read aright, the text will surely "accroistre vostre passetemps dadvantaige..." ("further increase your pastime..."). It will be a salutary text because the author has already perceived certain truths about struggle and fulfillment in time. He calls himself a "crotenotaire des martyrs amans et croquenotaire de amours" ("crotonotary of martyr-lovers and a crocked-notary of loves"): the medium of the saints' struggle and fulfillment. To make his stance even clearer, he quotes John's Gospel directly: "Quod vidimus testamur" (3.11) ("We testify to what we have seen"). The 1533 version adds a passage later deleted: "J'en parle comme sainct Jehan de l'Apocalypse. Quod vidimus testamur" ("I speak of it like St. John of the Apocalypse...")[18] Rabelais' Johannine tone is particularly concerned with the possibility that *this* kind of text, this written form of therapeutic mediation, may be lost and therefore unable to be successfully communicated to the future. Because he has a final end in view, the author is the more mindful of other violent, arbitrary endpoints which threaten to affect the future of his words: "...si d'adventure l'art de l'imprimerie cessoit, ou en cas que tous livres perissent..." ("...should the printer's art by chance disappear, or should all books perish..."). Of course, Rabelais' harangue is as funny as it is serious. As a defense against time's onslaught, he asks his readers to take hold of his text "par cueur," an absurd task on the face of it if what must be memorized is the "letter." The written or printed word, its structures and format, are less likely to perdure than is the "spirit" of the letter which, though rooted in the letter, is not exhausted by it. This spirit, like the oral tradition of the Caballah to which it is compared, may be passed on generationally by means of a succession of texts whose idiosyncrasy is not incompatible with a punctilious faithfulness to the original: "...on temps advenir un chascun les peust bien au net enseigner à ses enfans, et à ses successeurs et survivens..." ("...in times to come, each person can teach them most precisely to his children and to his heirs and survivors..."). Such faithfulness to a text,

---

[18] See the edition of P. Jourda, *Oeuvres complètes*, tome I (Paris, 1962), p. 218, f.n. 3. Cf. J. Plattard, "L'Ecriture saint et la littérature scripturaire dans l'oeuvre de Rabelais," *Revue des Etudes Rabelaisiennes* 8 (1910), 259.

as we have already seen, is a crux for the thematic material in *Apocalypse*, precisely because the text claims it will not survive without it. But Rabelais recalls as well a common theme in Old Testament eschatology which may be exemplified in the opening to the prophetic, apocalyptic book of *Joel*: "Super hoc filiis vestris narrate, et filii vestri filiis suis, et filii eorum generationi alterae" (1.3) ("Narrate these things to your children, and your children to their children, and their children to the succeeding generation").

Gargantua's famous letter to his son is just such a narrative; it hands over the spirit from one generation to the next by being faithful to the crisis of human time which is the characteristic of all Rabelaisian narrative. The father's advice is put in the context of an irenic apocalypse which must occur on the personal as well as on the cosmic level. Humanity will propagate itself until the final judgment:

> ...quand Jesu-Christ aura rendu à Dieu le pere son royaulme pacifique hors tout dangier et contamination de peché... veu que la paix tant desirée sera consumée et parfaicte, et que toutes choses seront reduites à leur fin et periode. (*Pan.* VIII)

> [...when Jesus Christ will have returned to God the Father his peaceful Kingdom free from any danger and contamination of sin... since peace, desired so much, will be achieved, perfected, and all things will be brought back to their end and period.]

This is exactly what Pantagruel is urged to do with the *royaulme* of his own life; its accomplishment is described by the same two verbs the author had applied to Christ's: *parfaire* and *consommer*. Macrocosmically, Christ exchanges their Spirit with his Father; it is a perfect union, by virtue of which the *royaulme* of time and creation may be brought back out of its exile to its Creator. Microcosmically, Gargantua's letter attempts to make their spirit present to his son Pantagruel; their union, imperfect because it is a production of seed, can aid a single life, a personal culture, to also "come back" to its source, even as that final return is materially and so movingly imaged in a father's wish to see his son in the flesh: "...retourne vers moy, affin que je te voye et donne ma benediction devant que mourir" ("...come back to me, so that I may see you and give you my blessing before I die"). Rabelais' is a touching, domestic but no less eschatological rephrasing of the patristic notion that *apokatastasis* (the movement of all creation out from and back to its origin) imitates *perichoresis* (the perfectly integrated, eternal, "circular" movement of Trinitarian life). Not only will "ce moyen de propagation seminale"—imperfect, biological generation—yield spiritual life, but a human father's imperfect semiotic structures will be interpreted pneumatically by his son. The nar-

126 *Irenic Apocalypse*

rator's "fin et periode" puns on the relationship between the "last things" and any narrative closure; his "propagation seminale" puns on the *propagatio semiotica* which is the text we and Pantagruel read.[19] The letter's concern to instill a humanist and evangelical wisdom refuses to alienate matter and spirit, body and soul. By virtue of his father's letter, Pantagruel interprets in a way which Rabelais denotes with the vocabulary of the Spirit. It is a little Pentecost:

> Ces lettres receues et veues, Pantagruel print nouveau courage, et feut *enflambé* à profitter plus que jamais; en sorte que, le voyant estudier et profitter, eussiez dict que tel estoit *son esperit entre les livres* comme est *le feu* parmy les brandes, tant il l'avoit *infatigable et strident*. (*Pan.* VIII; italics mine)

> [These letters received and seen, Pantagruel screwed up his courage anew, and was enflamed to profit (from his education) more than ever; so that seeing him studying and profiting, you might have said that his spirit was amidst the books like a fire amidst the brands, so incessant and vehement was it.]

The curious adjectives *infatigable* and *strident* which qualify Pantagruel's pentecostal *esprit*, seem the more opaque precisely because the rest of the text's referents are so transparent. But these words are, I suggest, just as much the vocabulary of Pentecost as are *feu* and *enflambé*. They are a Rabelaisian paraphrase of one of the principal liturgical texts of the feast, the *communio* at the Mass, which refers to a heavenly "sonus advenientis spiritus vehementis": the noise (*strident*) of the coming of a vehement or incessant (*infatigable*) spirit.[20]

But Rabelais is careful to distinguish between Pantagruel's spiritual gifts and the longed-for presence of Spirit in the rest of humanity. In the chapter which follows immediately upon the text of his father's letter, Pantagruel, rather than speaking effectively and in tongues as did the apostles after Pentecost, goes out to meet the multiplicity of language as a seemingly insurmountable hindrance to communication. The encounter with Panurge is, at least initially, Babelic rather than pentecostal. Though Pantagruel's spirit is surely still "strident," making a virtuous "noise," the sound of Panurge's stomach is just as insistent. The parallel "appetit *strident*" which Rabelais gives him

---

[19] For "periode," see Huguet, *Dictionnaire de la langue francaise du seizième siècle*, V, p. 728, who lists both meanings and quotes the "Ancien Prologue" to Book IV: "...toutes choses sublunaires ont leur fin et periode." The more serious punning on Latin *propagatio* (= propagation and propaganda) and Greek *Semeion*, both certainly known to Rabelais, is beyond the scope of Huguet's work. He fails to list "seminale," though Rabelais uses the word.

[20] For the entire text, see the *Graduale Romanum*, "in festo Pentecostes," a Solesmensibus monachis editus, Tournai, 1957.

(*Pan.* IX) underlines the problematic aspect of the everyday event of communicating one's desires and of understanding another's. That Panurge should articulate his hunger in fourteen languages indicates first of all that he is not physically starving. He has too much language for that. Rabelais seems to recall the apocalyptic trials in the book of *Amos*: "Ecce dies veniunt, dicit Dominus: / Et mittam famem in terram; / Non famem panis, neque sitim aquae; / Sed audiendi verbum Domini" (*Amos* 8.11). Yet Panurge seems to need bread, "now." The urgency of such need—of the Babelic situation—necessitates, for Rabelais, undercutting any too facile appropriation of the pentecostal solution of speaking in tongues.[21] The synchronicity which would have characterized the charism of tongues is broken down into the structures which might have constituted it. Because of the fall, the Babelic diachronicity of an awfully brilliant linguist asserts itself. Misunderstanding is the order of the day as Panurge keeps on trying to point linguistically to... bread. Though he knows he needs, simply, bread, the very complexity of his linguistic suffering sounds like a demand for a better and better bread, a bread which means more when (like a text) it is received, a bread which can be adequate to his polyglot appetite. On the one hand, Panurge's painful speech represents the psychic threat of an absolute "nominalism" over and against some possibility of coping with living in the world, of a process of orientation to which many lacking, insufficient and inefficient signs and sign systems contribute. On the other hand, what is "funny" is that language, to a certain degree, does manage to work. French, Panurge's "langue naturelle et maternelle" (*Pan.* IX) does get him his bread in the end. Between these two extremes of the possibilities of language, however, lies a process through which a different and unexpected meaning has occurred. Though Rabelais makes it clear that Pantagruel cannot decipher any of the linguistic systems he confronts, his having confronted them results in an interpretation which (like the manner in which we are forced to interpret most signs) is also a decision. "Doncques, dist Pantagruel,... je vous ay ja prins en amour si grand que... et vous et moy ferons un nouveau pair d'amitié..." (*Pan.* IX) ("Therefore, says Pantagruel, I've already come to love you so much... that both you and I shall make a new bond of friendship..."). Pantagruel's interpretation of Panurge's language amounts to a word of love; his verbal response to Panurge's demand for a "panem

---

[21] Panurge's appetite is at least on the way towards being irenically satisfied and reformed through Pantagruel. It is in this respect different from the apocalyptic fate of the carnal appetite which built Babel, as that fate is described, for example, in Philo, *De Confusione Linguarum*, pp. 107-54, in *Oeuvres*, ed. J. Kalim, vol. XIII (Paris, 1963).

quotidianum" promises to feed him constantly, superabundantly, from then on. The Babelic situation was rife with pneumatic possibilities all along. It is here that Pantagruel is most evangelical, his language most of all the "verbum Domini" of *Amos* 8. Rabelais has put the reader of his text in the curious position of knowing enough about this fictional world to know just how gratuitous the fortuitousness of Panurge's language can be. Part of our pleasure—even as we are befuddled by the languages heaped upon the pages—is that we already know, the "plot" makes it clear, that Panurge has happened upon someone who understands how to eat and how to drink.

Rabelais makes it clear, too, that drinking well and drinking ill often look very much alike. Once one drinks well, one cannot drink enough. Always drinking, though apparently as grotesque and threatening as the extraordinary physicality of the giants and the prolixity of their speech, indicates precisely what one must encounter if one encounter the real. Interpreting, or deciding, is always risky in such an encounter. It is relatively easy to conclude, for example, that any wine is *vin bon et frais*. It is one of the brawling "bien yvres," after all, who shouts: "Ce m'est eternité de beuverye, et beuverye de eternité" (*Gar.* V) ("For me this is an eternity of drinking, and a drinking of eternity"). The apostles who speak in tongues after Pentecost are accused of being drunks; Peter feels it necessary to reply, somewhat literalistically, that they are not drunk, that it's only nine o'clock in the morning.

Pantagruel's battle against the Dipsodes and Giants in *Pan.* XXVIff. makes the point in greatest detail. The brief description of the enemy camp provided Pantagruel by a prisoner of war echoes the rhetoric of doubles in *Apocalypse* where the Beasts of the Land and Sea imitate the Lamb and His followers *in malo*. Not only do the Giants resemble Pantagruel but their leader is as large as he. "Dipsode," it turns out, denotes "thirsty" and the "...vous ne veistes oncques gens tant alterez ny beuvans plus voluntiers..." (*Pan.* XXVI) ("...you've never seen any people as thirsty nor so willing to drink...") threatens to erase the differences between Pantagruelistes and Dipsodes. The battle itself recalls the defeat of the worshippers of the false Beast in *Apoc.* 14. Those idolators are forced to drink "the wine of God's wrath" and are "tortured by fire": a lake of blood—the wrathful wine harvested—pours out of their city *"per stadia mille sexcenta"* (14.29) ("for 1600 stadî"). In Rabelais, Anarch the King and his guards must drink wine constantly to relieve the thirst inflicted upon them by Pantagruel. Carpalim, like the "angelus... qui habebat potestatem super ignem" (14.18) ("the angel who had power over fire"), sets the city afire.

Pantagruel urinates on the city "et y eut deluge particulier *dix lieues à la ronde*" (*Pan.* XXVIII; italics mine) ("and there was a flood for 10 leagues roundabout") which is mistaken for blood by the horrified onlookers.[22] These references to apocalyptic are finally made explicit: "Aulcuns disoient que c'estoit la fin du monde et le jugement final, qui doibt estre consommé par feu..." (*Pan.* XXVIII) ("Some said it was the end of the world and the last judgement, which is to be accomplished by fire"). When Pantagruel himself goes out against the giants, he is like the angel-reaper who cuts down the earth's crop of evil with his scythe (*falx*) in *Apoc.* 14.15. Pantagruel vindicates drinking *in bono* by making his double—the chief Giant, Loup Garou—into his apocalyptic weapon: "...à veoir Pantagruel, sembloit un fauscheur qui de sa *faulx* (c'estoit Loup-Garou), abbatoit l'herbe d'une pré (c'estoyent les gens)..." (*Pan.* XXIX; italics mine) ("...Pantagruel seemed a reaper who with his scythe, who was Loup-Garou, cut down the grass of a field, that is, the people..."). Epistemon is decapitated in battle but Panurge, using a "resuscitatif" (*Pan.* XXX), revives him: his resurrection permits Epistemon to narrate the infernal fates of the world's famous and great. The passage may be traced to several sources;[23] Rabelais' use of *Apocalypse* throughout these chapters, however, ought to tell us where we are to look first. In *Apoc.* 20.4, among those who sit in judgment after the great battle against the false Beast are "animas decollatorum propter testimonium Iesu, et propter verbum Dei..."[24] They share an irenic "resurrectio prima" (20.5) which Rabelais appropriates and Panurge accomplishes in the fiction.

The narrative of Pantagrueline "esprit" identifies itself, in the Prologue to the *Tiers Livre*, with an ancient commonplace of the irenic genre: repose in the midst of struggle or *otium in bono*. We have already described the topos in detail in the chapter on Petrarch's prose and shown how the Senecan *pingue otium* (even after it is Christianized) is not easily distinguishable in its external manifestations from a destructive, parasitic, "drunken" laziness. Rabelais holds up the example of the philosopher Diogenes and claims that this model of virtue simultaneously did nothing and did everything. Because he does not wish to appear "ocieux" as his fellow citizens make ready for war, Diogenes proceeds to thrash his tub—the occasion for an im-

---

[22] "Ilz sont tous mors cruellement, voyez le sang courir" (*Pan.* XXVIII) ("They all died cruelly; see the blood run").
[23] See the Jourda edition, vol. I, p. 367, f.n. 1 for references to the diverse readings of Epistemon's descent into hell.
[24] "...propter verbum Dei": Pantagruel has specifically vowed to restore God's word to its evangelical integrity if he win the battle. See *Pan.* XXX.

mense, Rabelaisian outpouring of verbs, of actions. "...He twirled it, whirled it, scrambled it, bungled it, frisked it, jumbled it, tumbled it, wheedled it, scratched it, stroked it, churned it, beat it, bumped it, banged it..."[25] Because the narrator's voice says: "je pareillement..." ("and I in like manner...") and makes its enterprise—the narrative—correspond to that of Diogenes, the reader is provided with an explicit gloss which claims for the fiction a confidence, constancy and peace which is apt to be misinterpreted and is certainly a cause for scandal. Diogenes' thrashing his tub is as scandalous and apparently useless as was the woman's anointing Christ's feet or David's dancing naked before the Ark. Scripture makes the point that both Christ's disciples and David's wife Mical are horrified by what they see. But the Rabelaisian narrator makes a clear choice to "consommer ce rien, mon tout, qui me restoit" ("to accomplish this nothing, my everything, which remained for me"). "Prins ce choys et election, ay pensé ne faire exercice inutile et importun si je remuois mon tonneau Diogenic qui seul m'est resté du naufrage faict par le passé on far de Mal'encontre" (*T.L.*, Prologue) ("Having chosen, having decided, I've thought it would not at all be a useless, importunate exercise if I beat up my Diogenic tub which alone remains for me after the shipwreck in the Strait of Bad Luck"). The text is the tub; and it is being thrashed with respect to its spiritual as well as to its literal possibilities because Diogenes thrashes his "en grande vehemence d'esprit," the pentecostal "spiritus vehementis" to which Rabelais has already referred obliquely and which is here literally translated from the Latin.[26] Meaning in this passage seems not readily available in the inundation of words; the words themselves occasion a question as to their function: "A ce triballement de tonneau, que feray-je en vostre advis?... je ne scay encores" ("What shall I do, according to you, in this thropping of tub?... I don't know as yet"). The reader is invited to wait upon meaning, "Attendez un peu..." ("Wait a bit..."), or at least to note that the narrator, at such an impasse, turns to irenic drinking. The narrator's own recomposition of meaning seems to lay outside the text entirely: in the fictional "Apres l'epilogue," "after the afterword"; but it lies as well in the coincidence of the text's own participial and indicative moods: a semiotic paradigm for the fiction of drinking and action over time. "Icy beuvant je delibere, je discours, je resoulz et concluds" ("Drinking here, I deliberate, I discourse, I resolve and I conclude").

The voice of the narrator in the Prologue echoes what the author has pointed to all along: true repose exists as a function of struggle

---

[25] I quote from J.M. Cohen's translation (Baltimore: Penguin Books, 1970), p. 283.
[26] See note 20 above.

and not in spite of it. A grotesque prose, its violence towards an accepted style, could conceivably be read as that only, its effect as univocal and tumultuous as may be the initial effect of apocalyptic. But the Diogenes allusion defines an irenic text which sets itself as a sign of contradiction against the style of the world's fitful, illusory "praeparatio." Jean Leclercq's remarks about a Christian *otium in bono* perfectly describe the Rabelaisian Diogenes as well:

> Le repos spirituel est souvent présenté comme l'enjeu d'un combat: il faut le conquérir de haute lutte, et l'on en jouira comme on fait de la paix acquise sur un champ de bataille. Le loisir a des ennemis qui essaient de la détourner à leur profit. L'une des tentations du démon consiste à faire abandonner le repos; c'est alors qu'il faut faire preuve de constance, de tranquillité, d'une persévérance qui sera une imitation de l'éternité de Dieu. Ceci requiert un grand courage. Le repos sera le fruit de ce labeur, sa récompense.[27]

The kind of war Diogenes fights is a war which helps those who detest war to survive its inevitability. The narrator's parallel struggle is against what Rabelais implies to be France's own feverish concern with offense and defense. It is Rabelais' eschatology which permits him to reveal, by punning and parody, that the French attempts to prepare for the future are short-sighted, full of pride, and too ready to claim a falsely irenic repose: "...le tout... à profit tant evident pour l'advenir (car desormais sera France *superbement* bournée, seront Francois *en repous asceurez*)..." (italics mine) ("...everything with such a clear benefit for the future, for hence forward France will be proudly swelled out, the French will have a sure repose..."). Both Diogenes in his thrashing and the narrator in his telling provide an aesthetic/ascetic antiphrase of the accepted moral order; rather than "Dulce et decorum est pro patria mori," it is "pro patria vivere" or, in Pantagrueline, "pro patria bibere."[28]

---

[27] *Otia Monastica*, Etudes sur le vocabulaire de la contemplation au Moyen-Age, *Studia Anselmiana* fasc. LI (Roma, 1963), p. 106.

[28] Though it fail to recognize the fact, the morally and physically beleaguered "city" is threatened most of all, in the Prologue to the *Tiers Livre*, by another group of falsely irenic doubles of the Pantagrueline saints. Rabelais makes their duplicity explicit in language which recalls the war against the Dipsodes:

> Des caphars encores moins, quoy que tous soient beuveurs oultrez tous verollez croustelevez, guarniz de alteration inexstinguible et manducation insatiable. Pourquoy? Pource qu'ilz ne sont de bien, ains de mal [Note the necessity of a clear distinction] et de ce mal duquel journellement à Dieu requerons estre delivrez, quoy qu'ilz contrefacent quelquez foys des gueux.

> [(Speak to me) still less of the hypocrites, though they be all outrageous boozers, all marked by the pox, armed with an inextinguishable thirst and an insatiable appetite. Why? Because they are not good; they are, rather, evil, and of that evil from which we daily ask God to deliver us, though they may at times mask as the poor.]

Diogenes' reading of the problem of his contemporary history results in an act of interpretation which looks like a decision which, in its turn, looks like inaction. The text proposes such a model for interpretation at several points, nowhere more outrageously than in Pantagruel's defense of the old lawyer Bridoye in the *Tiers livre*. Bridoye decides a case by letting it "mature"; it remains open-ended for a time: "...je temporize, attendant la maturité du procès, et sa perfection en tous membres..." (*T.L.*, XLII) ("...I temporize, awaiting the trial's maturity, its perfection in all its parts..."). He insists he acts, in this wise, "comme vous aultres, messieurs" ("like all of you, gentlemen"). It is a *captatio benevolentiae* but it is also the author's way of underlining the inevitability of process; what happens as we temporize (notice the participle, *attendant*) becomes part of the decision we make. But Bridoye's heuristics are none the less radical for all this. After waiting for a time, he finally judges by the toss of the dice. Epistemon's attempt to articulate the cause of Bridoye's forty-year history of overwhelmingly fair and reasonable judgements makes the case for an eschatological hermeneutics as the *reasonable* foundation for such a method. Bridoye's throw of the dice is contextualized by making the fortuitous (though necessary) violence of "this or that" wholly subject to an irenic understanding of time's closure which will involve a single and completely satisfactory judgement. Bridoye "...se

---

The martial goings on of the French/Corinthians are a "tragicque comédie" (*T.L.*, Prologue), a term which is defined in the lexicon published in the 1552 edition. The definition is as eschatological as is the term's use in the *Tiers livre*: "farce plaisante au commencement, triste en la fin." See Jourda's edition, vol. II, p. 249, f.n. 1 and p. 253.

I have attempted so far to understand the precise function of apocalyptic in Rabelais, and, as I have said, the effort seems to me in harmony with M.A. Screech's thesis about Rabelais' fundamentally "evangelical" orientation. I am as indebted in this chapter to Bahktin's understanding of the grotesque (*Rabelais and His World*, tr. H. Iswolsky, Boston, 1968) and to Thomas Greene's notion of "comic courage" (*Rabelais: A Study in Comic Courage*, Englewood Cliffs, 1970). Bahktin makes the point that comedy in Rabelais is a function of the degradation of the higher to the lower orders. I would add only that the source of festive comedy (as opposed to dark comedy, "angry satire": Bahktin, p. 38) is the fact that the higher orders lose none of their fascination or value by being so lowered. J. Paris gets it wrong, I think, when he says that alimentary imagery is less used eucharistically than "pour leur pouvoir de minimiser l'oeuvre, de l'apparenter métaphoriquement aux produits matériels" (*Rabelais au Futur, op. cit.*, p. 14). I agree with M. Paris that the bulk of the imagery is not specifically eucharistic. But the specifically eucharistic, which is *implicit* in the narrative's metaphoric structure, is precisely a meeting with, a coming to terms with material products and human artifacts. In Rabelais' fictional world, as opposed to Paris' world-view, the possibilities of human *oeconomia* run the gamut from the manipulation of money and food to the manipulation of spirit. If a greater symbiosis is indeed achieved by Rabelais between the "poles" of a world *experienced as* dualistic (higher/lower), then the result is, in Christian terms, as revolutionary as Bahktin would have it be in Marxist terms. The tactic is incarnational.

recommenderoit humblement à Dieu le juste juge, invocqueroit à son ayde la grace celeste, se deporteroit en l'esprit sacrosainct du hazard et perplexité de sentence definitive, et, par ce sort, exploreroit son decret et bon plaisir, que nous appellons Arrest..." (*T.L.*, XLIV) ("...humbly would commend himself to God the just judge, invoking heavenly grace in his aid, he would avoid in a most holy spirit the hazard, the perplexity of a definitive Sentence; by the die-cast, he would find out [God's] ordinance and pleasure, which we call the Great Judgement"). Irenic interpretation, in other words, as it does in the text of *Apocalypse*, both acts in terms of and in some sense consciously defers to the one act of interpretation in which there can be definitive solution.[29] To use an even more anthropomorphic language, the "violence" of God's judgement cannot, according to such a model, be unconsciously imitated or appropriated without causing real harm or causing a type of ambiguity which, rather than being neutral, really does harm. Such harm seems to be what Rabelais points to in Panurge's destruction of the sheep-dealer and his entire flock in the *Quart livre*, V-VIII. Both parties to the dispute—Panurge and Dindenault—make use of evangelical expressions to respond to each other: Panurge, the apocalyptic "patience" as he gets angrier and angrier, Dindenault, the gospel "mon voisin" as he drives a harder and harder bargain. But the rhetoric of their growing violence towards each other blurs any ability on the reader's part to understand who is "right" and who is "wrong." The reader can only notice that Rabelais' text constantly calls up an entire New Testament narrative, because of which Panurge sounds like the Antichrist who kills the saints,[30] or like Judas,[31] or like the high priest's servant at

---

[29] To use another Rabelaisian example, Gargantua's not knowing whether to weep for his wife, dead in childbirth, or to rejoice for his newborn son is as much an eschatological problem as is Tertullian's not knowing whether to pray for the destruction of the sin-ridden world or for the merciful delay of the same. Tertullian "decided" to do both. The Gargantuan "solution" retains the problem's terms, its crisis, while it seizes upon an irenic action appropriate to both fulfillment and lack: "...il vault mieulx pleurer moins, et boire dadvantage!" (*Pan.* III) ("...it would be better to cry less and to drink on!"). For Tertullian's "mora finis," see Jaroslav Pelikan, *The Finality of Jesus Christ in an Age of Universal History*, A Dilemma of the Third Century (Richmond, 1966), pp. 15-17.

The Holy Spirit gets into Bridoye's decision by the punning "l'esprit sacrosainct." Bridoye is really a type of paraclete in Rabelais; the author knows that "paraclete" is Greek for "lawyer" and Epistemon contrasts Bridoye's discernment with the evils of all the demonic, "pervers advocatz" in France.

[30] The merchant jibes at the bespectacled Panurge: "O lunetier de l'Antichrist, responds si tu est de Dieu" (*Q.L.*, V) ("O spectacles of the Anti-Christ, answer me: are you in God's camp?").

[31] Weighed against the merchant's most valuable sheep, for which he bargains, Panurge will be found so wanting that: "serez quelque jour suspendu et pendu" (*Q.L.*, VI) ("You'll someday be pulled up and hung").

Gethsemane, or like Christ.[32] Dindenault seems either a Judas or Christ's disciple who "lives by the sword."[33] The sheep are either Christ or the saints, as they figure in *Apocalypse*, or are merely very stupid beasts. "Comme vous sçavez estre du mouton le naturel, tous jours suyvre le premier, quelque part qu'il aille. [See *Apoc.* 14.4: "Hi sequuntur Agnum quocumque ierit."] Aussi le dict Aristoteles... estre le plus sot et inepte animant du monde" (*Q.L.*, VIII) ("As you know, the nature of the sheep is always to follow the leader wherever he may go. Aristotle calls him the stupidest, most inept animal in the world"). Though the two litigants have just exchanged a "signe de perfaicte reconciliation" (*Q.L.*, V: a mutual Judas-kiss?), Panurge suddenly kills both merchant and sheep. Frère Jean, who has witnessed Panurge's violent seizing of the prerogative to judge finally, at least judges unambiguously when he quips: "Tu... te damne comme un vieil diable. Il est escript: *Mihi vindictam, et caetera* Matiere de breviaire" (*Q.L.*, VIII). "Vengeance is mine, saieth the Lord..."[34]

But interpretation is ours whether we like it or not. The famous chapters on *parolles degelées* in the *Quart livre* put the problem in the most extreme relief. Words become things here because they are, in fact, existants in the world. Much has been written about a conquest, in the Renaissance, over a supposedly medieval "realist" theory of language; it is a debate which needs to be engaged, at greater length than is possible in this study, on the level of the relevance of the language of ontology to the process of referentiality.[35] But Rabelais,

---

[32] Dindenault threatens Panurge as they haggle over the sheep: "Je te donneroys... un coup d'espée sus cette aureille luneticrre, et te tueroys comme un belier" (*Q.L.*, V) ("I'ld give you a sword-clout on this bespectacled ear of yours, and I'ld slaughter you like a sheep"). The "belier," of course, could as easily apply to Christ as does the ear-cutting to Malchas the servant.

[33] See f.n. 31, above. Dindenault, of course, puts a price on the head of the lovely sheep. Panurge, in an exclamation, will relate his own death-dealing to money, even to "silver": "C'est, dit Panurge, bien chié pour l'argent!" (*Q.L.*, VIII) ("Said Panurge, 'It was well-shit for the money!'").

[34] *Rom.* 12.19

[35] J. Paris, to cite his *Rabelais au futur* as an example of the debate, attacks what he calls in the Western tradition a "métaphysique logocentrique." He presumes a certain action to be proposed by that tradition for language—either as "parole" or "écriture": "...où le souffle manifeste la présence divine, la voix la conscience, le nom l'identité..." (p. 15). The word is indeed privileged in the West, but not to the exclusion of all other human activities. And because, in Christianity at least, the word must be understood pneumatically, all actions *occasion* "présence," "conscience" (in the epistemological sense before the ethical sense), "identité." But they do not necessarily occasion *this* or *that* experience, as Paris' definite articles imply. "To manifest" is actually not a bad way of putting it; language and gesture always permit such experience to be "at hand," which is not far from Pantagruel's "...que tous jours on a en main."

who certainly does not believe that words are what they signify, takes the risk of seeming the most naïve of "realists" when he pictures the flying phonemes as visible, tangible *things*. The episode forces the reader to interpret several attitudes toward the very facticity of language as he goes about using words and word-derived concepts in interpreting. Panurge fears the words, which he believes are being produced in the present, because they are "on their own turf." "D'adventaige ilz sont sus leurs fumiers, nous ne congnoissons le pays" (*Q.L.*, LV). What is fearful is not the concept of language—nor is it the concept of humanity—but rather these words, here and now, which constitute a text or topography whose referents do not seem as obscure ("...ce sont, par Dieu! coups de canon" (*Q.L.*, LV) ("...by God, these are cannon shots!") as does any intentionality which can be associated with it. Pantagruel's initial reaction is to quiet Panurge's fear with the idealist hope—certainly based in the theories of antiquity and the Middle Ages, *pace* Ockham—that the voyagers may have stumbled upon the very forms, ideas and universals themselves: miraculously tangible proofs, in other words, of what we commonly posit about intentionality and referentiality.[36] Pantagruel seems all too willing to embrace a comfortable millenium in which his compatriots may "have" the certitude they hope for. He adduces a text which states that when the ideas and universals appear among men, they will "part là rester reservée pour l'advenir, jusques à la consommation du siecle" (*Q.L.*, LV) ("remain there reserved for the future, until the consummation of the world"). He hopes he has found "telles parolles" and not others; if not, he fantasizes that they may be an eternal pastoral: the melancholy, disembodied poetry issuing from Orpheus' severed head. But they are neither. They are just *these* words or sounds which, though in an incomprehensible "languaige barbare" (*Q.L.*, LVI), are univocally interpreted by the voyagers as "parolles horrificques": the words and sounds of a terrible, bloody battle, their physical presence a text "mal plaisante[s] à veoir" (*Q.L.*, LVI) ("not at all nice to see"). Among the sounds are "goth, magoth" which point less ambiguously than the others to the eschatological battle in both the Old and New Testaments and to the excluded enemies of an eschatologically oriented Thélème.[37] But the episode stresses, first of

---

[36] Pantagruel says they are like the "dew on Gideon's fleece" (*Q.L.*, LV). In *Judges* 6.37, the tangible dew is requested twice by a skeptical Gideon as proof of God's intention to save Israel.

[37] Florence Weinberg, in her *The Wine and the Will* (Detroit, 1972), pp. 41-42, sees Thélème here and discerns "the lurking apocalyptic character of the entire parable," though her version of the struggle comes out sounding Manichaean. "Our Rabelaisian

all, that words uttered are simply existants. Pantagruel learns to modify his falsely irenic, millenialist desire for sublime words by realizing he must put down the fictional narrator's desire to "keep on ice" the sublimated sounds of "gay quips" among the battle. Words, says Pantagruel, are ordinarily at hand; though they always threaten not to satisfy, there is always a daily abundance of them: "...disant estre follie faire reserve de ce dont jamais l'on n'a faulte et que tous jours on a en main, comme sont motz de gueule entre tous bons et joyeulx Pantagruelistes" (*Q.L.*, LVI) ("...saying it was mad to keep in reserve that which one never lacks, which one always has at hand, like gay quips among good and happy Pantagruelists"). Holding on even to irenic-apocalyptic linguistic structures ("gay quips") would do violence to the ongoing activity of irenic communication among Pantagruelists which, as we know from the text, is always superabundant and lacking at the same time.[38]

The *Cinquième Livre*, as is well known, presents as yet unresolvable problems of attribution. Rather than take up in detail the several episodes of interest here (including the finale in which, appropriately, "toutes choses se meuvent a leur fin" ("all things move toward their end") and Panurge is made to drink the book of revelation as had Ezekiel and John), I shall mention one in particular because it is—whoever its author may be—a satire upon the very irenic stance which Rabelais incorporates into the first four books. This could, obviously, be an argument both for or against attribution.

The church on Ringing Island thoroughly satirizes the irenic life which Apocalypse proclaims, the *ecclesia* claims to embody, and Pantagruelists enjoy throughout the Rabelaisian fiction. The satire misses very few of the terms and ideas which have come to signify, in a most precise way, the irenic-apocalyptic state both in Rabelais and in the tradition he manipulates. The premise in Book Five is that *this* church must be falsely irenic and that the Pantagruelists must differentiate themselves from it. After being greeted by a hermit—an epitome, that is, of the irenic life—the voyagers meet the beedle Editus who wishes

---

heroes glimpse... the actual final battle of the millenium which takes place 'out of time', since the struggle between the dark and the light is eternal." Weinberg's excellent pages on eating and drinking recognize in these both apocalyptic violence and a type of fulfillment. She makes explicit, in addition, much of the text's "pentecostal" language. For "goth, magoth," see also "Rabelasiana," in *Revue des Etudes Rabelaisiennes* 8 (1910), 148.

[38] F. Rigolot discusses this apparent "duality" of Rabelais' language in Platonic terms in "Cratylisme...," *op. cit.*, p. 132. I would call irenic apocalypse the seemingly contradictory attitude toward language by which, for Rigolot, Rabelais avoids the danger of total *aporia*.

only to share with others his own irenic paradise: "...paradis en ceste vie, et en l'aultre pareillement avoir" (*C.L.*, VI) ("to have paradise in this life and likewise in the other"). Lest his new friends suspect the millenialist error, he assures them that eating and drinking and singing here are an *otium in bono*, fully responsive to the crisis of the times and of time itself. "Partant n'estimez icy temps ocieusement perdre" (*C.L.*, VI); "...rien n'est si cher ne si précieux que le temps; employons-le à bonnes oeuvres" (*C.L.*, V) ("Do not however think time lost lazily here;" "...nothing is so dear or precious as time; let us use it in good works"). Despite all of the structures of an irenic apocalypse which seem like all the structures of good Pantagruelism, Pantagruel is unaccountably saddened in the face of Editus' generosity.[39] One irenic commonplace mentioned only very peripherally in this study is the hierarchical, productive and chaste life of the beehive.[40] The text mentions on three occasions how similar the island's inhabitants seem to bees, above all because hierarchies, ranks and orders appear here as they do in the hive: "sans compagnie charnelle" (*C.L.*, III) ("without carnal relations"). It is a truly revolutionary moment and, if Rabelais' own, his most profound break with the tradition. What is finally lacking on the island is ordinary sexual generation. Celibacy is, ordinarily, too limiting; it can dehumanize, so that the very necessity for struggle in the midst of peace no longer seems even relevant. Editus' beautiful, sacred orders of birds are a thing unto themselves, requiring special treatment. As Thomas Greene has written, "The biological distinction between bird inhabitants and human visitors on the Ringing Island represents an ethical distinction in which reasonable good sense remains exceptional and alien."[41] In

---

[39] "Pantagruel monstroit face triste, et sembloit non content du sejour [quatridien] que nous terminoit Editus;..." (*C.L.*, VI) ("Pantagruel showed a sad face and seemed discontented with the four-day sojourn which Editus spelled out for us..."). The alternative reading for "quatridien" is "cotidien"—which would direct the satire at that most evangelical of irenic ideas upon which Rabelais' entire alimentary metaphor plays, as does this chapter's title.

Other irenic apocalyptic commonplaces: the island's "chans infatigables," a singing "sans cesse," Editus' Pantagrueline truism "...qui dort, si boit"; the voyagers "repose" in the singing, "du tout... y vacquer." The hive-delights are threatened by an apocalyptic plague of "Cagotz" who will "tout manger et tout gaster," mimicking good eating as they destroy it.

[40] The bee-topos is omnipresent in Western literature, from Vergil to Philo to Prudentius, from Luther to Hobbes to Nietzsche, from Dante to Swift to Valéry. See Thomas of Chantimpré, *Bonum universale de apibus* (Douai, 1627).

[41] *Rabelais: a Study in Comic Courage*, *op. cit.*, p. 105. The text reads: "...beuvoyent, mangeoyent comme hommes et emeutissoyent comme hommes, dormoyent et roussinoyent comme hommes; bref, à les voyre, eussiez dit que c'estoyent hommes; hommes toutefois

perhaps the most sober lines, the most like Rabelais in the entire farce, Pantagruel refuses the kind offer of the Cardinjays' baths and unguents. "Mais Pantagruel dist qu'il ne boiroit que trop sans cela" (*C.L.*, V) ("But Pantagruel said that he would drink only too much without that"). They would add nothing to his already irenic state.

n'estoyent mye, selon l'institution de maistre Editus..." (*C.L.*, II) ("...they drank and ate like men, and they let go their droppings like men, they slept and stood at stud like men; in short, to see them, you'ld have said that they were men: but they weren't men at all, according to the statement of master Editus,..."). Rabelais' story resembles closely the "paradisus avium" or garden of birds discovered in the *Navigatio S. Brendani* and its many vernacular translations. As John Freccero has shown ("Dante's 'Per Sé' Angel: the Middle Ground in Nature and in Grace," *Studi danteschi* 39 [1962], 5-38), the tradition gives every reason to suspect the quality of such birds' satisfaction.

Selected Bibliography

Adriani, Maurilio. "Apocalisse e insecuritas," in *Apocalisse e insecuritas. Archivio di Filosofia*, ed. Enrico Castelli. II (1954), pp. 21-33.

Alighieri, Dante. *The Divine Comedy*. Translated, with a commentary by Charles S. Singleton. 6 vols. Princeton: Princeton University Press, 1975.

———. *Epistolae*. Ed. Paget Toynbee. Second edition. Oxford: The Clarendon Press, 1966.

Altheim, Franz. "L'Apocalittica di oggi," in *Apocalisse e insecuritas. Archivio di Filosofia*, ed. Enrico Castelli. II (1954), pp. 77-92.

Antiphonale Romanum... pro diurnis horis. A Solesmensibus monachis editum. Tornaci: Desclée, 1949.

Apocalypses et théologie de l'espérance. Association Catholique Française pour l'Etude de la Bible. Congrès de Toulouse, 1975. Paris: Editions du Cerf, 1977.

Aquinas, Thomas. *Scriptum Super Sententiis Magistri Petri Lombardi*. Ed. R.P. Mandonnet and M.F. Moos. 4 vols. Paris: Lethielleux, 1929-1947 and 1956.

Auerbach, Erich. *Lingua letteraria e pubblico nella tarda antichità latina e nel medioevo*. Trans. F. Codino. Milano: Feltrinelli, 1960.

Augustinus, Aurelius. *Confessions*. Edited and translated by P. de Labriolle. 2 vols. Paris: Société Editions "Les Belles Lettres," 1954.

Avena, Antonio. "La composizione del *De Vita Solitaria*," *Rassegno Critico della Letteratura Italiana*. (Napoli) XII, 9-10 (1907), 193-202.

Babcock, Barbara. "Too many, too few: Ritual Modes of Signification," *Semiotica* 23 (1978), 291-302.

Baron, Hans. "Petrarch and the Humanistic Discovery of Man's Nature," in *Florilegium Historiale*. Eds J.G. Rowe and W.H. Stockdale. Toronto: University of Toronto Press, 1971.

Berdyaev, Nicolas. *The Beginning and the End*. New York: Harper Torchbooks, 1957.

Bernard of Clairvaux. *De Diligendo Deo*, in Migne, *Patrologia... Latina* CLXXXII, col. 973ff.

Bertaud, Emile. "Horloges spirituelles," in *Dictionnaire de spiritualité* VII (fasc. 46-47), col. 745-63.
Besret, Bernard, S.O.Cist. *Incarnation ou eschatologie?* Paris: Editions du Cerf, 1964.
Biblia Vulgata. Ed. Colunga-Turrado. 4th edition. Biblioteca de Autores Cristianos. Madrid: Editorial Católica, 1965.
Bleeth, Kenneth A. "Narrator and Landscape in the *Commedia*: an Approach to Dante's Earthly Paradise," *Dante Studies* 88 (1970), 31-49.
Bloomfield, Morton. *Piers Plowman as a Fourteenth-Century Apocalypse*. New Brunswick: Rutgers University Press, 1961.
Casel, Odo. *Das Christliche Kultmysterium*. Regensburg: F. Pustet, 1960.
Castelli, Enrico. "Premessa," in *Apocalisse e insecuritas. Archivio di Filosofia* II (1954), pp. 3-5.
Charity, A.C. *Events and Their Afterlife*. Cambridge: Cambridge University Press, 1966.
Chenu, M.-D. "Spiritus: le vocabulaire de l'âme au XIIe siècle," *Revue des Sciences Philosophiques et Théologiques* 41 (1957), 209-32.
Congar, Yves. "Pneumatologie et théologie de l'histoire," in *Herméneutique et eschatologie*. Ed. E. Castelli. Paris: Aubier-Editions Montaigne, 1971.
Constable, Giles. "The Popularity of Twelfth Century Spiritual Writers in the Late Middle Ages," in *Renaissance Studies in Honour of Hans Baron*. Ed. A. Molho and J. Tedeschi. DeKalb, Illinois: University of Illinois Press, 1971.
Costa, Dennis. "Dante as a Poet-Theologian," *Dante Studies* 89 (1971), 61-72.
Crocco, Antonio. *Simbologia gioachimita e simbologia dantesca*. Napoli: Edizioni Empireo, 1962.
Danièlou, Jean. *Bible et liturgie*. Paris: Editions du Cerf, 1951.
Davy, M.-M. *Théologie et mystique de Guillaume de St.-Thierry*. Etudes de théologie et d'histoire de la spiritualité, 14. Paris: Vrin, 1954.
Debognie, Pierre, C.SS.R. *Jean Mombaer de Bruxelles, abbé de Livry: ses écrits et ses réformes*. Louvain, 1928.
Déchanet, J.-M. "Aux sources de la doctrine de Guillaume de St.-Thierry," *Collectanea Ordinis Cisterciensis Reformatae* 5 (1938-39), 187-98, 262-78.
———. "Seneca Noster. Des Lettres à Lucilius à la Lettre aux frères du Mont-Dieu," in *Mélanges Joseph de Ghellinck S.J. Museum Lessianum*, section historique no. 14. Gembloux: Duclot, 1951, pp. 753-66.
Dempf, Alois. "L'Apocalittica di Dante," in *Apocalisse e insecuritas. Archivio di Filosofia*. Ed. Enrico Castelli. II (1954), pp. 93-102.
Doignon, J. "L'Esprit souffle où il veut... dans la plus ancienne tradition patristique latine," *Revue des Sciences Philosophiques et Théologiques* 62 (1978), 350-57.
Eco, Umberto. *Apocalipticos e integrados ante la cultura de masas*. Trans. A. Boglar. Barcelona: Lumen, 1968.
———. *Opera Aperta*. Forma e indeterminazione nelle poetiche contemporanee. Milano: Bompiani, 1962.
Eliade, Mircea. *Cosmos and History*. The myth of the eternal return. New York: Harper Torchbooks, 1959.
Focillon, Henri. *L'An Mil*. Paris: A. Colin, 1952.

Franceschini, Ezio. "La figura dell'eremita nella letteratura latina medioevale," *Miscellanea del Centro di Studi Medioevali*, IV (1962), 560-69.
von Franz, Marie Louise, ed. *Aurora Consurgens*. A document attributed to Thomas Aquinas on the problem of opposites in chemistry. New York: Pantheon, 1966.
Freccero, John. "Dante's Pilgrim in a Gyre," *PMLA* 76 (1961), 168-81.
―――. "Paradiso x: The Dance of the Stars," *Dante Studies* 86 (1968), 85-111.
Frye, Northrop. *Fearful Symmetry*. Boston: Beacon Press, 1962.
Funk, Robert W., ed. *Apocalypticism*, in *Journal for Theology and the Church* no. 6. New York: Herder and Herder, 1969.
―――. *Language, Hermeneutic, and the Word of God*. New York: Harper and Row, 1966.
Gans, Eric. "Pour une esthétique triangulaire," *Esprit* 11 (November, 1973), 564ff.
Garin, Eugenio, et al. *L'Attesa dell'età nuova nella spiritualità della fine del medioevo*. Todi, 1962.
Girard, René. "Discussion avec René Girard," *Esprit* 11 (November, 1973), 528ff.
―――. "Les Malédictions contre les Pharisiens et la Révélation évangélique," *Bulletin du Centre Protestant d'Etudes* 3 (June, 1975), 3-29.
―――. *La Violence et le sacré*. Paris: Grasset, 1971.
Guillaume de St.-Thierry. *The Golden Epistle*. Tr. Theodore Berkeley, OCSO. Cistercian Fathers Series, 12. Spencer, Massachusetts: Cistercian publications, 1971.
―――. *On Contemplating God*. Tr. Sister Penelope, CSMV. Cistercian Fathers Series, 3. Spencer, Massachusetts: Cistercian publications, 1971.
―――. *Un Traité de la vie solitaire (Epistola ad Fratres de Monte-Dei)*. Ed. M.-M. Davy. Paris: Vrin, 1940.
Joachim of Flora. *Concordia Novi ac Veteris Testamenti*. Venetia: Simonis de Luere, 1519.
―――. *Expositio magni prophetae Abbatis Joachim in Apocalipsin*. Venetia: Franciscus Bindonus, 1527.
―――. *Il libro delle figure dell'Abate Gioacchino da Fiore*. Ed. Luigi Tondelli. 2 vols. 2nd edition. Torino: Società Editrice Internazionale, 1953.
Kaske, R.E. "Dante's DXV," in *Dante. A Collection of Critical Essays*. Ed. John Freccero. Englewood Cliffs: Prentice-Hall, 1965, pp. 122-40.
―――. "Sì si conserva il seme d'ogni giusto (*Purg.* xxxii.48)," *Dante Studies* 89 (1971), 49-54.
Kermode, Frank. *The Sense of an Ending*. Studies in the theory of fiction. New York: Oxford University Press, 1968.
Kimmerle, Heinz. "Hermeneutical Theory or Ontological Hermeneutics," in R.W. Funk, ed. *History and Hermeneutic*. New York: Harper Torchbooks, 1967, pp. 107-21.
Koch, Klaus. *The Rediscovery of Apocalyptic*. Studies in Biblical Theology. Second series, no. 22. London: SCM Press, 1972.
Kristeller, Paul Oskar. *Eight Philosophers of the Italian Renaissance*. Stanford: Stanford University Press, 1964.

Lawrence, D.H. *Apocalypse*. New York: Viking Press, 1966.
Leclercq, Jean. *L'Amour des lettres et le désir de Dieu*. Initiation aux auteurs monastiques du moyen age. Paris: Editions du Cerf, 1957.
_____. *Otia Monastica*. Etudes sur le vocabulaire de la contemplation au Moyen-Age. Studia Anselmiana (fasc. LI). Rome: Herder, 1963.
de Lubac, Henri. *Exégèse médiévale*. 4 vols. Paris/Liguge: Aubier, 1959-64.
_____. *Histoire et esprit*. L'Intelligence de l'écriture d'après Origène. Paris/Liguge: Aubier, 1950.
Marcel, Gabriel. *Being and Having*. New York: Harper Torchbooks, 1965.
Marinelli, Francesco. *Personalismo trinitario nella storia della salvezza*. Rapporti tra la SS.ma Trinità e le opere ad extra nello scriptum super sententiis di S. Tommaso. Collectio: Spiritualitas. Roma: Pontificale Università Lateranense, 1969.
Mineo, Nicolò. *Profetismo e Apocalittica in Dante*. Catania: Università di Catania, 1968.
Ockham, William of. *Philosophical Writings*. Ed. Philotheus Boehner. New York: Bobbs-Merrill, 1964.
Paris, Jean. *Rabelais au futur*. Paris: Editions du Seuil, 1970.
Parker, Patricia. "The Progress of Phaedria's Bower: Spenser to Coleridge," *ELH* 40, no. 3 (Fall, 1973), 372ff.
Pelikan, Jaroslav. *The Finality of Jesus Christ in an Age of Universal History*. A dilemma of the third century. Ecumenical Studies in History, no. 3. Richmond, Virginia: John Knox Press, 1966.
_____. *The Light of the World*. New York: Harper Brothers, 1962.
Petrarca, Francesco. *The Life of Solitude*. Translated with introduction and notes by Jacob Zeitlin. Urbana, Illinois: University of Illinois Press, 1924.
_____. *Prose*. A cura di G. Martellotti, P.G. Ricci, et al. Milano-Napoli: Ricciardi, 1955.
Peuch, Henri-Charles. "La Gnose et le Temps," *Eranos-Jahrbuch* 15 (1951), 57-114.
Prigent, Pierre. *Apocalypse et liturgie*. Cahiers théologiques, 52. Neuchâtel: Delachaux et Niestlé, 1964.
_____. *Flash sur l'Apocalypse*. Neuchâtel: Delachaux et Niestlé, 1974.
Reeves, Marjorie. *The Influence of Prophecy in the Later Middle Ages*. Oxford: The Clarendon Press, 1969.
Richard of St.-Victor. *In Apocalypsim libri septem*. In Migne, *Patrologia... Latina* CXCVI, cols. 683ff.
Ricoeur, Paul. "The Model of the Text: Meaningful Action Considered as a Text," *New Literary History* 5 (Autumn, 1973), 91-117.
Rissi, Mathias. *The Future of the World*. An exegetical study of *Revelation* 19.11-22.15. Studies in Biblical Theology, second series, no. 23. London: SCM Press, 1972.
Rupert of Deutz. *De Operibus Spiritus Sancti*. Tome II. Edited by Jean Gribomont and Elizabeth de Solms. In *Sources Chrétiennes*, no. 165. Paris: Editions du Cerf, 1970.
Ryan, Patrick OCSO. "The Witness of William of St.-Thierry to the Spirit and Aims of the Early Cistercians," in *The Cistercian Spirit: a Symposium*. Ed. M. Basil Pennington OCSO. Shannon, Ireland, 1970.

Sachot, M. Review of *La Théologie face au défi herméneutique* by J.-P. Resweber, in *Revue des Sciences Réligieuses*. Université des sciences humaines de Strasbourg. 50, no. 2 (April, 1976), 169-73.

Sarolli, Gianroberto. *Prolegomena alla Divina Commedia*. Firenze: L. Olschki, 1971.

Seneca, L. Annaeus. *Ad Lucilium Epistolae Morales*. Recog. L.D. Reynolds. 2 vols. Oxford: The Clarendon Press, 1965.

Serpagli, Francesco. *Prolegomeni al "De Vita Solitaria" di Francesco Petrarca*. Parma: Scuola Tipografia Benedettina, 1966.

Simon, Alfred. "La Masque de la violence," *Esprit* 11 (November, 1973), 515ff.

Singleton, Charles. *Dante Studies* I, II (*Commedia*: Elements of Structure; *Journey to Beatrice*). Cambridge, Massachusetts: Harvard University Press, 1965-67.

Snyder, Graydon F. "The Litteralization of the Apocalyptic Form in the New Testament Church," *Biblical Research* 14 (1969), 5-18.

Sollers, Philippe. "Dante et la traversée de l'écriture," in *L'Ecriture et l'expérience des limites*. Paris: Editions du Seuil, 1968.

Straus, Erwin W. "Psychiatry and Philosophy," in *Psychiatry and Philosophy*. Ed. Maurice Natanson. New York: Springer-Verlag, 1969.

Tardieu, Michel. "Psychaios Spinther: Histoire d'une métaphor dans la tradition platonicienne jusqu'à Eckhart," *Revue des Etudes Augustiniennes* 21, no. 3 (1975), 225-55.

Tromp, Sebastianus, ed. *De Spiritu Sancto anima corporis mystici*. Testimonia selecta e patribus graecis et latinis. Pontificia Universitas Gregoriana, Textus et Documenta, Series Theologica, no. 1, 7. Romae: apud aedes Pontificiae Universitatis Gregorianae, 1932.

Viller, M. "Le *Speculum Monachorum* et la 'Dévotion Moderne'," *Revue d'Ascètique et de Mystique* 3 (1922), 45-56.

de Vrégille, Bernard. "L'Attente des saints d'après St. Bernard," *Nouvelle Revue Théologique* 70 (1948), 225-44.

Wilkins, Ernest Hatch. *Petrarch's Later Years*. Cambridge: Harvard University Press, 1959.

Wittgenstein, Ludwig. *Über Gewissenheit/On Certainty*. Ed. G.E.M. Anscombe and G.H. von Wright. New York: Harper Torchbooks, 1972.